2008
Britain's Best
Leisure &
Relaxation
Guide

Hotels, Spas, Leisure Breaks, Golfing & Activities, Guesthouses,
Inns, Self-Catering and Caravan & Camping Holidays

FHG
K·U·P·E·R·A·R·D

Maps: ©MAPS IN MINUTES™ / Collins Bartholomew 2007

Typeset by FHG Guides Ltd, Paisley.
Printed and bound in Malaysia by Imago.

Distribution. Book Trade: ORCA Book Services, Stanley House,
3 Fleets Lane, Poole, Dorset BH15 3AJ
(Tel: 01202 665432; Fax: 01202 666219)
e-mail: mail@orcabookservices.co.uk
Published by FHG Guides Ltd., Abbey Mill Business Centre,
Seedhill, Paisley PA1 ITJ (Tel: 0141-887 0428 Fax: 0141-889 7204).
e-mail: admin@fhguides.co.uk

Britain's Best Leisure & Relaxation Guide is published by FHG Guides Ltd,
part of Kuperard Group.

Cover design: FHG Guides
Cover Pictures: With thanks to
right; Hoar Cross Hotel, near Yoxall, Staffordshire
left; Langstone Cliff Hotel, Dawlish, South Devon

Visit the FHG website
www.holidayguides.com
for details of the wide choice of accommodation
featured in the full range of FHG titles

Contents

How to use this guide

The entries in **Britain's Best Leisure & Recreation Guide** are divided into five sections.

The new and colourful **Spas** and the **Golf and Activity** sections can be found at the start of the guide, with the entries being listed in *Country* and *County* order. The rest of the guide is split into three main sections: **Board** (hotels, guesthouses, farms, bed and breakfast, etc), **Self-catering,** and **Caravans** (including camping). The entries in these sections are classified under Country, Region, County and Town and the headings on each page indicate this. Most display advertisers also have a descriptive review in the appropriate section, and this is always preceded by a row of symbols, largely self-explanatory. A list is given below, and regularly throughout the guide.

Within each section the same symbol appears in the same position so that you can run your eye down each page and tell at a glance whether or not a particular service or amenity is available. You can identify very quickly which entries do, or do not meet your needs. You can then read the detailed review for further information and how to book.

symbols
used in this guide

Months open (eg:4/10 means April to October)

- Pets Welcome
- Children Welcome
- Suitable for Disabled
- Totally non-smoking
- Licensed

board

Months open (eg:4/10 means April to October)

- Pets Welcome
- Children Welcome
- Suitable for Disabled
- Linen provided

Min/Max no of persons in one unit (eg:2/6)

self catering

Months open (eg:4/10 means April to October)

- Pets Welcome
- Shop on site
- Restaurant/Takeaway on site
- Showers/hot water
- Licensed Bar

caravans & camping

Ratings & Awards

For the first time ever the AA, VisitBritain, VisitScotland, and the Wales Tourist Board will use a single method of assessing and rating serviced accommodation. Irrespective of which organisation inspects an establishment the rating awarded will be the same, using a common set of standards, giving a clear guide of what to expect. The RAC is no longer operating an Hotel inspection and accreditation business.

Accommodation Standards: Star Grading Scheme

Using a scale of 1-5 stars the objective quality ratings give a clear indication of accommodation standard, cleanliness, ambience, hospitality, service and food, This shows the full range of standards suitable for every budget and preference, and allows visitors to distinguish between the quality of accommodation and facilities on offer in different establishments. All types of board and self-catering accommodation are covered, including hotels,
B&Bs, holiday parks, campus accommodation, hostels, caravans and camping, and boats.

VisitBritain and the regional tourist boards, enjoyEngland.com, VisitScotland and VisitWales, and the AA have full details of the grading system on their websites

The more stars, the higher level of quality

★★★★★
exceptional quality, with a degree of luxury

★★★★
excellent standard throughout

★★★
very good level of quality and comfort

★★
good quality, well presented and well run

★
acceptable quality; simple, practical, no frills

National Accessible Scheme

If you have particular mobility, visual or hearing needs, look out for the National Accessible Scheme. You can be confident of finding accommodation or attractions that meet your needs by looking for the following symbols.

 Typically suitable for a person with sufficient mobility to climb a flight of steps but would benefit from fixtures and fittings to aid balance

 Typically suitable for a person with restricted walking ability and for those that may need to use a wheelchair some of the time and can negotiate a maximum of three steps

 Typically suitable for a person who depends on the use of a wheelchair and transfers unaided to and from the wheelchair in a seated position. This person may be an independent traveller

 Typically suitable for a person who depends on the use of a wheelchair in a seated position. This person also requires personal or mechanical assistance (eg carer, hoist).

OXFORD

The City of Dreaming Spires

OXFORD offers a slice of English culture and history dating back to the eighth century. It is most famous as home of the oldest university in the English-speaking world. Scholars have been writing and researching at Oxford University since the 1100s.

Poet, Mathew Arnold deemed Oxford 'the city of dreaming spires' in reference to the architecture of the college buildings that make up Oxford University. Standing at the foot of Carfax Towers at the very centre of the city, you are surrounded by walls that have stood for 800 years. And extending up from the hidden buildings beyond the walls are the spires that top the college cathedrals and make up the city's skyline.

Long before Oxford served as a classic example of the English heritage, the city actually grew up at the union of two rivers, the Thames and the Cherwell. The very reason for Oxfords existence was the presence of a ford on the Thames for oxen crossing the river. The Thames is also known as the Isis within the Oxford boundaries.

Walking along the Thames path can be refreshing as you get a glimpse to the beautiful nature and wildlife. A walk along the Oxford's rowing river and the rural reaches to Abingdon is a thrilling event in itself. You can also join the Thames at Osney Bridge, walk past the Waterman's Arms and Iffley Lock to Folly Bridge. It is home to famous Salter Brothers, boat Hire Company and two popular riverside pubs.

The Thames bids farewell to Oxford at Sandford Lock. The Old World King's Arm is the last riverside pub until Abingdon. The walk is an exhilarating experience as it captures the beauty of nature at its best and invites us all to enjoy life at its own pace.

Punting and rowing are very popular activities. A trip down to Cherwell or the Isis where boating and punting provides tantalising views of the dreaming spires. Magdalen Bridge Boathouse, on the High Street offers punts, chauffeured punts, rowing boats and pedalos for hire on the River Cherwell. The most popular circular route, past the Botanic Garden and Christ Church Meadow takes approx. 30 minutes – to an hour. The other direction offers a magnificent rural landscape and challenging route towards the University Parks.

Cherwell Boathouse at Bardwell Road offers punts, rowing boats and Canadian canoes for hire on the River Cherwell, in a secluded part of the city. Salter Steamers Ltd at Folly Bridge offers punts, day and rowing boat hire on the Thames (Thames is also know as Isis within Oxford boundaries). Boat Trips are available on the Thames as well as daily trips from Folly Bridge, Oxford, to Iffley Lock (20 minutes each way), Sandford and Abingdon (2 hours each way).

For those who want to relax and enjoy the beautiful river and its surroundings, hop aboard Oxford River Cruises. They offer a range of luxurious lunch, tea and dinner cruises in a 12-seater Edwardian boat, from Christ Church to the Trout at Wolvercote. They follow the same stretch of the River Thames taken by Lewis Carroll and Alice Liddell in a small rowing boat almost 150 years ago. Other theme trips include Wind in the Willows and Narnia. Trips run from March, leaving from the landing stage in the centre of the city opposite Christ Church College. Also, College Cruisers, Combe Road Wharf has residential narrow boats for hire on the Oxford Canal.

If you are looking to indulge in some good food, then there are some very good choices of restaurants along the river. They include Cherwell Boathouse Restaurant and Aqua Vitae, at Folly Bridge/ St Aldates. Riverside pubs include The Head of the River in St Aldate's, The Trout at Wolvercote, The Perch at Binsey and The Victoria Arms at Old Marston.

A visit to old beautiful college and university buildings, or idyllic river trips to the Thames and Cherwell. A visit to the University museums brings history into perspective. Following the literary

trials, discovering the secret gardens or shopping. Wining and dining from student's pubs to the city's chic venues, Oxford City captures and displays its characteristics in style.

Oxford never fails to impress, if you are a first time visitor or an avid traveller to the region. There is a surprise around every corner. Along with the beautiful historic architecture, which is one of a kind, the city is youthful, full of buzz and vibrant.

For more information on events and news on River Thames go to
www.visitthames.co.uk

England and Wales · Counties

NORTHUMBERLAND

TYNE & WEAR

DURHAM

43

CUMBRIA

42 41 40 39

ISLE OF MAN

NORTH YORKSHIRE

38

LANCASHIRE

EAST RIDING OF YORKSHIRE

34

WEST YORKSHIRE

37

33

GREATER MANCHESTER

36

S. YORKSHIRE

35

32

30

31

ISLE OF ANGLESEY

CONWY

b

CHESHIRE

DERBYSHIRE

LINCOLNSHIRE

a

NOTTINGHAMSHIRE

c

GWYNEDD

29

27

26

STAFFORDSHIRE

28

LEICESTERSHIRE

RUTLAND

25

24

NORFOLK

SHROPSHIRE

WEST MIDLANDS

CEREDIGION

POWYS

WORCESTERSHIRE

NORTHAMPTONSHIRE

CAMBRIDGESHIRE

SUFFOLK

HEREFORDSHIRE

WARWICKSHIRE

CARMARTHENSHIRE

23

BEDFORDSHIRE

PEMBROKESHIRE

GLOUCESTERSHIRE

BUCKINGHAMSHIRE

22

HERTFORDSHIRE

ESSEX

h l o

OXFORDSHIRE

d e g m

12 11

GREATER LONDON

9 10

f k n

21

17

16 15 14 13

8

i j

20

19 18

WILTSHIRE

SURREY

KENT

SOMERSET

HAMPSHIRE

DEVON

5

WEST SUSSEX

EAST SUSSEX

DORSET

3 4

6 7

ISLE OF WIGHT

CORNWALL

1 2

Unitary Authorities – England & Wales

1. Plymouth
2. Torbay
3. Poole
4. Bournemouth
5. Southampton
6. Portsmouth
7. Brighton & Hove
8. Medway
9. Thurrock
10. Southend
11. Slough

12. Windsor & Maidenhead
13. Bracknell Forest
14. Wokingham
15. Reading
16. West Berkshire
17. Swindon
18. Bath & Northeast Somerset
19. North Somerset
20. Bristol
21. South Gloucestershire
22. Luton

23. Milton Keynes
24. Peterborough
25. Leicester
26. Nottingham
27. Derby
28. Telford & Wrekin
29. Stoke-on-Trent
30. Warrington
31. Halton
32. Merseyside
33. Blackburn with Darwen

34. Blackpool
35. N.E. Lincolnshire
36. North Lincolnshire
37. Kingston-upon-Hull
38. York
39. Redcar & Cleveland
40. Middlesborough
41. Stockton-on-Tees
42. Darlington
43. Hartlepool

NORTH WALES
a. Denbighshire
b. Flintshire
c. Wrexham

SOUTH WALES
d. Swansea
e. Neath & Port Talbot
f. Bridgend
g. Rhondda Cynon Taff
h. Merthyr Tydfil
i. Vale of Glamorgan
j. Cardiff
k. Caerphilly
l. Blaenau Gwent
m. Torfaen
n. Newport
o. Monmouthshire

Spas

Penventon Hotel

Cornwall's Premier Independent Hotel, The Penventon offers superb facilities at "affordable" prices for every social or business occasion Central for touring Cornwall, our inspirational breaks can be arranged for 2 to 7 days.

Bedrooms
• All appointed to a high standard, with bath or shower en suite.
• Colour TV, direct dial telephone, controllable central heating and tea/coffee making facilities.
• Suites offer one or two bedrooms with lounge areas, some with patios. • Special weekend and weekly rates available.

Dining
• AA Rosetted menus • Choose from over 100 classic French, Italian and English dishes in the Dining Galleries.
• Local fish, shellfish and meat traditionally served.
• Favourite melodies played on piano grande each evening.

Leisure
• Centrally heated Aphrodite's Health and Leisure Complex.
• Large sauna, steam bath, spa hydrobath, fitness suite.
• Luxury robes and towels always provided
• STATZ "VERTICLE" sun room, allowing the fastest tan available.
• Poolside bar and menu.
• Open 7 days a week, normally adults only.
• Resident beautician and masseuse for health and beauty treatments.

AA ROSETTED

★★★ HOTEL

The Penventon Hotel
Redruth, West Cornwall TR15 1TE
Telephone: 01209 20 3000 • Fax: 01209 20 3001
e-mail: manager@penventon.com
www.penventon.com

Standing in four acres of mature subtropical gardens, overlooking two miles of sandy beach, yet within easy reach of Dartmoor and Exeter, Devoncourt provides an ideal base for a family holiday.

BEDROOMS
The accommodation is in 49 single, double or family rooms, all with private bathroom, colour TV, tea and coffee making facilities and telephone.

LEISURE
Swimming pool, sauna, steam room, whirlpool spa, solarium and fitness centre, snooker room, hair and beauty salon. For those who prefer to be out of doors there is a tennis court, croquet lawn, attractive outdoor heated pool, 18 hole putting green and golf practice area, all within the grounds.

DINING
Attractive lounge bar and restaurant overlooking the fabulous gardens, with fantastic sea views from the large picture windows. Children's menus and vegetarian options available.

DEVONCOURT HOTEL Douglas Avenue, Exmouth, Devon EX8 2EX
Tel: 01395 272277 • Fax: 01395 269315
E-mail: enquiries@devoncourt.com • www.devoncourt.com

Devoncourt is the ideal base for a holiday,
giving the whole family the opportunity
to relax and enjoy themselves at any time of the year.
The hotel is beautifully situated in four acres of mature grounds,
with palm trees and uninterrupted sea views.

Within easy reach of Dartmoor and the city of Exeter, and only
a short walk from the beach and promenade.
There is also a large park with picnic and barbecue areas.
Sporting facilities such as golf, sea fishing, sailing, ten pin bowling and
horse riding are nearby. Devon enjoys an exceptionally mild climate
and is often referred to as The English Riviera.

LOCAL ATTRACTIONS
Bicton Botanical Gardens • Woodbury Common • Dartmoor.

DIRECTIONS
M5 Motorway, Junction 30 – 8km, 8 miles from Exeter, and just three
hours' drive from London, The Midlands and South Wales.

at Puckrup Hall

The Escape Spa:

The new Escape Spa offers a luxurious range of Espa face and body treatments. With 3 treatment rooms, relaxation room and outdoor terrace, this is the perfect place for all your pampering needs. From an eyebrow shape to full spa days the choices are endless.

Livingwell Healthclub:

Our Livingwell Healthclub has excellent facilities including swimming pool, steam room, sauna, jacuzzi and fully equipped gymnasium.

Golf Club:

Our 18 hole par 70 championship golf course provides the perfect challenge for both the novice and experienced golfers, with undulating fairways and strategically placed bunkers. You'll find the Pro-shop and clubhouse bar situated within the golf facility where you can enjoy a relaxing drink after your round.

Bars And Restaurants:

The terrace bar offers a wide range of beverages along with a light menu served throughout the day. Enjoy a drink or two before entering the elegant Balharries restaurant, with its sophisticated surroundings, relaxed ambience and beautiful views over the golf course. The table d'hote menu with à la Carte choices provides the perfect finish to your days relaxation.

**Hilton Puckrup Hall Golf Club & Spa, Tewkesbury,
Gloucestershire GL20 6EL
TEL: 01684 296200
FAX: 01684 850788**

Situated in a quiet residential area, The Glenorleigh is 10 minutes' walk from both the sea front and town centre.

AA
★★★★
Guest Accommodation

• Bedrooms
All bedrooms are en suite, and have central heating, tea making facilities, colour TV and child listening. The rooms are beautifully decorated and refurbished, with your comfort in mind. Four-poster room available, and some rooms overlook the pool.

• Leisure
There is a heated swimming pool, and a games room with pool table, darts and solarium.

• Dining
The elegant dining room provides a delightful setting in which to enjoy a four-course dinner, or full English Breakfast, with a varied and interesting choice of menu daily.

The Glenorleigh, 26 Cleveland Road, Torquay, Devon TQ2 5BE
Tel: 01803 292135 • Fax: 01803 213717
E-mail: glenorleigh@btinternet.com • www.glenorleigh.co.uk

The Glenorleigh is a 15 bedroom family-run guest accommodation with a friendly and relaxed atmosphere, and guests can be sure of good food and service.

The Victorian villa has been extensively refurbished over the last few years, and offers all the facilities required by today's discerning guest whilst retaining the style and elegance of the original building.

One of the hotel's finest features is the garden and heated swimming pool, which is totally secluded and where you cannot fail to feel relaxed. There is a Mediterranean feel to the sun terrace and garden, a fact which many guests have commented upon.

The cosy bar overlooking the pool area (illuminated at night) is the ideal setting for a relaxing evening, to meet old friends or make new ones. There is a wide selection of wines, draught beers and spirits available.

The hotel is within easy reach of Torquay's seafront, theatre, harbour and shops. All are accessible on foot and the area is relatively flat. Torquay offers all the facilities expected of a modern seaside resort, including The Riviera Centre with its range of bars, pool, wave machine and constant year round temperature.

LOCAL ATTRACTIONS
• Kents Cavern • Babbacombe Model Village • Paignton Zoo • Quaywest Water Park
• Torre Abbey • Woodlands Leisure Park

DIRECTIONS
Follow the A3022 Newton Abbot to Torquay Road until you reach the traffic lights at Torre Station. Bear right here into Avenue Road. Cleveland Road is the first turning on your left.

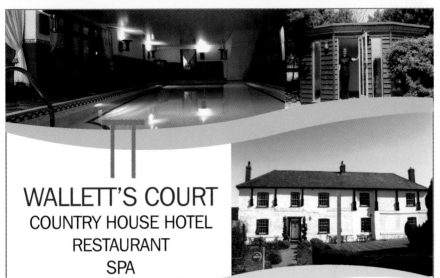

WALLETT'S COURT
COUNTRY HOUSE HOTEL
RESTAURANT
SPA

Four hundred years of history exude from the walls of the ancient manor house nestling in wild open landscape in the heart of White Cliffs Country ninety minutes from the city of London, and ten minutes from the port of Dover.

Bedrooms • Climb the Jacobean staircase to one of the three four-poster bedrooms or stroll across the courtyard to one of fourteen contemporary rooms housed in converted Kentish hay barns, stables and cowsheds surrounding the manor. Twenty-first century comforts abound, crisp cotton linen, digital channel flat screen TVs, DVD and CD players, broadband wireless internet. Lose yourself in bubbles at bath time or get energised in the shower with luxurious Essential Elements bath treats. Double/twin from £129; Single from £109.

Leisure • Chill, feel alive, de-stress, shine and glow with a massage or beauty treatment in your own cabin in the woods on the edge of the grounds overlooking the rolling hills. **Wallett's Relax** – Energise, uplift, restore and feel the energy flow through your body in the sauna, steam room and hydrotherapy pool. **Wallett's Active** – Dip into the indoor swimming pool and feel the force of the counter-current swim trainer and hydrotherapy jet. Invigorate with a session in the gym. Breathe in the sea air on the all-weather floodlit tennis court, on the croquet lawn, boules court, or on the clay shooting range.

Conference • Get together for a pow-wow, private meeting, party or brainstorming session in the Adam Room or the Conservatory. There are two rooms available, each accommodating up to 15. From £49 per person per day. Rates include morning coffee, buffet lunch, afternoon tea, meeting room and mineral water.

Dining • Eat in the conservatory, the library or in bed at breakfast, take lunch in the lounge by the fire in winter or on the terrace in summer and dine in the oak-beamed restaurant in the evening. Drink where and when you like, champagne in the bath, sundowners at cocktail hour, great whites and elegant reds with dinner.

Directions • From London and The North: Point yourself at Dover on the M2/A2 or M20/A20, when you get close to Dover follow signs for A258 Deal. Once on the A258 take the first right turn for Westcliffe and St. Margaret's-at-Cliffe, find Wallett's Court 1 mile on the right. From Dover Docks: Follow signs for A258 Deal on the flyover to the top of the cliffs. Once on the A258 take the first right turn for Westcliffe and St Margaret's-at-Cliffe, find Wallett's Court 1 mile on the right.

WALLETT'S COURT COUNTRY HOUSE HOTEL • RESTAURANT • SPA
St Margaret's-at-Cliffe, near Dover, Kent CT15 6EW
Tel: 01304 852424 • Fax: 01304 853430 • FREEPHONE (UK only) 0800 0351628
E-mail: mail@wallettscourt.com • www.wallettscourt.com

Searles Leisure Resort offers a warm welcome and superb facilities

Searles Leisure Resort has been providing quality holidays on the North West Norfolk Coast for over 50 years, and our experience shows through our excellent facilities and friendly staff.

There is a superb choice of accommodation, from luxury lodges to comfy caravans, and an award-winning Tent and Touring Park. Many of our guests return time and time again.

■ Entertainment

In the evenings you can relax with a drink in the Sundowner Bar for the resident entertainment team's main show or enjoy a quieter evening in the Mariners Bar.

There are four bars, three restaurants and a Country Club to choose from, and a selection of themed breaks, including music and dance, is also available.

■ Leisure

Our Indoor and Outdoor Pools with Spa and Sauna make relaxing after treatments easy, for the more active a fully equipped gym is also available. For those who enjoy outdoor sports there are tennis courts, bowls green, 9 hole golf course and driving range, with golf shop and Country Club.

■ Eating and Drinking

Guests on Half Board will dine in the Mariners Restaurant, which provides quality food to satisfy all tastes. During the day the Plaza café or the Country Club provide light lunches and snacks.

■ Golf Breaks

Golf Breaks can be arranged and bookings co-ordinated at the championship courses at Hunstanton and King's Lynn.

■ Local attractions

Hunstanton's sandy bathing beach just 200 metres away and the North Norfolk coast just on the doorstep for you to explore. Searles runs daily coastal trips and tours to Seal Island, other attractions include, Sandringham House, Norfolk Lavender, Houghton Hall and RSPB nature reserves.

■ Directions

Excellent road links ensure an easy journey to Hunstanton from all parts of the country. Take the A149 from King's Lynn. As you enter Hunstanton the B1161 is well signposted to the South Beach at the 1st roundabout. On reaching the 2nd roundabout carry on a further 20 metres and turn left into Searles.

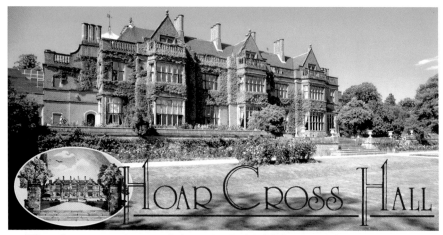

The only spa resort in a stately home in England. This graceful residence has been restored to its former glory and offers a unique combination of traditional elegance and first class service, along with the extensive facilities of a modern spa resort.

Bedrooms

There are 100 bedrooms, all with private bathroom. The range of luxury accommodation includes Superior Rooms, Masters, which have spa baths, suites with separate lounge areas and Penthouses with balconies overlooking the treetops - some have private saunas. The magnificent Royal Suite has lounge, dining hall, two separate en suite bedrooms, three balconies, private massage room and sauna.

Leisure

Two swimming pools ★ Three saunas ★ Three steam rooms ★ Two saunariums ★ Water grottos ★ Aerobics ★ Yoga ★ Large gymnasium. There is a choice of over 100 beauty treatments and therapies designed to ease the aches and pains of modern living. For day bookings contact the Reservations Team on **01283 575 678, www.edenspa.co.uk**

Golf

Golf Academy with a PGA Professional 9 Hole course, driving range and practice areas. Other activities include tennis, croquet and archery.

Conference

Residential, daily and half-day conferences catered for. Facilities include OHP, screen and flip chart. ISDN line, TV & video, and film projector and screen can all be hired.

Dining

Tasty cuisine is a top priority, with two restaurants to choose from. Enjoy à la carte dining in the evening in the original Ballroom, with its gilded ceilings and William Morris wallpaper. The extensive buffet lunch and breakfast are served in the Plantation Restaurant overlooking the pool. In the evening you can enjoy a glass of champagne, a fine brandy or your choice of drinks from the Champagne Bar which overlooks the formal gardens and terrace.

Hoar Cross Hall Spa Resort
Hoar Cross, near Yoxall, Staffordshire DE13 8QS
Reservations & Enquiries Tel: 01283 575 671
Spa Reception Tel: 01283 575 747 • Fax: 01283 575 748
email: info@hoarcross.co.uk • www.hoarcross.co.uk

Flackley Ash
Hotel and Restaurant

Georgian Country House Hotel set in beautiful countryside with croquet and putting lawns. 45 well appointed, en suite rooms including four-posters and garden suites. Warm and friendly atmosphere, fine wines and fresh local food. Visit castles, gardens, seaside and the ancient Cinque Port of Rye.

AA
★★★

• Bedrooms •

Individually furnished in the style of a traditional English country house, with double, twin rooms and suites available. Everything has been arranged for your comfort with a full range of modern facilities including:
• En suite bathroom • Remote control TV & radio
• Direct dial telephone • Trouser press • Internet Access
• Tea / Coffee making facilities • Hairdryer.

• Leisure •

• Enjoy a swim in the indoor pool, a work out in the gym and finish up by unwinding with a sauna and a session in the steam room • Gym • Spa Bath • Indoor Swimming Pool • Sauna• Steam Room
• Beauty Suite Experience a programme of soothing beauty treatments and feel tensions and stress drain away with Facials, Manicures, Pedicures, Reflexology & Aromatherapy massage from our fully trained and highly experienced therapists. We are committed to giving hotel residents priority on beauty treatments.

• Conference •

• Two Large Function Rooms • Five Meeting / Training Rooms
• Extensive free parking • Gardens and grounds of 5 acres
• Team building activities available, private and corporate.

• Dining •

• Award-winning Restaurant • Bar and Lounge areas • Conservatory dining area
Savour the delicious taste of our traditional and international cuisine cooked to perfection. Fresh local fish and seafood, home made soups, roasts and where possible locally grown seasonal vegetables. Our award-winning restaurant with views of the gardens is the perfect setting to enjoy good food and our wide choice of splendid wines. Relax, unwind and be pampered.

Peasmarsh, Rye, East Sussex TN31 6YH • Tel: 01797 230651
e-mail: enquiries@flackleyashhotel.co.uk • www.flackleyashhotel.co.uk

Flackley Ash
Hotel and Restaurant

This Georgian Country House Hotel and Restaurant is nestled deep in the South of England's countryside near Rye in East Sussex, and situated close to the historic towns and ports of Tunbridge Wells, Tenterden, Hastings, Winchelsea and Brighton. Set in the peace and quiet of beautiful countryside, yet within reach of London, the Channel Tunnel and Ferry Ports.

There are five acres of grounds for guests to enjoy.

For relaxation and spa breaks, we can boast a gym, beauty suite, sauna, steam room, spa bath and indoor swimming pool for those looking to tone up or relax in comfort.
We are happy to cater for special occasions and business events, with two large, elegantly designed and thoughtfully laid out function rooms, licensed for Civil Weddings, and a further five purpose-built meeting / syndicate rooms. We take great pride in offering professional serving staff and catering from our award-winning kitchens for up to 130 people, for business or pleasure.

Eating, meeting, marrying or touring – whatever brings you to this historic part of England, our staff will make you feel comfortable, relaxed and at home. We pride ourselves on the facilities and friendly service provided to all those visiting or staying with us.

LOCAL ATTRACTIONS

- Rye Historic Port, 3 miles
- Winchelsea, 3 miles
- Hastings Old Town, 8 miles
- Bodiam Castle, 10 miles
- Battle Abbey, 13 miles
- Leeds Castle, 30 miles
- Canterbury Cathedral, 35 miles
- Hever Castle, 38 miles
- Great Dixter Gardens, 5 miles
- Sissinghurst Manor, 15 miles

DIRECTIONS

From the North
From the M25 orbital motorway take Junction 5 on to the A21 signposted Tunbridge Wells/Hastings. Follow this until you come to Flimwell. At the traffic lights turn left onto the A268 and continue to Newenden. 500 yards after the narrow bridge in Newenden, take the left turn signposted Rye (A268). Flackley Ash is on the left hand side when entering Peasmarsh.

From the South
When coming from Rye take the A268 towards London - the hotel is on the right side in the village of Peasmarsh. Free parking is available at the hotel.
Ashford International Station 22 miles; Channel Tunnel 34 miles; Heathrow Airport 84 miles; Gatwick Airport 48 miles.

Best Western
THE BELL in DRIFFIELD

16 individually styled suites and bedrooms
with free internet access, including
three disabled-friendly rooms.
Non-smoking rooms and room service
available. Other facilities include parking and lifts

❖ Leisure

The hotel offers an unrivalled range of leisure facilities including swimming pool, sauna, steam room, jacuzzi and full Nautilus Gym. Classic, Luxury and De luxe Spa Days are available. Refreshments and lunch included. Robes, towels and slippers provided.

Other treatments available: Rasul Steam Treatment, Physioacoustic Chair to alleviate pain and stress, and Floatation Chamber for deep relaxation. The Fragrant Retreat offers additional spa, reflex and beauty treatments. Discounts available on Spa Facilities for hotel guests.

❖ Conferences

As a venue full of character, The Bell is hard to beat. This 18th century Listed coaching inn is furnished with antiques, and its meeting rooms are of architectural importance. Can accommodate up to 150 delegates. Equipment includes LCD Projector, Fax, Flip chart, OHP, Photocopier, Screen, Video.

❖ Dining

Beautiful oak panelled restaurant offering fine dining, morning coffee a speciality, unrivalled carvery lunch, traditional Sunday lunch and evening bar meals, and The Oak Bar featuring around 300 malt whiskies and hand pulled cask-conditioned real ales.

**Best Western
Bell in Driffield Hotel
Market Place, Driffield,
East Yorkshire YO25 6AN
Tel: 01377 256661
Fax: 01377 253228
e-mail: bell@bestwestern.co.uk
www.bw-bellhotel.co.uk**

AA
★★★
HOTEL

Best Western
THE BELL in DRIFFIELD

❖ Welcome...

An 18th century Listed hotel, situated in the centre of Driffield, 'The Capital of the Wolds', tastefully furnished with antiques and fine arts. Tardis-like in appearance it boasts 16 individually styled suites and bedrooms, a beautiful oak panelled dining room offering fine dining in elegant surroundings, The Oak Bar, where you can choose a tipple from a Whisky Menu featuring 300 malt whiskies, or choose from a range of hand pulled-cask-conditioned real ales. Situated within easy reach of historic York and Beverley.

Driffield Spa welcomes you to a world of calm and relaxation. Relax, unwind and get away from all the constraints and pressures with a revitalising Spa Day at our luxurious health spa. We aim to improve your health, well-being and physical condition by means of water, heat, massage and treatments. Spa Days include refreshments, lunch, towels, robes, slippers, and soaps, and usually last around 5 to 8 hours.

There is an unrivalled range of leisure facilities, including floatation tank, indoor swimming pool, full Nautilus gym, an Holistic Beauty Salon, squash court and snooker room etc.

Spa Day Rates range from £50 to £100 per person, and rooms are from £80 single and from £100 double/twin, superior rooms from £112.

Special Cleansing Spa Break £340 – two nights Dinner, Bed and Breakfast based on two people sharing, includes use of swimming pool, Jacuzzi, steam room, sauna, super spa and full Nautilus gym.

The Hotel is not suitable for children under 16 years old.

❖ Local Attractions

Driffield is considered to be the Capital of the beautiful and peaceful Yorkshire Wolds which stretch lazily from the chalk cliffs at Flamborough to the Humber Estuary at Hessle, taking in a huge area rich in history, colour, interesting people and beautiful buildings. There are some of the most picturesque villages and lively market towns in the country in this area, some well known, some well off the beaten track

There is an excellent array of Sporting Facilities, and the town plays host to many regional fixtures including Rugby, Golf, Hockey, Bowls, Swimming, Running and Show Jumping.

❖ Directions

Exit M62, Junction 37 A614 to Bridlington, left at roundabout to Driffield, and continue into town centre.
Humberside Airport 31 miles, Leeds/Bradford Airports 46 miles. Driffield Railway Station close by.

highland *escape*

If your heart beats for the Highlands...

Enjoy all that's best in the Highlands in comfortable and relaxing surroundings.

Overlooking the mouth of River Brora, the Royal Marine is a charming country house hotel designed by renowned Scottish architect Sir Robert Lorimer in 1913. Great care has been taken in the restoration of the original antique furniture, and the building's woodwork and panelling glow with the warmth of log fires and convivial company. Passing under the wooden arches of the entrance hall and ascending the grand staircase, guests step back in time to refined living of a bygone era.

The hotel is especially attractive to sportsmen: Golf can be arranged on the best of Highland links courses, including Brora, Royal Dornoch, Golspie and Tain. The Highland Wildcat Trails in Golspie offer purpose-built single track for mountain bikers of all skill levels. For the fishermen, the hotel has boats on Loch Brora and can arrange fly fishing on the tidal stretches of both Brora and Helmsdale rivers, together with nearby lochs. The surrounding hills provide excellent walking and the hotel's leisure club includes an indoor pool, sauna, steam room, Jacuzzi, solarium and gym. Massages and beauty treatments can also be arranged.

Also available are luxury two-bedroom apartments at the new development at The Links with magnificent views across Brora golf course and the Dornoch Firth. Guests in the apartments enjoy the best of both worlds, either self-catering or access to the hotel's restaurants, bars and leisure club.

LOCAL ATTRACTIONS:

Brora is ideal as a centre for touring the Northern Highlands and the Orkney Islands. The sparsely populated region abounds with birds and wildlife, and the rock formations are of particular interest to geologists and fossil collectors. There are miles of sandy beach with seals and dolphins. Clynelish and Glenmorangie Malt Whisky Distilleries offer daily tours and just five miles south lies Dunrobin Castle and Gardens with daily falconry displays.

DIRECTIONS:

Situated midway between Inverness and John o'Groats on the main A9, Brora is easily reached by car, train, bus or direct flights into Inverness from most major UK cities

We are 1 hour's drive north of Inverness on the A9. Take first right after the bridge over the River Brora. Continue for 200 metres until you get to the hotel.

• Inverness airport - 72 miles • Brora train station - $\frac{1}{2}$ mile

• Inverness - 56 miles • Aberdeen - 150 miles • Glasgow 220 miles

Looking for Holiday Accommodation?

for details of hundreds of properties throughout the UK, visit our website

www.holidayguides.com

Golfing
Holidays

where
eagles
dare

At the heart of Royal Deeside there is a special place where buzzards soar with eagles and the land rises and falls gracefully.

In the foothills of the Scottish Highlands near Aberdeen, Inchmarlo's spectacular 18-hole Laird's course follows the natural twists and turns of the undulating countryside creating a truly breath-taking golfing experience.

INCHMARLO
GOLF CLUB
ROYAL DEESIDE

- **Stunning Laird's 18-hole championship course**
- **Challenging Queen's 9-hole course**
- **Floodlit 30-bay driving range**
- **Fully stocked golf shop**
- **Professional tuition**
- **Corporate event management**
- **Accommodation available nightly/weekly etc**
- **Gillies Restaurant - Open to the public**
- **Golf Societies welcome Monday - Friday (prior booking essential)**

Inchmarlo • Banchory • Royal Deeside • AB31 4BQ • Scotland
Tel: 01330 826424 • www.inchmarlo.com • info@inchmarlo.com

GOLF CLUB

Mere

Mere Golf & Country Club

From the welcoming yet peaceful grounds, the friendly service, the five star food and wines and the fact that you are spoilt for choice when it comes to an unusually large venue with superb leisure facilities, including a fitness studio, swimming pools and tennis court, a golfing experience at Mere will be a memorable occasion.

For an exhilarating round of golf, it's hard to beat the 6,817 yard, par 71 course created out of 150 acres of Cheshire parkland in 1934 by none other than Open Champions James Braid and George Duncan.

It would be hard to find a more picturesque course than Mere, with its parkland setting alongside the beautiful lake which gives the course its name. Mere offers cleverly sited hazards and some of the best greens in Britain.

Over the years Mere has hosted several major events, including the 2001 Dan Technology Seniors and the Tournament of Champions, and is a regional qualifying course for the 2009 Open at Turnberry.

- Individual and Corporate Golfing Packages.
- Clubs, Trolleys and Buggies for hire. Caddies available.
- Unique Floating Golf Ball Range.
- Extensively stocked Professional Shop. • Resident Professional.
- First class Restaurant and Conference & Banqueting facilities

One of the most exclusive leisure and sporting facilities in the North West.

**Mere Golf
& Country Club**
Chester Road, Mere
Knutsford, Cheshire WA16 6LJ
Telephone: 01565 830 155
Fax: 01565 830 713
E-mail: enquiries@meregolf.co.uk
www.meregolf.co.uk

HOTEL

21 individually
decorated bedrooms

Superb food using
fresh local produce

Overlooking
Studland Bay

Private path to beaches

Pets welcome
& beautiful walks

2 all-weather
Tennis Courts

Golf Course
& Riding Stables nearby

Manor House Hotel
STUDLAND BAY DORSET

★ ★ ★

Old fashioned charm & service

3, 5 & 7 day Bargain Breaks

" *Welcome to one of the most beautiful places in England. I can't take the credit for the glorious views and the beaches. But I am proud to provide a comfortable and relaxing hotel with good food and attentive but informal service, to give you the break you deserve.* '
Andrew Purkis

WINNER OF CLUBHOUSE OF THE YEAR 2007

the ultimate golf experience...

Whittlebury Park

Near Towcester,
Northamptonshire.
NN12 8WP
Tel:　01327 850000
Email: enquiries@whittlebury.com
Web:　www.whittlebury.com

36 Holes of Championship Golf
Indoor Golf & Tuition Centre
2 Tier Floodlit Driving Range
Individual & Corporate Memberships
Corporate & Society Events
Summer & Winter Green Fees 7 days/week
Open to all Visitors and Guests every day

Artists, photographers, birders, walkers, cyclists, fishermen, golfers and especially families, find Berwick an architectural gem, an ideal centre for basing their holiday. On a clear day you can see no fewer than three magnificent castles, suggesting exciting days out, from the ramparts which surround the old part of the town and which form an excellent source for enjoyable walks. Our secluded quality maisonette and studio flat (first and second floors, sleeping up to 12) offer a comfortable choice of accommodation, amazingly within a few minutes' easy walk of shops, restaurants, golf course, beaches etc. See our website for more details and ideas.

**2 The Courtyard, Church Street,
Berwick-upon-Tweed TD15 1EE • Tel: 01289 308737
www.berwickselfcatering.co.uk**

Visit the FHG website
www.holidayguides.com
for details of the wide choice of accommodation
featured in the full range of FHG titles

GOLF CLUB

Trentham Park Golf Club
Trentham Park, Trentham, Stoke-on-Trent ST4 8AE

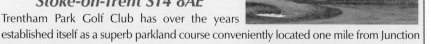

Trentham Park Golf Club has over the years established itself as a superb parkland course conveniently located one mile from Junction 15 on the M6, approximately halfway between Birmingham and Manchester.

It is set in the former grounds of Trentham Hall, once the seat of the Duke of Sutherland. It is an 18-hole, Par 71 course. The greens have been resdesigned and re-bunkered by Steve Marnoch, the international golf course expert. The club has a reputation for making societies and visitors welcome, and the food is as good as the course. The clubhouse has been refurbished and offers first-class facilities for its members and visitors.

Society Packages from £30 per player • All enquiries welcome

Tel: 01782 658800
www.trenthamparkgolfclub.com
admin@trenthamparkgolfclub.com

HOTEL

ROUND OFF A PERFECT DAY

Enjoy a break on the invigorating Heritage Coast. Play the challenging, mature 18-hole seaside course designed by the legendary James Braid. Guests in the hotel can enjoy concessionary rates at Aldeburgh Golf Club, one of the top 100 courses in the British Isles or play the Suffolk Tour including Ipswich, Woodbridge and Felixstowe Ferry. A warm welcome, comfortable en suite rooms and good food.

The Thorpeness Hotel, Thorpeness, Aldeburgh, Suffolk IP16 4NH
Tel: 01728 452176 • Fax: 01728 453868
e-mail: info@thorpeness.co.uk • www.thorpeness.co.uk

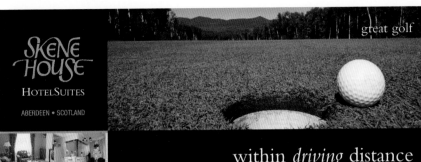

Publisher's note

While every effort is made to ensure accuracy, we regret that FHG Guides cannot accept responsibility for errors, misrepresentations or omissions in our entries or any consequences thereof. Prices in particular should be checked.
We will follow up complaints but cannot act as arbiters or agents for either party.

Unwind and enjoy beautiful Portpatrick in style and comfort

Once you have experienced the magic of Portpatrick, you will be sure to return. Situated on the beautiful Galloway coast, this friendly place has something for everyone. Many superb golf courses including Portpatrick Dunskey.

Our three cottages form a most elegant and private complex, a few minutes' walk from the sea. With modern fittings and decor, plus extensive decked terracing and barbecue facilities, the accommodation is a must for the discerning visitor.

Ben Ma Cree

Fully renovated and extended, the property enjoys fabulous sea views and has a spiral staircase between the main floors.
4 bedrooms • sleeps 7/9

Clanna Susàidh

New cottage with full disabled access, gas central heating. Decked patio area with barbecue and seating.
2 bedrooms • sleeps 4/6

All properties have
- TV, video
- Washer, dryer
- Dishwasher
- Fridge, freezer
- CD player
- Microwave

Cots/high chairs available

Linen provided

Graeme An Tiaoseach

Newly built in traditional style, with central heating and log-burning stove.
2 bedrooms • sleeps 4/6

For details contact **Graham and Sue Fletcher, 468 Otley Road, Leeds LS16 8AE 0113 230 1391 or 07976 671926 info@gscottages.co.uk www.gscottages.co.uk**

STB ★★★★

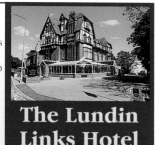

Readers are requested to mention this FHG
guidebook when seeking accommodation

The FHG Directory of Website Addresses

on pages 157-179 is a useful quick reference guide for
holiday accommodation with e-mail and/or website details

Visit the FHG website
www.holidayguides.com
for details of the wide choice of accommodation
featured in the full range of FHG titles

HOTEL

Fit4All Wexford is located in a tranquil waterside setting by the River Slaney in Ferrycarrig, Wexford. This purpose-built facility features a modern, customised Training Studio and a lodge for individuals on overnight programmes or fitness breaks.

The studio complex has been designed to the highest specifications with modern décor throughout. There is a wide range of equipment and facilities, carefully designed for fitness purposes but with privacy, relaxation and luxury.

Reception area • Relaxation area • Shiatsu Massage Chair
Private Consultation Rooms • Sauna • Steam room
Canadian Hot Tub • Training Studio • Kinesis Wall by Technogym

The Holiday Lodge is located in the idyllic tranquil waterside setting of Ferrycarrig, Wexford and is the perfect relaxation sanctuary for holiday breaks, overnight packages and fitness and spa breaks. The modern decor and high standard of comfort are designed to provide perfect relaxation as a stand-alone break or as part of a fitness and spa break. No pets or children under 14.

Two double/twin rooms with en suite shower • High spec kitchen and appliances
CD system • LCD TV • PC connectivity • Disabled access throughout

Knockahone
Barntown
Wexford
Ireland
00 353 (0)53 9172313
info@fit4all.ie
www.fit4all.ie

Other specialised holiday guides from **FHG**

Recommended **INNS & PUBS** OF BRITAIN

Recommended **COUNTRY HOTELS** OF BRITAIN

Recommended **SHORT BREAK HOLIDAYS** IN BRITAIN

The bestselling and original **PETS WELCOME!**

The **GOLF GUIDE,** Where to Play, Where to Stay IN BRITAIN & IRELAND

COAST & COUNTRY HOLIDAYS

SELF-CATERING HOLIDAYS IN BRITAIN

BED & BREAKFAST STOPS

CARAVAN & CAMPING HOLIDAYS

CHILDREN WELCOME! Family Holiday & Days Out Guide

Published annually: available in all good bookshops or direct from the publisher:
FHG Guides, Abbey Mill Business Centre, Seedhill, Paisley PA1 1TJ
Tel: 0141 887 0428 • Fax: 0141 889 7204
E-mail: admin@fhguides.co.uk • Web: www.holidayguides.com

Ratings & Awards

For the first time ever the AA, VisitBritain, VisitScotland, and the Wales Tourist Board will use a single method of assessing and rating serviced accommodation. Irrespective of which organisation inspects an establishment the rating awarded will be the same, using a common set of standards, giving a clear guide of what to expect. The RAC is no longer operating an Hotel inspection and accreditation business.

Accommodation Standards: Star Grading Scheme

Using a scale of 1-5 stars the objective quality ratings give a clear indication of accommodation standard, cleanliness, ambience, hospitality, service and food, This shows the full range of standards suitable for every budget and preference, and allows visitors to distinguish between the quality of accommodation and facilities on offer in different establishments. All types of board and self-catering accommodation are covered, including hotels, B&Bs, holiday parks, campus accommodation, hostels, caravans and camping, and boats.

VisitBritain and the regional tourist boards, enjoyEngland.com, VisitScotland and VisitWales, and the AA have full details of the grading system on their websites

The more stars, the higher level of quality

★★★★★
exceptional quality, with a degree of luxury

★★★★
excellent standard throughout

★★★
very good level of quality and comfort

★★
good quality, well presented and well run

★
acceptable quality; simple, practical, no frills

National Accessible Scheme

If you have particular mobility, visual or hearing needs, look out for the National Accessible Scheme. You can be confident of finding accommodation or attractions that meet your needs by looking for the following symbols.

 Typically suitable for a person with sufficient mobility to climb a flight of steps but would benefit from fixtures and fittings to aid balance

 Typically suitable for a person with restricted walking ability and for those that may need to use a wheelchair some of the time and can negotiate a maximum of three steps

 Typically suitable for a person who depends on the use of a wheelchair and transfers unaided to and from the wheelchair in a seated position. This person may be an independent traveller

 Typically suitable for a person who depends on the use of a wheelchair in a seated position. This person also requires personal or mechanical assistance (eg carer, hoist).

England Board

London

London
(Central & Greater)

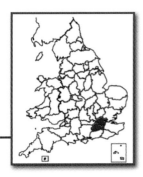

FHG Guides

publish a large range of well-known accommodation guides.
We will be happy to send you details or you can use the order form
at the back of this book.

London

Stavrou Hotels

Gower Hotel

129 SUSSEX GARDENS,
HYDE PARK, LONDON W2 2RX

Tel: 0207 262 2262
Fax: 0207 262 2006

E-Mail: gower@stavrouhotels.co.uk
Website: www.stavrouhotels.co.uk

The Gower Hotel is a small family-run Hotel, centrally located, within two minutes' walk from Paddington Station, which benefits from the Heathrow Express train "15 minutes to and from Heathrow Airport". Excellently located for sightseeing London's famous sights and shops, Hyde Park, Madame Tussaud's, Oxford Street, Harrods, Marble Arch, Buckingham Palace and many more close by. All rooms have private shower and WC, radio, TV (includes satellite and video channels), direct dial telephone and tea and coffee facilities. All recently refurbished and fully centrally heated. 24 hour reception.

All prices are inclusive of a large traditional English Breakfast & VAT

Single Rooms from £30-£79 • Double/Twin Rooms from £60-£89 • Triple & Family Rooms from £80
Discount available on 3 nights or more if you mention this advert

Queens Hotel

33 Anson Road, Tufnell Park,
LONDON N7
Tel: 0207 607 4725
Fax: 0207 697 9725

E-Mail: queens@stavrouhotels.co.uk
Website: www.stavrouhotels.co.uk

The Queens Hotel is a large double-fronted Victorian building standing in its own grounds five minutes' walk from Tufnell Park Station. Quietly situated with ample car parking spaces; 15 minutes to West End and close to London Zoo, Hampstead and Highgate. Two miles from Kings Cross and St Pancras Stations. Many rooms en suite. **All prices include full English Breakfast plus VAT. Children at reduced rates. Discounts on longer stays.**

Single Rooms from £30-£55 • Double/Twin Rooms from £40-£69 • Triple & Family Rooms from £20 per person

Stavrou Hotels is a family-run group of hotels.
We offer quality and convenience at affordable rates.
A VERY WARM WELCOME AWAITS YOU

Our hotels accept all major Credit cards, but some charges may apply.

The Athena

110-114 SUSSEX GARDENS, HYDE PARK, LONDON W2 1UA
Tel: 0207 706 3866; Fax: 0207 262 6143
E-Mail: athena@stavrouhotels.co.uk www.stavrouhotels.co.uk

TREAT YOURSELVES TO A QUALITY HOTEL AT AFFORDABLE PRICES

The Athena is a newly completed family run hotel in a restored Victorian building. Professionally designed, including a lift to all floors and exquisitely decorated, we offer our clientele the ambience and warm hospitality necessary for a relaxing and enjoyable stay. Ideally located in a beautiful tree-lined avenue, extremely well-positioned for sightseeing London's famous sights and shops; Hyde Park, Madame Tussaud's, Oxford Street, Marble Arch, Knightsbridge, Buckingham Palace and many more are all within walking distance.

Travel connections to all over London are excellent, with Paddington and Lancaster Gate Stations, Heathrow Express, A2 Airbus and buses minutes away.
Our tastefully decorated bedrooms have en suite bath/shower rooms, satellite colour TV, bedside telephones, tea/coffee making facilities. Hairdryers, trouser press, laundry and ironing facilities available on request. Ample car parking available.

Stavrou Hotels is a family-run group of hotels.
We offer quality and convenience at affordable rates.
A VERY WARM WELCOME AWAITS YOU.

Single Rooms from £50-£89
Double/Twin Rooms from £64-£99
Triple & Family Rooms from £25 per person
All prices include full English breakfast plus VAT.

Our hotels accept all major Credit cards, but some charges may apply.

HOTELS

HOLLYBUSH HOTELS (Reservations 0845 88 00 211).

Ther perfect destination to enjoy short breaks and holidays with like minded people. Hollybush hotels offers some of the best location in the South and South West for you to take a short break. Our dedicated sales department are there to help you arrange the perfect holiday. Contact our reservations hotline or visit our website for more information or to order your brochure. SEE ALSO COLOUR ADVERT AT THE START OF THE GUIDE..

Rates: from £25 to £40 single, £40 to £50 double, £55 to £65 triple and £75 for a quad room.
www.hollybushhotels.co.uk

B&B

1/12

CENTRAL LONDON. Manor Court Hotel, 7 Clanricarde Gardens, London W2 4JJ (020 7792 3361 or 020 7727 5407; Fax: 020 7229 2875).
Situated off the Bayswater Road, opposite Kensington Palace. Family-run B&B Hotel within walking distance of Hyde Park and Kensington Gardens. Very near to Notting Hill underground. All rooms have colour TV and telephone. We accept Visa, Mastercard, Diners Club and American Express Cards.
Rates: from £25 to £40 single, £40 to £50 double, £55 to £65 triple and £75 for a quad room.
• Open all year.
ETC ◆
e-mail: enquiries@manorcourthotel.com

HOTEL

LONDON. Elizabeth Hotel, 37 Eccleston Square, Victoria, London SW1V 1PB (020 7828 6812; Fax: 020 7828 6814).
Quiet, convenient town house overlooking the magnificent gardens of Eccleston Square. Only a short walk from Buckingham Palace and other tourist attractions. Easy access to Knightsbridge, Oxford Street and Regent Street. Extremely reasonable rates in a fantastic location. Visa, Mastercard, Switch, Delta and JCB are all accepted. SEE ALSO COLOUR ADVERT.
ETC/AA ★★★
e-mail: info@elizabethhotel.com
www.elizabethhotel.com

HOTEL

1/12

LONDON. Athena Hotel, 110-114 Sussex Gardens, Hyde Park, London W2 1UA (020 7706 3866; Fax: 020 7262 6143).
Treat yourselves to a quality hotel at affordable prices. The Athena is a family-run hotel which is newly completed in a restored Victorian building, professionally designed, including a lift to all floors, and exquisitely decorated. We offer our clientele the ambience and warmth necessary for relaxing and an enjoyable stay with our warm hospitality. Ideally located in a beautiful tree-lined avenue, extremely well positioned for sight-seeing London's finest sights. Our tastefully decorated bedrooms have en suite bath/shower rooms, satellite colour TV, bedside telephones, tea/coffee making facilities. Hairdryers, trouser press, laundry and ironing facilities available on request. Ample car space. SEE ALSO INSIDE FRONT COVER.
RATES: Single room £50 - £65. Double /twin £64 - £95, triple/family room from £28 per person. All prices include a full traditional breakfast + VAT.
ETC ◆◆◆
e-mail: athena@stavrouhotels.co.uk   www.stavrouhotels.co.uk

FREE or REDUCED RATE entry to Holiday Visits and Attractions – see our
READERS' OFFER VOUCHERS on pages 181-218

London

HOTEL
1/12 🐴 ♿

LONDON. Queens Hotel, 33 Anson Road, Tufnell Park, London N7 (020 7607 4725; Fax: 020 7697 9725).
Family-run hotel in large double-fronted Victorian building four minutes walk to the underground and sightseeing attractions. London Zoo, Regent's Park, Hampstead and Highgate villages, the canals and much more of historic London easily reached. Most rooms have en suite facilities and are clean and well maintained. Central heating, TV lounge and facilities for tea/coffee. Garden at rear. SEE ALSO COLOUR ADVERT.
Rates: Singles from £30-£55, double/twin rooms from £40-£69; triple and family rooms from £20 per person, depending on season. Includes full English breakfast and VAT. Children half-price.

ETC ◆◆
e-mail: queens@stavrouhotels.co.uk   www.stavrouhotels.co.uk

HOTEL
1/12 🐴 ♿

LONDON. Gower Hotel, 129 Sussex Gardens, Hyde Park, London W2 2RX (020 7262 2262; Fax: 020 7262 2006).
The Gower is a small family-run hotel centrally located within two minutes of Paddington Station which benefits from the Heathrow Express train - "15 minutes to and from Heathrow Airport". Excellently located for sightseeing London's famous sights and shops, Hyde Park, Madame Tussauds, Harrods, Oxford Street, Marble Arch, Buckingham Palace and many more all nearby. All rooms have private shower and WC, radio, TV (satellite and video channels), direct dial telephones, tea/coffee making facilities. All are recently refurbished and fully centrally heated. 24 hour reception. We look forward to seeing you. SEE ALSO COLOUR ADVERT.
Rates: Single rooms from £30 to £79, double/twin from £60 to £89, triple and family rooms from £80. All prices are per person and are inclusive of VAT and a large traditional English breakfast. Credit cards welcome.

ETC ◆◆
e-mail: gower@stavrouhotels.co.uk   www.stavrouhotels.co.uk

symbols

Months open (eg:4/10 means April to October)

🐕 Pets Welcome
🐎 Children Welcome
♿ Suitable for Disabled
🚭 Totally non-smoking
🍷 Licensed

board

Cornwall

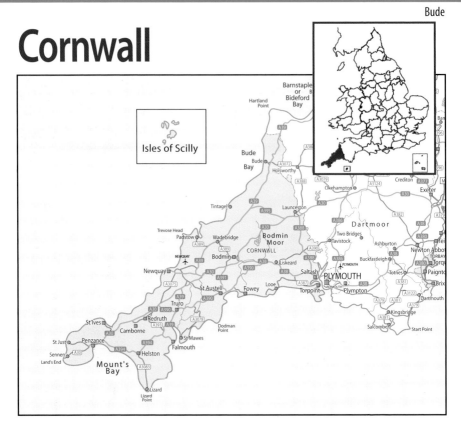

Trencreek Farmhouse - 01840 230219

Comfortable farmhouse offering homely and relaxed family atmosphere. Situated in quiet and peaceful surroundings yet within easy reach of Crackington Haven. Well placed for easy access to coastal and countryside walks. Family, double and twin-bedded rooms, most en suite, all with tea/coffee making facilities. Two comfortable lounges. Games room. Separate diningroom. Generous portions of freshly prepared, home-cooked farmhouse food.
Children welcome, special rates for under 12s.
Spring and Autumn breaks available. Non-smoking.

**Margaret and Richard Heard,
Trencreek Farmhouse, St Gennys, Bude EX23 0AY**

Looking for holiday accommodation?

for details of hundreds of properties
throughout the UK including
comprehensive coverage of all areas of Scotland try:

www.holidayguides.com

Family-friendly hotel set in 4 acres of Cornish countryside

Wringford Down

Hat Lane, Cawsand,
Cornwall PL10 1LE
Tel: 01752 822287

Located on the Rame peninsula in an Area of Outstanding Natural Beauty with tiny Cornish fishing villages, dramatic cliff top walks and secluded sandy bays.

- 11 suites, some within main building and others in adjacent chalets. All have private bathrooms.

- Well stocked bar, and restaurant serving excellent home-cooked food.

- Well equipped indoor and outdoor play areas with swings, slides, soft toys, ride-on toys, ball pool, playhouse etc; pool and table tennis tables for the older children. There is also a tennis court, which can be used for playing tennis, but which spends most of its time as a playground.

- Indoor pool and a smaller paddling pool, kept at a nicely warm 29 deg C. The pool is open from just before Easter until just after the October half term break.

- Television lounge and a playroom with books, board games and a piano.

- Courtyard room with a pool table and an adults-only room off the bar with a bar billiards table and dartboard.

FARMHOUSE B&B

BUDE. Margaret and Richard Heard, Trencreek Farmhouse, St Gennys, Bude EX23 0AY (01840 230219).
Comfortable farmhouse offering homely and relaxed family atmosphere. Situated in quiet and peaceful surroundings yet within easy reach of Crackington Haven. Well placed for easy access to coastal and countryside walks. Family, double and twin-bedded rooms, most en suite, all with tea/coffee making facilities. Two comfortable lounges. Games room. Separate diningroom. Generous portions of freshly prepared, home-cooked farmhouse food. SEE ALSO COLOUR ADVERT.
Rates: Spring and Autumn breaks available
• Children welcome, special rates for under 12s • Non-smoking

HOTEL   1/12

CAMELFORD. Bowood Park Hotel & Golf Course, Camelford PL32 9RF (01840 213017).
Set in 230 acres of ancient deer park in fashionable North Cornwall. 3 Star hotel with 31 luxury en suite rooms. Championship golf course, winner of Golf Monthly's 'Gold Award'. Visitors welcome – reduced green fees for hotel guests. Fine dining restaurant with a daily-changing menu. Room, breakfast, dinner and golf packages available at competitive rates. SEE ALSO COLOUR ADVERT IN GOLF SECTION.
ETC/AA ★★★ *HOTEL*
e-mail: info@bowoodpark.org   www.bowoodpark.org

HOTEL   1/12

CAWSAND. Wringford Down Hotel, Hat Lane, Cawsand PL10 1LE (01752 822287).
Located on the Rame peninsula in an Area of Outstanding Natural Beauty with tiny Cornish fishing villages, dramatic cliff top walks and secluded sandy bays. 11 suites, some within main building and others in adjacent chalets. All have private bathrooms. Well stocked bar, and restaurant serving excellent home-cooked food. Well equipped indoor and outdoor play areas with swings, slides, soft toys, ride-on toys, ball pool, playhouse etc; pool and table tennis tables for the older children. There is also a tennis court, which can be used for playing tennis, but which spends most of its time as a playground. Indoor pool and a smaller paddling pool, kept at a nicely warm 29 deg C. The pool is open from just before Easter until just after the October half term break. Television lounge and a playroom with books, board games and a piano. Courtyard room with a pool table and an adults-only room off the bar with a bar billiards table and dartboard. SEE ALSO COLOUR ADVERT.
AA ★★★
e-mail: accommodation@wringforddown.co.uk   www.cornwallholidays.co.uk

GUEST HOUSE   1/12

NEWQUAY. Karen and John, Pensalda Guest House, 98 Henver Road, Newquay TR7 3BL (Tel & Fax: 01637 874601).
Take a break in the heart of Cornwall. A warm and friendly welcome awaits at Pensalda. Situated on the main A3058 road, an ideal location from which to explore the finest coastline in Europe. Close to airport and the Eden Project. Double and family rooms available, all en suite, all with TV, tea/coffee making facilities, including two chalets set in a lovely garden. Fire certificate. Large car park. Licensed. Central heating. SEE ALSO COLOUR ADVERT
Rates: Bed and Breakfast from £23. Special offer breaks November to March (excluding Christmas and New Year).
• Non-smoking
ETC ★★★
e-mail: karen_pensalda@yahoo.co.uk   www.pensalda-guesthouse.co.uk

GUEST HOUSE   1/12

ST AGNES. Dorothy Gill-Carey, Penkerris, Penwinnick Road, St Agnes TR5 0PA (Tel & Fax: 01872 552262).
A creeper-clad B&B hotel/guest house with lawned garden in unspoilt Cornish village. A home from home offering real food, comfortable bedrooms with facilities (TV, radio, kettle, H&C). Dining room serving breakfast, with dinner available by arrangement. Bright cosy lounge with a log fire in winter - colour TV, video and piano. Licensed. Ample parking. Dramatic cliff walks, sandy beaches, surfing - one km/10 minutes' walk. Easy to find on the B3277 road from big roundabout on the A30 and just by the village sign. SEE ALSO COLOUR ADVERT.
Rates: Bed and Breakfast from £20 to £35 per night; Dinner available from £17.50.
• Open all year • Self-catering also available in Perranporth
ETC/AA ★★
e-mail: info@penkerris.co.uk   www.penkerris.co.uk

Readers are requested to mention this FHG guidebook when seeking accommodation

Devon

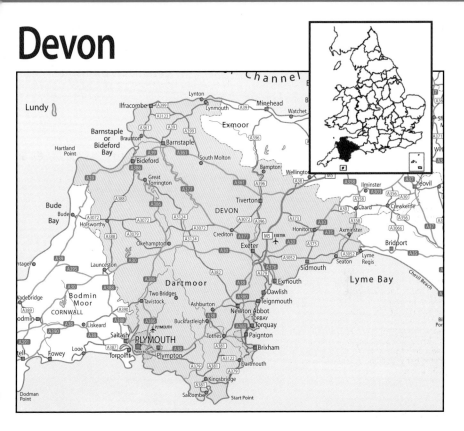

Devon is unique, with two different coastlines: bare rugged cliffs, white pebble beaches, stretches of golden sands, and the Jurassic Coast, England's first natural World Heritage Site. Glorious countryside: green rolling hills, bustling market towns and villages, thatched, white-washed cottages and traditional Devon longhouses. Wild and wonderful moorland: Dartmoor, in the south, embraces wild landscapes and picture-postcard villages; Exmoor in the north combines breathtaking, rugged coastline with wild heather moorland. Step back in time and discover historic cities, myths and legends, seafaring characters like Drake and Raleigh, and settings for novels by Agatha Christie and Conan Doyle.

Devon is home to an amazing and diverse range of birds. Enjoy special organised birdwatching trips, perhaps on board a RSPB Avocet Cruise or a vintage tram. Devon is the walking county of the South West – imagine drifts of bluebells lit by dappled sunlight, the smell of new mown hay, the sound of the sea, crisp country walks followed by a roaring fire and hot 'toddies'! If pedal power is your choice, you will discover exciting off-road cycling, leisurely afternoon rides, and challenging long distance routes such as the Granite Way along Dartmoor, the Grand Western Canal and the coastal Exmouth to Budleigh Circuit.

Please mention **BRITAIN'S BEST HOLIDAYS**
when making enquiries about accommodation featured in these pages

Umberleigh

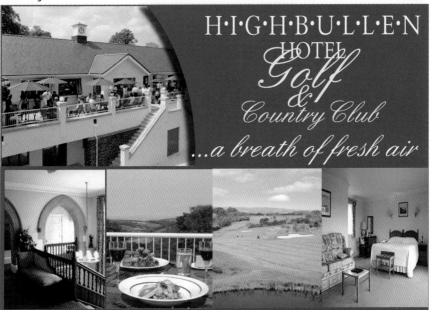

Highbullen Hotel, Golf & Country Club is beautifully set in a richly wooded 200 acre parkland estate. Boasting breathtaking views towards the romantic Devon landscapes of Exmoor and Dartmoor, the 42 bedroom hotel is truly a hidden treasure, nestling between the Mole and Taw valleys in mature wooded seclusion. Few establishments in the South of England can match the wealth of sporting and leisure facilities available on site at Highbullen.

• Double or twin-bedded room with private bath, central heating, TV and direct dial telephone. Seasonal Breaks available from November to March.

• Elegant Restaurant... Terraced Brasserie, offering a wealth of dining options, Highbullen is synonymous with fine food.

• Superb award-winning 18 hole par 68 golf course, five miles of salmon and trout-fishing, indoor and outdoor tennis courts, including four new grass courts to Wimbledon specifications. Fitness suite, aerobics studio, indoor and outdoor swimming pools, health and beauty spa, squash, indoor bowls, croquet, indoor putting green, golf simulator, boules, snooker, sauna, steam room, jacuzzi – the list goes on... our sporting and leisure professionals are there to cater for your every need.

• The whole ethos at Highbullen is to let you decide exactly what you want from your stay, whether it's lazing in the quiet spot on the river with a cold bottle of Chablis, or playing three hard sets of tennis before a light Brasserie lunch.

Highbullen Hotel, Chittlehamholt, Umberleigh, North Devon EX37 9HD
Tel: 01769 540 561 Fax: 01769 540 492 • E-mail: info@highbullen.co.uk
www.highbullen.co.uk

HOTEL

1/12 🐕 🪀 ♿ 🚭 🍷

DAWLISH. Langstone Cliff Hotel, Mount Pleasant Road, Dawlish Warren, Dawlish EX7 0NA (01626 868000)

The South Devon Hotel with a different outlook. Wonderful situation overlooking the sea and magnificent red cliffs, with a public footpath down to the sandy beach. Within the hotel grounds there are also some pleasant woodland walks. All the hotel rooms include en suite bathroom, remote-control TV with satellite, radio, telephone (with modem point), tea and coffee facilities, trouser press, hairdryer; baby listening available. Bedrooms and all public areas have free broadband wireless internet access. Leisure facilities include tennis, outdoor swimming pool, indoor swimming pool, fitness room, therapy room and hairdressing salon. Snooker and table tennis. Nearby is 18 hole Warren Golf Course where hotel guests have concessionary fees; golf practice area in the hotel grounds. SEE ALSO COLOUR ADVERT.

AA ★★★

e-mail: cch@langstone-hotel.co.uk **www.langstone-hotel.co.uk**

HOTEL

EXMOUTH. Devoncourt Hotel, Douglas Avenue, Exmouth EX8 2EX (01395 272277; Fax: 01395 269315)

Standing in four acres of mature subtropical gardens, overlooking two miles of sandy beach, yet within easy reach of Dartmoor and Exeter, Devoncourt provides an ideal base for a family holiday. Single, double and family suites, all en suite, well furnished and well equipped; attractive lounge bar and restaurant. Indoor & outdoor heated pools, sauna, steam room, spa & solarium, snooker room, putting, tennis and croquet, golf, sea fishing, horse riding nearby SEE ALSO COLOUR ADVERT.

ETC/AA ★★★★

e-mail: enquiries@devoncourt.com **www.devoncourt.com**

HOTEL

UMBERLEIGH. Highbullen Hotel, Golf & Country Club, Chittlehamholt, Umberleigh EX37 9HD (01769 540561; Fax: 01769 540492)

Highbullen Hotel, Golf & Country Club is beautifully set in a richly wooded 200 acre parkland estate. Boasting breathtaking views towards the romantic Devon landscapes of Exmoor and Dartmoor, the 42 bedroom hotel is truly a hidden treasure, nestling between the Mole and Taw valleys in mature wooded seclusion. Superb award-winning 18 hole par 68 golf course, five miles of salmon and trout-fishing, indoor and outdoor tennis courts, including four new grass courts to Wimbledon specifications. Fitness suite, aerobics studio, indoor and outdoor swimming pools, health and beauty spa, squash, indoor bowls, croquet, indoor putting green, golf simulator, boules, snooker, sauna, steam room, jacuzzi – the list goes on... our sporting and leisure professionals are there to cater for your every need. SEE ALSO COLOUR ADVERT.

e-mail: info@highbullen.co.uk **www.highbullen.co.uk**

symbols

Months open (eg:4/10 means April to October)

🐕 Pets Welcome

🪀 Children Welcome

♿ Suitable for Disabled

🚭 Totally non-smoking

🍷 Licensed

board

Dorset

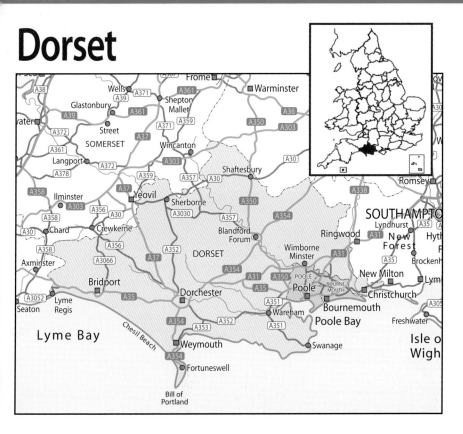

HOLLYBUSH HOTELS (Group Reservations: 0845 450 4596).
The perfect venue for group holidays and special events. Hollybush Hotels offers some of the best locations in the West for groups of all sizes to take a short break. We can cater for groups of 20-600 people. Our dedicated Group Sales Department is there to arrange the perfect holiday. Let us take the stress and worry away, allowing you to relax and enjoy your time with us. SEE ALSO COLOUR ADVERT AT START OF THE SECTION.
www.hollybushhotels.co.uk

HOTEL

STUDLAND BAY. Manor House Hotel, Studland Bay BH19 3AU (01929 450288; Fax: 01929 452255) National Trust hotel set in 20 acres on cliffs overlooking Studland Bay. Superb food and accommodation. Log fires and four-posters. Tennis, horse-riding, golf and walking. SEE ALSO COLOUR ADVERT IN GOLF SECTION.
e-mail: info@themanorhousehotel.com   **www.themanorhousehotel.com**

The FHG Directory of Website Addresses

on pages 157-179 is a useful quick reference guide for

holiday accommodation with e-mail and/or website details

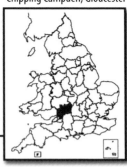

Gloucestershire

FHG Guides

publish a large range of well-known accommodation guides.
We will be happy to send you details or you can use the order form
at the back of this book.

FREE or REDUCED RATE entry to Holiday Visits and Attractions – see our
READERS' OFFER VOUCHERS on pages 181-218

Tewkesbury

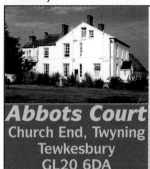

B&B

CHIPPING CAMPDEN. 'Brymbo', Honeybourne Lane, Mickleton, Chipping Campden GL55 6PU (01386 438890; Fax: 01386 438113).
A warm and welcoming farm building conversion with large garden in beautiful Cotswold countryside, ideal for walking and touring. All rooms are on the ground floor, with full central heating. The comfortable bedrooms all have colour TV and tea/coffee making facilities. Sitting room with open log fire. Breakfast room. Parking. Two double, two twin, one family. Bathrooms: three en suite, two private or shared. Brochure available. Credit Cards accepted. Close to Stratford-upon-Avon, Broadway, Chipping Campden and with easy access to Oxford and Cheltenham.
Rates: Bed and Breakfast: single £27 to £42; double £45 to £60.
• Children welcome. • Dogs welcome.
ETC ★★★★
e-mail: enquiries@brymbo.com   **www.brymbo.com**

B&B

GLOUCESTER. S.J. Barnfield, "Kilmorie Smallholding", Gloucester Road, Corse, Staunton, Gloucester GL19 3RQ (Tel & Fax: 01452 840224; Mobile 07840 702218).
Quality all ground floor accommodation. "Kilmorie" is Grade II Listed (c1848) within conservation area in a lovely part of Gloucestershire. Double, twin, family or single bedrooms, all having tea tray, colour digital TV, radio, mostly en suite. Very comfortable guests' lounge, traditional home cooking is served in the separate diningroom overlooking large garden. Perhaps walk waymarked farmland footpaths which start here. Children may "help" with our pony, and "free range" hens. Rural yet perfectly situated to visit Cotswolds, Royal Forest of Dean, Wye Valley and Malvern Hills. Ample parking. SEE ALSO COLOUR ADVERT.
Rates: Bed and full English Breakfast from £24 per person
• Children over five years welcome. • No smoking, please.
ETC ★★★★ *GUEST ACCOMMODATION.*
e-mail: sheila-barnfield@supanet.com

HOTEL

TEWKESBURY. Hilton Puckrup Hall Golf Club & Spa, Puckrup, Tewkesbury GL20 6EL (01684 296200; Fax: 01684 850788)
Hilton Puckrup Hall is the ideal country house location, set in 140 acres of glorious parkland on the edge of the Cotswolds, with panoramic views over the Malvern Hills. With a championship golf course, Livingwell Healthclub, the Escape Spa, 112 bedrooms and 16 conference and banqueting suites, it is the perfect retreat whether you're here on business or leisure. Situated just 40 minutes from Birmingham, 50 minutes from Bristol and just 1 hour and 50 minutes from London. SEE ALSO COLOUR ADVERT.
www.hilton.co.uk/tewkesbury

FARMHOUSE B&B

TEWKESBURY. Mrs Bernadette Williams, Abbots Court Church End, Twyning Tewkesbury GL20 6DA (Tel & Fax: 01684 292515).
A large, quiet farmhouse on a working farm set in 350 acres, built on the site of monastery between the Malverns and Cotswolds, half a mile M5-M50 junction. Six en suite bedrooms with colour TV and tea making facilities. Centrally heated. Open all year except Christmas. Large lounge with open fire and colour TV. Lawn. Cot and high chair available. Laundry facilities. Coarse fishing available on the farm. Ideally situated for touring with numerous places to visit • Swimming, tennis, sauna, golf within three miles. SEE ALSO COLOUR ADVERT.
Rates: Bed and Breakfast from £21 to £25. Reduced rates for children and Senior Citizens.
ETC ★★★ *FARMHOUSE*
e-mail: abbotscourt@aol.com

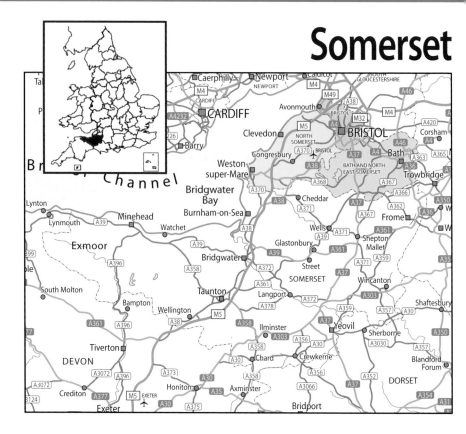

Somerset

INN

EXFORD. The Exmoor White Horse Inn, Exford TA24 7PY (01643 831229).
A dream of an Olde Worlde 16th Century Inn, with log fires, standing on a green by the side of a trickling stream in one of Exmoor's most beautiful villages. 28 sumptious en suite rooms with TV, tea and coffee making and direct dial telephones. Five course candlelit dinner prepared with fresh local produce. Spend days exploring Exmoor and its spectacular coast, riding, walking, fly fishing available. SEE ALSO COLOUR ADVERT.
www.exmoor-whitehorse.co.uk

Visit the FHG website

www.holidayguides.com

for details of the wide choice of accommodation

featured in the full range of FHG titles

Berkshire

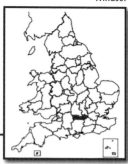

BLUEBELL HOUSE

LOVEL LANE, WINKFIELD, WINDSOR SL4 2DG

Tel & Fax: 01344 886828

Charming ex-coaching inn on the outskirts of Windsor and Ascot, and close to Bracknell and Maidenhead. Traditional rooms offering classic accommodation with an added touch of class. All rooms tastefully furnished and have TV, hairdryer, trouserpress, iron, mini-fridge and toaster/food warmer, one room has a four-poster bed.
A very full Continental breakfast is taken in your room. Private off-road parking.

e-mail: registrations@bluebellhousehotel.co.uk • www.bluebellhousehotel.co.uk

B&B

WINDSOR. Bluebell House, Lovel Lane, Winkfield, Windsor SL4 2DG (Tel & Fax: 01344 886828)
Charming ex-coaching inn on the outskirts of Windsor and Ascot, and close to Bracknell and Maidenhead. Traditional rooms offering classic accommodation with an added touch of class. All rooms tastefully furnished and have TV, hairdryer, trouser press, iron, mini-fridge and toaster/food warmer, one room has a four-poster bed. A very full Continental breakfast is taken in your room. Private off-road parking. SEE ALSO COLOUR ADVERT.
ETC ★★★★
e-mail: registrations@bluebellhousehotel.co.uk   www.bluebellhousehotel.co.uk

symbols

Months open (eg:4/10 means April to October)

🐕   Pets Welcome

🐎   Children Welcome

♿   Suitable for Disabled

🚭   Totally non-smoking

🍷   Licensed

board

Lymington

Hampshire

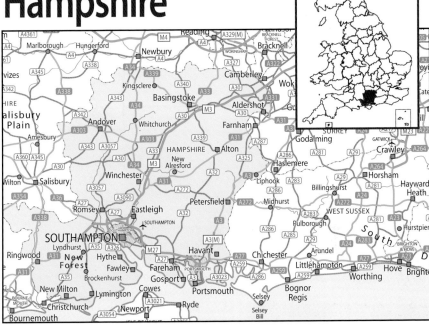

B&B　　　　　　　　　　　　　　　　　　　1/12　　

LYMINGTON. Harts Lodge, 242 Everton Road, Everton, Lymington S041 0HE (01590 645902).
Bungalow set in three acres. Large garden with small lake. Quiet location, three miles west of Lymington. Friendly welcome. Double, twin and family en suite rooms, each with tea/coffee making facilities and colour TV. Delicious four-course English breakfast. The sea and forest are five minutes away by car. Horse riding, golf and fishing are nearby. The village pub, half-a-mile, serves excellent meals. SEE ALSO COLOUR ADVERT.
Rates: Bed and Breakfast from £27.50 per person.
• Non-smoking
AA ★★★★

Isle of Wight

The Isle of Wight has several award-winning beaches, including Blue Flag winners, all of which are managed and maintained to the highest standard. Sandown, Shanklin and Ryde offer all the traditional delights; or head for Compton Bay where surfers brave the waves, fossil hunters admire the casts of dinosaur footprints at low tide, kitesurfers leap and soar across the sea and paragliders hurl themselves off the cliffs

Newport is the commercial centre of the Island with many famous high street stores and plenty of places to eat and drink. Ryde has a lovely Victorian Arcade lined with shops selling books and antiques. Cowes is great for sailing garb and Godshill is a treasure chest for the craft enthusiast. Lovers of fine food will enjoy the weekly farmers' markets selling home-grown produce and also the Garlic Festival held annually in August.

Many attractions are out of doors to take advantage of the Island's milder than average temperatures. However, if it should rain, there's plenty to choose from. There are vineyards offering wine tasting, cinemas, theatres and nightclubs as well as sports and leisure centres, a bowling alley and an ice skating rink, home to the Island's very own ice hockey team – the Wight Raiders.

The Island's diverse terrain makes it an ideal landscape for walkers and cyclists of all ages and abilities. Pony trekking and beach rides are also popular holiday pursuits and the Island's superb golf courses, beautiful scenery and temperate climate combine to make it the perfect choice for a golfing break.

Ventnor

HOTEL

SANDOWN. Sandhill Hotel, 6 Hill Street, Sandown PO36 9DB (01983 403635; Fax: 01983 403695)
Kathy, Stacey and Steve welcome you to our friendly family hotel situated in a pleasant residential area of Sandown. The beach, town centre and railway station are all within easy walking distance. All bedrooms (single, double and family) are en suite, with tea/coffee making facilities, direct-dial telephone, free wifi access and colour TV. We have a comfortable licensed bar, lounge and sun lounge, and our spacious restaurant offers a selection of evening meals and snacks to cater for all tastes, with a substantial varied breakfast menu. Limited car parking spaces available. SEE ALSO COLOUR ADVERT.
Rates: Bed and Breakfast from £27pppn.
ETC ★★★
e-mail: sandhillsandown@aol.com　　　　**www.sandhill-hotel.co.uk**

HOTEL

TOTLAND. Frenchman's Cove Country Hotel, Alum Bay Old Road, Totland PO39 0HZ (01983 752227)
Our delightful family-run guesthouse is set amongst National Trust downland, not far from the Needles and safe sandy beaches. Ideal for ramblers, birdwatchers, cyclists and those who enjoy the countryside. We have almost an acre of grounds. Cots and high chairs are available. All rooms are en suite, with colour TV and tea/ coffee making facilities. Guests can relax in the attractive lounges. Also available is the Coach House, a well appointed self-catering apartment for two adults and two children. No smoking. No pets.
Please contact Sue or Chris Boatfield for details. SEE ALSO COLOUR ADVERT IN GOLF SECTION.
www.frenchmanscove.co.uk

HOTEL　　　　　　　　　　　　　　　　　　　1/11

VENTNOR. Best Western Ventnor Towers Hotel, 54 Madeira Road, Ventnor PO38 1QT (01983 852277; Fax: 01983 855536)
A country house hotel on the Isle of Wight in a spectacular clifftop location with panoramic sea views. 30 bedrooms, all with TV, internet access, hairdryer etc. Set in four acres of gardens.Pitch and putt, heated outdoor pool, tennis. Children welcome - baby listening, family rooms available. Pets welcome by arrangement. An ideal base for exploring the island or for a relaxing break. SEE ALSO COLOUR ADVERT.
EnjoyEngland ★★★ AA ★★★
www.ventnortowers.com

symbols

Months open (eg:4/10 means April to October)

🐕　Pets Welcome
🐴　Children Welcome
♿　Suitable for Disabled
🚭　Totally non-smoking
🍸　Licensed

board

Kent

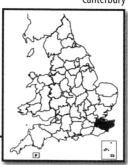

FARMHOUSE B&B

1/12

CANTERBURY. Great Field Farm, Stelling Minnis, Canterbury CT4 6DE (01227 709223)
Situated in beautiful countryside, 10 minutes' drive from Canterbury, Channel Tunnel and Folkestone, our spacious farmhouse provides friendly, comfortable accommodation. Full central heating and double glazing. Hearty breakfasts with home-grown produce. All rooms en suite with colour TV, courtesy tray and free internet access. Cottage suite with its own entrance. Both annexe suite (sleeps 2) and new detached ground floor geo-thermally heated Sunset Lodge (sleeps 4/5) are ideal for B&B or self-catering. SEE ALSO COLOUR ADVERT.
Rates: Bed and Breakfast from £30 per person.
• Non-smoking establishment • Self-catering also available
ETC ★★★★ *SILVER AWARD*
www.great-field-farm.co.uk

HOTEL

DOVER. Walletts Court Country House Hotel, St Margaret's-at-Cliffe, Near Dover CT15 6EW (01304 852424; Fax: 01304 853430)
Four hundred years of history exude from the walls of the ancient manor house nestling in wild open landscape in the heart of White Cliffs Country ninety minutes from the city of London, and ten minutes from the port of Dover. Three four-poster bedrooms and fourteen contemporary rooms housed in converted Kentish hay barns, stables and cowsheds surrounding the manor. Massage or beauty treatment in your own cabin. Sauna, steam room and hydrotherapy pool. Indoor swimming pool, gym. All-weather floodlit tennis court, croquet lawn, boules court, clay shooting range. Eat in the conservatory, the library or in bed at breakfast, lunch in the lounge or dine in the oak-beamed restaurant in the evening. SEE ALSO COLOUR ADVERT IN SPA SECTION.
e-mail: mail@wallettscourt.com   www.wallettscourt.com

HOTEL

TENTERDEN. London Beach Country Hotel & Golf Club, Tenterden TN30 6HX (01580 766279; Fax: 01580 763884)
Tenterden's Premier Hotel and Conference Venue. The London Beach Country Hotel is located in the beautiful Weald of Kent, just two minutes from the historic market town of Tenterden and 20 minutes from Ashford International Station. The hotel offers outstanding facilities with top-class catering by award-winning chefs. The perfect venue for weddings, conferences and team building activities, including golf, archery and clay pigeon shooting. Our friendly staff will see to your every need. Set in 97 acres of beautiful Wealden countryside, one mile from Tenterden. Parkland golf course. 26-bedroom hotel. Three large function rooms. Superb restaurant. Spike bar. SEE ALSO COLOUR ADVERT.
AA ★★★
e-mail: enquiries@londonbeach.com   www.londonbeach.com

Oxfordshire

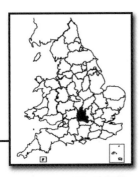

Arden Lodge

Modern detached house in select part of Oxford,
within easy reach of Oxford Centre.
Excellent position for Blenheim Palace and for
touring Cotswolds, Stratford, Warwick etc.
Close to river, parks, country inns and golf course.
Easy access to London. All rooms have tea/coffee
making and private facilities. Parking.
Bed and Breakfast from £25 per person per night.

Mr and Mrs L. Price, Arden Lodge, 34 Sunderland Avenue (off Banbury Road), Oxford OX2 8DX
Tel: 01865 552076 • Fax: 01865 512265 • mobile: 07702 068697

ATTRACTION

BURFORD. Cotswold Wildlife Park and Gardens, Burford OX18 4JP (01993 825728).
Situated mid-way between Oxford and Cheltenham, Cotswold Wildlife Park is set in 160 acres of landscaped
parkland containing everything from Ants to Rhinos. Adventure playground, children's farmyard, picnic areas and
cafeteria. Narrow gauge railway running from April to October. Open daily from 10am. SEE ALSO COLOUR ADVERT.
www.cotswoldwildlifepark.co.uk

GUEST HOUSE   1/12

**OXFORD. Mr and Mrs L. Price, Arden Lodge, 34 Sunderland Avenue (off Banbury Road), Oxford OX2
8DX (01865 552076; mobile: 07702 068697; Fax: 01865 512265).**
Modern detached house in select part of Oxford, within easy reach of Oxford Centre. Excellent position for
Blenheim Palace and for touring Cotswolds, Stratford, Warwick etc. Close to river, parks, country inns and golf
course. Easy access to London. All rooms have tea/coffee making and private facilities. Parking. SEE ALSO
COLOUR ADVERT.
Rates: Bed and Breakfast from £25 per person per night.

Looking for holiday accommodation?
for details of hundreds of properties
throughout the UK including
comprehensive coverage of all areas of Scotland try:
www.holidayguides.com

Surrey

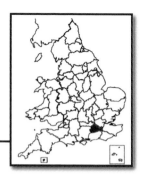

HOTEL

SOUTH CROYDON. Selsdon Park Hotel & Golf Club, Addington Road, Sanderstead, South Croydon CR2 8YA TN33 (0208 6578811; Fax: 0208 6516171).
Set in 205 acres of spectacular parkland including an 18-hole championship golf course, this Neo-Jacobean building provides you with serenity and seclusion. Only 13 miles from London it is the ideal base from which to visit the capital. 204 de luxe en suite bedrooms Pay & Play parkland course, designed by J H Taylor. 18 holes, 6473 yards/5854 metres, Par 73. S.S.S. 71 Practice ground. Buggy hire. Pre-bookable tee times. Green fees. Corporate Golf Days, Society Meetings, Golfing Breaks. Restaurant, grill and private dining Golf Academy Golf Tuition. PGA Professional. SEE ALSO COLOUR ADVERT IN GOLF SECTION.
VisitBritain ★★★★ AA★★★★
www.principal-hotels.com/selsdonpark

Luton

Bedfordshire

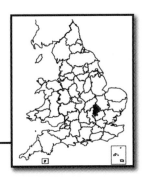

Wicks
B&B

Bed and Breakfast accommodation situated just 10 minutes from Luton Airport, just off the M1 Junction 10 and close to the A505. Near town centre and railway stations (Town Centre and Parkway); 25 minutes' train journey to Central London. Large bungalow with double rooms; tea/coffee making equipment and colour TV. Overnight parking available. Close to local pubs, restaurants and shops. Children welcome. A warm welcome awaits.

Mr and Mrs Wicks, 19 Wigmore Lane, Stopsley, Luton LU2 8AA • Tel: 01582 423419 Mobile: 07972 214929
e-mail: wicks-bandb@hotmail.co.uk

B&B
LUTON. Mr and Mrs Wicks, 19 Wigmore Lane, Stopsley, Luton LU2 8AA (01582 423419; Mobile: 07972 214929).
Bed and Breakfast accommodation situated just 10 minutes from Luton Airport, just off the M1 Junction 10 and close to the A505. Near town centre and railway stations (Town Centre and Parkway); 25 minutes' train journey to Central London. Large bungalow with double rooms; tea/coffee making equipment and colour TV. Overnight parking available. Close to local pubs, restaurants and shops. Children welcome. A warm welcome awaits. SEE ALSO COLOUR ADVERT.
e-mail: wicks-bandb@hotmail.co.uk

symbols

Months open (eg:4/10 means April to October)

🐕 Pets Welcome
🐎 Children Welcome
♿ Suitable for Disabled
🚭 Totally non-smoking
🍷 Licensed

board

Norfolk

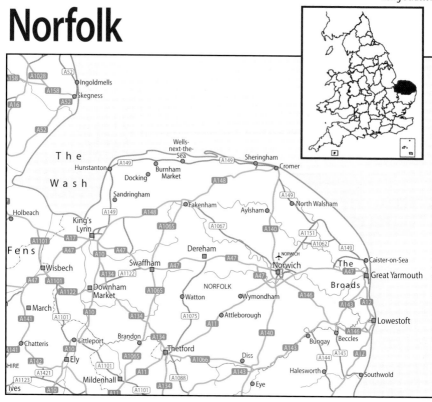

Greenacres Farmhouse

Woodgreen, Long Stratton, Norwich NR15 2RR
Period 17th century farmhouse on 30 acre common with ponds and natural wildlife, 10 miles south of Norwich (A140). The beamed sittingroom with inglenook fireplace invites you to relax. A large sunny dining room encourages you to enjoy a leisurely traditional breakfast. All en suite bedrooms (two double/twin) are tastefully furnished to complement the oak beams and period furniture, with tea/coffee facilities and TV. Full size snooker table and all-weather tennis court for guests' use. Jo is trained in therapeutic massage, aromatherapy and reflexology and is able to offer this to guests who feel it would be of benefit. Come and enjoy the peace and tranquillity of our home.Bed and Breakfast from £25. Reductions for two nights or more. Non-smoking.

Tel: 01508 530261 • www.abreakwithtradition.co.uk

B&B/GUESTHOUSE   1-12

LONG STRATTON. Greenacres Farmhouse, Woodgreen, Long Stratton, Norwich NR15 2RR (01508 530261).
Period 17th century farmhouse on 30 acre common with ponds and natural wildlife, 10 miles south of Norwich (A140). The beamed sittingroom with inglenook fireplace invites you to relax. A large sunny dining room encourages you to enjoy a leisurely traditional breakfast. All en suite bedrooms (two double/twin) are tastefully furnished to complement the oak beams and period furniture, with tea/coffee facilities and TV. Full size snooker table and all-weather tennis court for guests' use. Jo is trained in therapeutic massage, aromatherapy and reflexology and is able to offer this to guests who feel it would be of benefit. Come and enjoy the peace and tranquillity of our home.
SEE ALSO COLOUR ADVERT
Rates: Bed and Breakfast from £25. Reductions for two nights or more.
• Non-smoking
ETC ★★★★ *B&B*
www.abreakwithtradition.co.uk

Felixstowe, Framlingham

Suffolk

Visit the FHG website
www.holidayguides.com
for details of the wide choice of accommodation
featured in the full range of FHG titles

HOTEL
1/12

ALDEBURGH. The Thorpeness Hotel, Thorpeness, Aldeburgh IP16 4NH (01728 452176; Fax: 01728 453868).
Enjoy a break on the invigorating Heritage Coast. Play the challenging, mature 18-hole seaside course designed by the legendary James Braid. Guests in the hotel can enjoy concessionary rates at Aldeburgh Golf Club, one of the top 100 courses in the British Isles or play the Suffolk Tour including Ipswich, Woodbridge and Felixstowe Ferry. A warm welcome, comfortable en suite rooms and good food. SEE ALSO COLOUR ADVERT IN GOLF SECTION.
e-mail: info@thorpeness.co.uk   **www.thorpeness.co.uk**

GUEST HOUSE

FELIXSTOWE. Geoffrey and Elizabeth Harvey, The Grafton Guest House, 13 Sea Road, Felixstowe IP11 2BB (01394 284881; Fax: 01394 279101).
Situated by the sea front, the Grafton offers quality Bed and Breakfast accommodation. All en suite and standard rooms have colour TV, clock radio, hairdryer and tea/coffee making facilities. Owners Geoffrey and Elizabeth are committed to providing a first class service and extend a warm welcome to all guests. throughout. SEE ALSO COLOUR ADVERT.
Rates: single rooms from £30, double from £50, per night, including breakfast.
• Non-smoking
ETC ★★★★ *GUEST ACCOMMODATION.*
e-mail: info@grafton-house.com   **www.grafton-house.com**

B&B
1/12

FRAMLINGHAM. Mrs Jennie Mann, Fiddlers Hall, Cransford, Near Framlingham, Woodbridge IP13 9PQ (01728 663729).
Signposted on B1119, Fiddlers Hall is a 14th century, moated, oak-beamed farmhouse set in a beautiful and secluded position. It is two miles from Framlingham Castle, 20 minutes' drive from Aldeburgh, Snape Maltings, Woodbridge and Southwold. A Grade II Listed building, it has lots of history and character. The bedrooms are spacious; one has en suite shower room, the other has a private bathroom. Use of lounge and colour TV. Plenty of parking space. Lots of farm animals kept. Traditional farmhouse cooking. SEE ALSO COLOUR ADVERT.
Rates: Bed and Breakfast terms from £65 per room.
www.fiddlershall.co.uk

Winster

Derbyshire

Ample private parking • Non-smoking throughout
Bed and Breakfast from £23 per person

**Mrs Jane Ball, Brae Cottage,
East Bank, Winster DE4 2DT
Tel: 01629 650375**

In one of the most picturesque villages in the Peak District National Park this 300-year-old cottage offers independent accommodation across the paved courtyard. Breakfast is served in the cottage. Rooms are furnished and equipped to a high standard; both having en suite shower rooms, tea/coffee making facilities, TV and heating. The village has two traditional pubs which provide food. Local attractions include village (National Trust) Market House, Chatsworth, Haddon Hall and many walks from the village in the hills and dales.

  'WHICH?' GOOD BED & BREAKFAST GUIDE
'WHICH?' GUIDE TO GOOD HOTELS

WINSTER. Mrs Jane Ball, Brae Cottage, East Bank, Winster DE4 2DT (01629 650375).
In one of the most picturesque villages in the Peak District National Park this 300-year-old cottage offers independent accommodation across the paved courtyard. Breakfast is served in the cottage. Rooms are furnished and equipped to a high standard; both having en suite shower rooms, tea/coffee making facilities, TV and heating. The village has two traditional pubs which provide food. Local attractions include village (National Trust) Market House, Chatsworth, Haddon Hall and many walks from the village in the hills and dales. Ample private parking. SEE ALSO COLOUR ADVERT.
Rates: Bed and Breakfast from £23 per person
• Non-smoking throughout
ETC ★★★★ *GUEST ACCOMMODATION, SILVER AWARD.*

The FHG Directory of Website Addresses

on pages 157-179 is a useful quick reference guide for

holiday accommodation with e-mail and/or website details

FREE or REDUCED RATE entry to Holiday Visits and Attractions – see our

READERS' OFFER VOUCHERS on pages 181-218

HOTEL

BRANSTON. Branston Hall Hotel, Lincoln Road, Branston, Lincoln LN4 1PD (01522 793305).
Only five minutes' drive from historic Lincoln, our beautiful hotel dates back to 1885, and is set in 88 acres of wooded parkland and lakes. 50 en suite bedrooms and Lakeside Restaurant. Leisure and Conference facilities. Wedding specialists. Open to non-residents. A venue for all seasons. SEE ALSO COLOUR ADVERT.
AA ★★★ *AND ROSETTE*
www.branstonhall.com

HOTEL

SUTTON-ON-SEA. The Grange and Links Hotel and Sandilands Golf Club, Sandilands, Sutton-on-Sea LN12 2RA (01507 441334; Fax: 01507 443043)
The Grange and Links Hotel has a reputation for quality accommodation, fine food and good service. This privately run hotel, situated just two minutes walk from the Lincolnshire beach, is part of a complex which includes Sandilands Golf Club – an 18 Hole Links Course.The Grange and Links is an AA three-star hotel specialising in activity golfing holidays, midweek and weekend breaks for golfers (including two games on a Saturday) and offers those who enjoy a game of golf a tranquil break in a beautiful setting. Our own privately owned 18 hole (Par 70, SSS 69) links golf course. Two tennis courts, 4-acre garden, gymnasium, 2 snooker tables, croquet lawn.SEE ALSO COLOUR ADVERT IN GOLF SECTION.
e-mail: enquiries@GrangeandLinksHotel.co.uk   **www.grangeandlinkshotel.co.uk**

symbols

Months open (eg:4/10 means April to October)

   Pets Welcome

    Children Welcome

&   Suitable for Disabled

⊘   Totally non-smoking

Ⴜ   Licensed

board

Oswestry

Shropshire

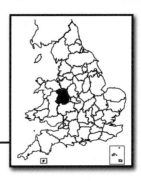

Shropshire is perhaps less well-known than other English counties. This is despite being the birthplace of Charles Darwin, home to the world's first iron bridge (now a World Heritage Site), having not one, but two of the finest medieval towns in England, inspiring the creation of the modern Olympics, and being the kingdom of the real King Arthur. After all, Shropshire is easy enough to find and get to from almost anywhere. (Hint: just north of Birmingham or south of Manchester depending on your direction of travel, and sitting snugly on the Welsh borders).

TOP FARM HOUSE Knockin, Near Oswestry SY10 8HN

Full of charm and character, this beautiful 16th century Grade 1 Listed black and white house is set in the delightful village of Knockin. Enjoy the relaxed atmosphere and elegant surroundings of this special house with its abundance of beams. Sit in the comfortable drawing room where you can read, listen to music, or just relax

with a glass of wine (please feel free to bring your own tipple). Hearty breakfasts from our extensive menu are served in the lovely dining room which looks out over the garden. The large bedrooms are all en suite, attractively decorated and furnished. All have tea/coffee making facilities, colour TV, etc. Convenient for the Welsh Border, Shrewsbury, Chester and Oswestry. Friendly hosts and great atmosphere. Bed and Breakfast from £27.50 to £35.

TELEPHONE: 01691 682582
E-MAIL: **p.a.m@knockin.freeserve.co.uk**

  Silver SILVER AWARD **AA**

B&B

OSWESTRY near. Top Farm House, Knockin, Near Oswestry SY10 8HN (01691 682582).
Full of charm and character, this beautiful 16th century Grade 1 Listed black and white house is set in the delightful village of Knockin. Enjoy the relaxed atmosphere and elegant surroundings of this special house with its abundance of beams. Sit in the comfortable drawing room where you can read, listen to music, or just relax with a glass of wine (please feel free to bring your own tipple). Hearty breakfasts from our extensive menu are served in the lovely dining room which looks out over the garden. The large bedrooms are all en suite, attractively decorated and furnished. All have tea/coffee making facilities, colour TV, etc. Convenient for the Welsh Border, Shrewsbury, Chester and Oswestry. Friendly hosts and great atmosphere. SEE ALSO COLOUR ADVERT.
Rates: Bed and Breakfast from £27.50 to £35.
ETC ◆◆◆◆ *SILVER AWARD,* **AA** *FOUR RED DIAMONDS.*
e-mail: **p.a.m@knockin.freeserve.co.uk**

A useful index of towns/counties appears at the back of this book

Staffordshire

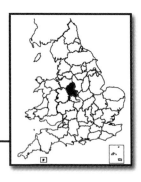

HOTEL

YOXALL. Hoar Cross Hall Spa Resort, Hoar Cross, Near Yoxall DE13 8QS (01283 575747; Fax: 01283 575748)
The only spa resort in a stately home in England. This graceful residence has been restored to its former glory and offers a unique combination of traditional elegance and first class service, along with the extensive facilities of a modern spa resort. 100 bedrooms, all with private bathroom. Two swimming pools, two saunariums, saunas, steam rooms, water grottos, aerobics, yoga, large gymnasium; Golf Academy with a PGA Professional, 9-hole course, driving range and practice areas. Other activities include tennis, croquet and archery. Plantation Restaurant overlooking pool; à la carte dining in the original ballroom; Champagne Bar. SEE ALSO COLOUR ADVERT IN SPA SECTION.
e-mail: info@hoarcross.co.uk   www.hoarcross.co.uk

Yorkshire

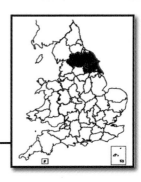

East Yorkshire

HOTEL   1/12   &   ♀

DRIFFIELD. Best Western The Bell in Driffield, Market Place, Driffield YO25 6AN (01377 256661; Fax: 01377 253228)

An 18th century Listed hotel, situated in the centre of Driffield, 'The Capital of the Wolds', tastefully furnished with antiques and fine arts. Tardis-like in appearance, it boasts 16 individually styled suites and bedrooms, and a beautiful oak panelled dining room offering fine dining in elegant surroundings. There is an unrivalled range of leisure facilities, including floatation tank, indoor swimming pool, full Nautilus gym, a Holistic Beauty Salon, squash court and snooker room etc. SEE ALSO COLOUR ADVERT IN SPA SECTION.

AA ★★★

e-mail: bell@bestwestern.co.uk   **www.bw-bellhotel.co.uk**

North Yorkshire

Danby

The Fox & Hounds Inn

Former 16th century coaching inn, now a high quality residential Country Inn & Restaurant set amidst the beautiful North York Moors. Freshly prepared dishes, using finest local produce, are served every lunchtime and evening, with selected quality wines and a choice of cask ales. Excellent en suite acccommodation is available. Open all year. Winter Breaks available November to March.

VisitBritain ★★★★ Inn   *Tel: 01287 660218*
Ainthorpe, Danby, Yorkshire YO21 2LD
E-mail: info@foxandhounds–ainthorpe.com
www.foxandhounds–ainthorpe.com

COUNTRY INN   1/12   🐕   ♀

DANBY. The Fox and Hounds Inn, Ainthorpe, Danby YO21 2LD (01287 660218; Fax: 01287 660030).

Former 16th century coaching inn, now a high quality residential Country Inn & Restaurant set amidst the beautiful North York Moors. Freshly prepared dishes, using finest local produce, are served every lunchtime and evening, with selected quality wines and a choice of cask ales. Excellent en suite acccommodation is available. SEE ALSO COLOUR ADVERT.

• Open all year. Winter Breaks available November to March.

VisitBritain ★★★★

e-mail: info@foxandhounds–ainthorpe.com   **www.foxandhounds–ainthorpe.com**

Cheshire

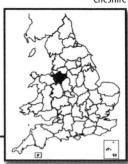

Cheshire - soak in the atmosphere of the historic city of Chester, created by an abundance of black-and-white buildings set in a circuit of glorious city walls, the most complete in the country. Chester's crowning glory is the 13th century Rows – two tiers of shops running along the main streets, offering a unique and sophisticated shopping experience. A leisurely walk along the finest city walls in Britain will take you past most of the city's delights like the stunning Eastgate Clock and the 1000-year-old Cathedral, a haven of reflective tranquillity in a lively, bustling, cosmopolitan centre. The biggest archaeological dig in Britain is currently underway at the 2000-year-old Roman Amphitheatre; there is architectural splendour to enjoy at every turn. The lush countryside surrounding Chester is peppered with stately homes, award-winning gardens and chic market towns featuring characteristic black-and-white half-timbered buildings. Tatton Park near Knutsford is one of Britain's finest Georgian manors, with acres of parklands and formal gardens, a perfect attraction to enjoy in every season, and the host of the RHS Flower Show in July. Or visit Arley Hall and Gardens near Northwich, with its stunning herbaceous borders and Country Fair and Horse Trials in May. For super chic in super villages and towns, breeze into Tarporley, Nantwich, Knutsford and Wilmslow where sophisticated shopping, fine cuisine and contemporary pleasures ensure an afternoon of indulgence and fine delights, with food and drink festivals being held throughout the year.

Vicarage Lodge, 11 Vicarage Road, Hoole, Chester CH2 3HZ

A late Victorian family-run guesthouse offering a warm welcome and peaceful stay. Situated in a quiet residential area just off the main Hoole Road, yet only one mile from the city centre. Double and twin rooms, en suite available.

All rooms have washbasins, central heating, hair dryers, shaver points, remote-control colour TV and tea/coffee facilities. Large selection of breakfast choices. Private car park on premises. Good-sized patio garden where guests can relax.

Bed and Breakfast from £25pp single, £45 twin/double. Weekly and winter terms available.

Tel & Fax: 01244 319533

GUESTHOUSE

CHESTER. **Vicarage Lodge, 11 Vicarage Road, Hoole, Chester CH2 3HZ (Tel & Fax: 01244 319533).** A late Victorian family-run guesthouse offering a warm welcome and peaceful stay. Situated in a quiet residential area just off the main Hoole Road, yet only one mile from the city centre. Double and twin rooms, en suite available. All rooms have washbasins, central heating, hair dryers, shaver points, remote-control colour TV and tea/coffee facilities. Large selection of breakfast choices. Private car park on premises. Good-sized patio garden where guests can relax. SEE ALSO COLOUR ADVERT.
Rates: Bed and Breakfast from £25pp single, £45 twin/double. Weekly and winter terms available.

Cumbria

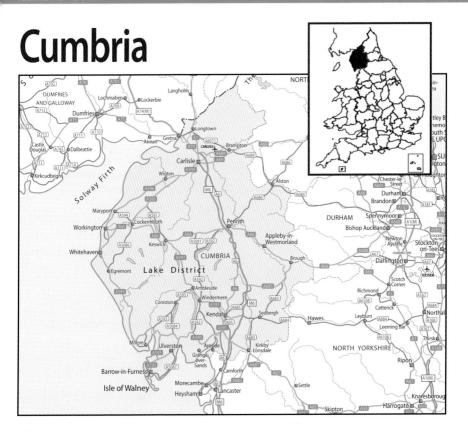

Cumbria - The Lake District is often described as the most beautiful corner of England, and it's easy to see why 15 million visitors head here every year. It is a place of unrivalled beauty, with crystal clear lakes, bracken-covered mountains, peaceful forests, quiet country roads and miles of stunning coastline.

At the heart of Cumbria is the Lake District National Park. Each of the lakes that make up the area has its own charm and personality: Windermere, England's longest lake, is surrounded by rolling hills; Derwentwater and Ullswater are circled by craggy fells; England's deepest lake, Wastwater, is dominated by high mountains including the country's highest, Scafell Pike. For those who want to tackle the great outdoors, Cumbria offers everything from rock climbing to fell walking and from canoeing to horse riding – all among stunning scenery.

Cumbria has many delightful market towns, historic houses and beautiful gardens such as Holker Hall with its 25 acres of award-winning grounds. There are many opportunities to sample local produce, such as Cumbrian fell-bred lamb, Cumberland Sausage, and trout and salmon plucked fresh from nearby lakes and rivers.

Cumbria is a county of contrasts with a rich depth of cultural and historical interest in addition to stunning scenery. Compact and accessible, it can offer something for every taste.

When making enquiries please mention FHG GUIDES

The Dower House

Lovely old house, quiet and peaceful, stands on an elevation overlooking Lake Windermere, with one of the most beautiful views in all Lakeland. Its setting within the 100-acre Wray Castle estate (National Trust), with direct access to the Lake, makes it an ideal base for walking and touring. Hawkshead and Ambleside are about ten minutes' drive and have numerous old inns and restaurants. Ample car parking; prefer dogs to sleep in the car. Children over five years welcome.

Wray Castle, Ambleside
Cumbria LA22 0JA
Tel: 015394 33211

Bed and Breakfast from £32.00pp
Dinner, Bed & Breakfast from £48.50pp
Open all year round

Pallet Hill
Farm

Pallet Hill Farm is pleasantly situated two miles from Penrith, four miles from Ullswater, with easy access to the Lake District, Scottish Borders and Yorkshire Dales.
- Good farmhouse food and hospitality with personal attention.
- An ideal place to spend a relaxing break.
- Golf club, swimming pool, pony trekking in the area.
- Double, single and family rooms; Children welcome.
- Sorry, no pets. • Car essential, parking.
- Open Easter to November.

Bed and Breakfast £16 (reduced weekly rates), reduced rates for children.

Penrith, Cumbria CA11 0BY
Tel: 017684 83247

Autumn Leaves Guest House

The Lake District is waiting for you to discover its natural beauty and Autumn Leaves is the ideal base, whether your break is a quiet 'get away from it all' or filled with activities, either way you will be assured of a warm welcome. The guest house, situated in a quiet but central road across from Ellerthwaite Park, is only 150 metres from Windermere's centre and 10 minutes' walk from the train and bus station. Lake Windermere is just a short walk down hill to Bowness. Public transport for the Lakes area also runs regularly from the end of our road. Some rooms are en suite and all have central heating, TV, radio alarm and tea/coffee making facilities. We have plenty of maps and information available and are happy to share our knowledge of the area. Pets welcome.

29 Broad Street, Windermere LA23 2AB
Tel: 01539 448410
e-mail: info@autumnleavesguesthouse.co.uk
www.autumnleavesguesthouse.co.uk

B&B from £26-£37pppn.

GUEST HOUSE   1/12

AMBLESIDE. The Dower House, Wray Castle, Ambleside LA22 0JA (015394 33211).
Lovely old house, quiet and peaceful, stands on an elevation overlooking Lake Windermere, with one of the most beautiful views in all Lakeland. Its setting within the 100-acre Wray Castle estate (National Trust), with direct access to the Lake, makes it an ideal base for walking and touring. Hawkshead and Ambleside are about ten minutes' drive and have numerous old inns and restaurants. Ample car parking. SEE ALSO COLOUR ADVERT.
Rates: Bed and Breakfast from £32.00pp; Dinner, Bed & Breakfast from £48.50pp
• Open all year round • Children over five years welcome • Prefer dogs to sleep in the car
ETC ★★★★

GUEST HOUSE   1/12

CARLISLE. Mrs G. Elwen, New Pallyards, Hethersgill, Carlisle CA6 6HZ (01228 577308).
Farmhouse filmed for BBC TV. Relax and see beautiful North Cumbria and the Borders. A warm welcome awaits you in our country farmhouse tucked away in the Cumbrian countryside, yet easily accessible from M6 Junction 44. In addition to the surrounding attractions there is plenty to enjoy, including hill walking, peaceful forests and sea trout/salmon fishing or just nestle down and relax with nature. Bed and Breakfast: Two double en suite, two family en suite rooms and one twin/single bedroom, all with tea/coffee making equipment. Menu choice. We are proud to have won a National Salon Culinaire Award for the "Best Breakfast in Britain".

Rates: Bed and Breakfast from £25 per person, Dinner £14; Dinner, Bed and Breakfast weekly rates from £170 to £180.
• Working farm. • Disabled facilities. • Self-catering offered.
ETC ◆◆◆◆ *GOLD AWARD WINNER.*
e-mail: newpallyards@btinternet.com   **www.4starsc.co.uk**

FARMHOUSE B&B   4/10

PENRITH. Pallet Hill Farm, Penrith CA11 0BY (017684 83247)
Pallet Hill Farm is pleasantly situated two miles from Penrith, four miles from Ullswater, with easy access to the Lake District, Scottish Borders and Yorkshire Dales. Good farmhouse food and hospitality with personal attention. An ideal place to spend a relaxing break. Golf club, swimming pool, pony trekking in the area. Double, single and family rooms. Car essential, parking. SEE ALSO COLOUR ADVERT.
Rates: Bed and Breakfast £16 (reduced weekly rates), reduced rates for children.
• Children welcome • Sorry, no pets • Open Easter to November

GUESTHOUSE

Windermere. Autumn Leaves Guest House, 29 Broad Street, Windermere LA23 2AB (01539 448410).
The Lake District is waiting for you to discover its natural beauty and Autumn Leaves is the ideal base, whether your break is a quiet 'get away from it all' or filled with activities, either way you will be assured of a warm welcome. The guest house, situated in a quiet but central road across from Ellerthwaite Park, is only 150 metres from Windermere's centre and 10 minutes' walk from the train and bus station. Lake Windermere is just a short walk down hill to Bowness. Public transport for the Lakes area also runs regularly from the end of our road. Some rooms are en suite and all have central heating, TV, radio alarm and tea/coffee making facilities. We have plenty of maps and information available and are happy to share our knowledge of the area.
• Pets welcome.
Rates: B&B from £26-£37pppn
ETC ★★★ *GUEST ACCOMMODATION*
e-mail: info@autumnleavesguesthouse.co.uk   www.autumnleavesguesthouse.co.uk

Lancashire

t:01253 712236
w:www.dalmenyhotel.co.uk
e:reservations@dalmenyhotel.co.uk
Dalmeny Hotel & Leisure, South Promenade,
St Annes on Sea, Lancashire, FY8 1LX

125 spacious bedrooms

Centrally located on St Annes'
famous promenade and sandy beach

With fabulous leisure facilities including:
Gymnasium with separate Cardio Theatre,
20m Pool, Jacuzzi, Sauna, Aromatic Steam Room

North West Decleor Gold Spa of the Year
Quality treatments and total relaxation

HOTEL
ST ANNES ON SEA. Dalmeny Hotel & Leisure, South Promenade, St Annes on Sea FY8 1LX (01253 712236).
Centrally located on St Annes' famous promenade and sandy beach. 125 spacious bedrooms. Fabulous leisure facilities including: gymnasium with separate cardio theatre, jacuzzi, sauna, aromatic steam room. North West Decleor Gold Spa of the Year. Quality treatments and total relaxation. SEE ALSO COLOUR ADVERT.
e-mail: reservations@dalmenyhotel.co.uk www.dalmenyhotel.co.uk

Merseyside

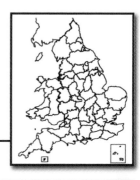

Visit the FHG website

www.holidayguides.com

for details of the wide choice of accommodation

featured in the full range of FHG titles

LIVERPOOL. Holme Leigh Guest House, 93 Woodcroft Road, Wavertree, Liverpool L15 2HG (0151-734 2216).
Recently fully refurbished. all rooms are comfortably furnished, complete with TV, tea and coffee and en suite facilities. Full central heating. Award-winning breakfast room. Close to Sefton Park, just two miles from the M62 and 20 minutes from the airport, 2½ miles from city centre. All rates include VAT and Continental breakfast. SEE ALSO COLOUR ADVERTISEMENT.
Rates: Single rooms available from £22 per night, doubles and twins from £44. Family rooms also available.
e-mail: info@holmeleigh.com   www.holmeleigh.com

SOUTHPORT. The Leicester, 24 Leicester Street, Southport PR9 0EZ (01704 530049; Fax: 01704 545561).
10 individually designed en suite bedrooms (single, double, twin), all with hospitality tray, ironing facilities, hairdryer, toiletries and room safe. Modern, spacious dining room serving choice of breakfast menu. Evening meals by arrangement. Lounge/bar area with comfortable sofas and 42" plasma TV. Currently in the process of being regraded as 4 Stars. SEE ALSO COLOUR ADVERTISEMENT.
www.theleicester.com

Scotland Board

Scotland · Regions

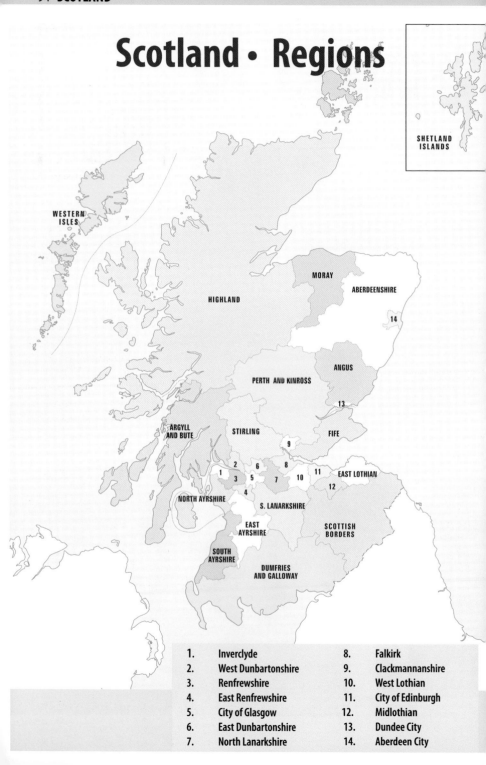

SHETLAND
ISLANDS

WESTERN
ISLES

MORAY

ABERDEENSHIRE

HIGHLAND

14

ANGUS

PERTH AND KINROSS

13

ARGYLL
AND BUTE

STIRLING

FIFE

9

EAST LOTHIAN

NORTH AYRSHIRE

S. LANARKSHIRE

EAST
AYRSHIRE

SCOTTISH
BORDERS

SOUTH
AYRSHIRE

DUMFRIES
AND GALLOWAY

1.	Inverclyde	8.	Falkirk
2.	West Dunbartonshire	9.	Clackmannanshire
3.	Renfrewshire	10.	West Lothian
4.	East Renfrewshire	11.	City of Edinburgh
5.	City of Glasgow	12.	Midlothian
6.	East Dunbartonshire	13.	Dundee City
7.	North Lanarkshire	14.	Aberdeen City

Aberdeenshire, Banff & Moray

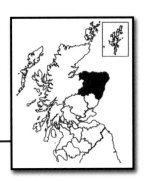

Aberdeenshire, Banff & Moray - one of the easiest ways to explore the area is by following one of the signposted tourist routes and theme trails. Perhaps the most famous of these is the Malt Whisky Trail around magnificent Speyside which links the award winning Speyside Cooperage and eight famous distilleries. Aberdeenshire is very much Scotland's "Castle Country" and 13 of the region's finest castles and great houses are located along Scotland's only Castle Trail. A lesser known feature of Scotland's North East is the fact that 10% of Scotland's Standing Stones are to be found here. Archaeolink, Scotland's prehistory park, interprets the early history of Grampian and promotes a journey through time for all ages. Royal Deeside has many attractions associated with Queen Victoria and a succession of British monarchs. There are many well known sites in this part of the region along the Victorian Heritage Trail including Balmoral Castle, home to royalty for 150 years, Crathie Church, Royal Lochnagar Distillery and Loch Muick. Around the Coastal Trail you will find some of Europe's best coastline, visually stunning, clean air and clear seawater. There are delightful villages such as the "Local Hero" village of Pennan, picturesque harbours, spectacular cliff formations, 150 miles of unspoilt beaches and fabulous golf courses such as Cruden Bay, Royal Tarlair, Duff House Royal and many more along the Moray Firth, as well as the company of the area's wildlife from dolphins to seals and seabirds.

HOTEL

**ABERDEEN. Skene House Hotel Suites. Skene House, Holburn (01224 580000).
Skene House, Whitehall (01224 646600). Skene House, Rosemount (01224 645971).**
A suite for the price of a hotel room. Relax into the warm welcoming atmosphere of Aberdeen's unique Skene House Hotel Suites and enjoy the luxury of our home from home comforts. Skene House Hotel Suites not only provide superb accommodation but can help plan sightseeing itineraries, golf itineraries, coach transportation, car hires and much more. They are an excellent choice if you are here with family. SEE ALSO COLOUR ADVERT IN GOLF SECTION.
Rates: from £29.50 per person per night based upon 6 sharing a 3 bedroom suite.
**e-mail: holburn@skene-house.co.uk
          whitehall@skene-house.co.uk
          rosemount@skene-house.co.uk
www.skene-house.co.uk**

RESIDENTIAL CLUB   1/12   ♀

**The Royal British Legion Scotland, Ravenswood Residential Club, Ramsay Road, Banchory AB31 5TS
(Secretary: 01330 822347).**
A warm welcome to Legion members and guests. Single and Double rooms available. Usual Club activities and entertainment. SEE ALSO COLOUR ADVERTISEMENT IN GOLF SECTION.
• Bed and Breakfast from £25
www.banchorylegion.com

Argyll & Bute

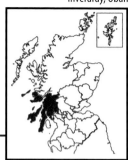

Minard Castle, Inveraray

Stay in style in our 19th Century Scottish castle which stands in its own grounds in beautiful countryside beside Loch Fyne, three-quarters-of-a-mile from the A83 Inveraray to Lochgilphead road. A peaceful location for a quiet break, you can stroll in the grounds, walk by the loch, explore the woods, or use Minard Castle as your base for touring this beautiful area with its lochs, hills, gardens, castles and historic sites. Breakfast in the Morning Room and relax in the Drawing Room. The comfortable bedrooms have colour television, tea/coffee making facilities and en suite bathrooms. *No smoking in the house* • *Evening Meals available within five miles.*
Bed and Breakfast £55-£60 per person, children half price • *Open April to October* • *We offer a warm welcome in a family home* • *Self-catering property also available, £150 to £370 per week.*
Reinold & Anne Gayre, Minard Castle, Minard PA32 8YB • **Tel & Fax: 01546 886272**
e-mail: reinoldgayre@minardcastle.com • **www.minardcastle.com**

HAWTHORN. A warm welcome awaits you in this delightful bungalow set in 20 acres of farmland where we breed our own Highland cattle which graze at the front. It is a peaceful location as we are set back from the road, and an ideal spot for touring, with the main ferry terminal at Oban just 10 minutes away. Our luxurious rooms have their own special sitting room attached where you can enjoy your coffee or a glass of wine in peace. We also have our own on-site restaurant.

Mrs J. Currie, Hawthorn, 5 Keil Crofts, Benderloch, Oban PA37 1QS • **01631 720452**
e-mail: june@hawthorncottages.com • **www.hawthorncottages.com**

symbols

Months open (eg:4/10 means April to October)

🐕	Pets Welcome
🐎	Children Welcome
♿	Suitable for Disabled
🚭	Totally non-smoking
🍷	Licensed

board

B&B   4/10   🐎 ♿ ⊘

INVERARAY. Reinold and Anne Gayre, Minard Castle, Minard PA32 8YB (Tel & Fax: 01546 886272).
Stay in style in our 19th Century Scottish castle which stands in its own grounds in beautiful countryside beside
Loch Fyne, three-quarters-of-a-mile from the A83 Inveraray to Lochgilphead road. A peaceful location for a quiet
break, you can stroll in the grounds, walk by the loch, explore the woods, or use Minard Castle as your base for
touring this beautiful area with its lochs, hills, gardens, castles and historic sites. Breakfast in the Morning Room
and relax in the Drawing Room. The comfortable bedrooms have colour television, tea/coffee making facilities and
en suite bathrooms. Evening Meals available within five miles. We offer a warm welcome in a family home.
SEE ALSO COLOUR ADVERT.
Rates: Bed and Breakfast £55-£60 per person per night, children half price.
• No smoking in the house • Open April to October • Self-catering property also available, £150 to £370 per week.
STB ★★★★ *B&B,* **STB ★★★** *SELF-CATERING.*
e-mail: reinoldgayre@minardcastle.com   **www.minardcastle.com**

B&B

OBAN. Mrs J. Currie, Hawthorn, 5 Keil Crofts, Benderloch, Oban PA37 1QS (01631 720452).
A warm welcome awaits you in this delightful bungalow set in 20 acres of farmland where we breed our own
Highland cattle which graze at the front. It is a peaceful location as we are set back from the road, and an ideal spot
for touring, with the main ferry terminal at Oban just 10 minutes away. Our luxurious rooms have their own special
sitting room attached where you can enjoy your coffee or a glass of wine in peace. We also have our own
restaurant on site. SEE ALSO COLOUR ADVERT.
e-mail: june@hawthorncottages.com   **www.hawthorncottages.com**

Borders

THE SCOTTISH BORDERS stretch from the rolling hills and moorland in the west, through gentler valleys to the rich agricultural plains of the east, and the rocky Berwickshire coastline with its secluded coves and picturesque fishing villages. Through the centre, tracing a silvery course from the hills to the sea, runs the River Tweed which provides some of the best fishing in Scotland. As well as fishing there is golf – 18 courses in all, riding or cycling and some of the best modern sports centres and swimming pools in the country. Friendly towns and charming villages are there to be discovered, while castles, abbeys, stately homes and museums illustrate the exciting and often bloody history of the area. It's this history which is commemorated in the Common Ridings and other local festivals, creating a colourful pageant much enjoyed by visitors and native Borderers alike.

One of the delights of travelling is finding gifts and keepsakes with a genuine local flavour, and dedicated souvenir hunters will find a plentiful supply of traditional delicacies, from drinks to baking and handmade sweets. Handcrafted jewellery, pottery, glass and woodwork, as well as beautiful tweeds and high quality knitwear can be found in the many interesting little shops throughout the area.

Scottish Borders eating establishments take pride in providing particularly good food and service and the choice of hotels, inns restaurants and cafes make eating out a real pleasure.

B&B   1/12

BIGGAR. South Mains Farm, Biggar ML12 6HF (01899 860226)
South Mains Farm is a working family farm, situated in an elevated position with good views, on the B7016 between Biggar and Broughton. An ideal place to take a break on a North/South journey. Edinburgh 29 miles, Peebles 11 miles. Well situated for touring the Border regions in general. A comfortable bed and excellent breakfast provided in this centrally heated and well furnished farmhouse. The lounge has a log fire and the bedrooms, two double and one single, have hand-basins, electric blankets and tea/coffee making facilities. Guest bathroom. Open all year. Car essential, parking. SEE ALSO COLOUR ADVERT.

Edinburgh & Lothians

EDINBURGH & LOTHIANS - Scotland's Capital is home to a wide range of attractions offering something for visitors of all ages. The Royal Mile holds many of the most historic sights, but within a short distance there are fine gardens to visit or the chance to sample the latest in interactive technology. A network of signposted paths allow walkers of all abilities to enjoy the contrasts of the area, whether for a leisurely stroll or at a more energetic pace. The annual Festival in August is part of the city's tradition and visitors flock to enjoy the performing arts, theatre, ballet, cinema and music, and of course "The Tattoo" itself. At the Festival Fringe there are free shows and impromptu acts, a jazz festival and book festivals. Other events take place throughout the year, including children's festivals, science festivals, the famous Royal Highland Show and the Hogmanay street party. East Lothian has beautiful countryside and dramatic coastline, all only a short distance from Edinburgh. Once thriving fishing villages, North Berwick and Dunbar now cater for visitors who delight in their traditional seaside charm. In Midlothian you can step back in time with a visit to Rosslyn Chapel or Borthwick and Crichton Castles, or seize the chance to brush up on your swing at one of the excellent courses in the area. The Almond Valley Heritage Centre in Livingston has a museum, friendly farmyard animals and children's activities, while the Butterfly and Insect World at Lasswade offers a fabulous tropical display.

A relaxed and friendly base is provided at Cruachan from which to explore central Scotland. The centre of Edinburgh can be reached by train in only 30 minutes from nearby Bathgate, and Glasgow is only 35 minutes by car. All rooms en suite/private facilities, full hospitality tray, fresh towels daily, colour TV and central heating. Hosts Kenneth and Jacqueline ensure you receive the utmost in quality of service, meticulously presented accommodation and of course a full Scottish breakfast. They look forward to having the pleasure of your company.

Bed and Breakfast from £29 per person per night.

78 East Main Street, Blackburn EH47 7QS
Tel: 01506 655221 • Fax: 01506 652395
e-mail: cruachan.bb@virgin.net • www.cruachan.co.uk

Cruachan B&B

AA ★★★

INTERNATIONAL GUEST HOUSE • EDINBURGH

Conveniently situated 1½ miles south of Princes Street on the main A701, on the main bus route. Private parking. All bedrooms en suite, with direct-dial telephone, colour television and tea/coffee making facilities. Some rooms enjoy magnificent views across to the extinct volcano of Arthur's Seat. The full Scottish breakfasts served on the finest bone china are a delight. Contact Mrs Niven for details. *AA* ★★★★

B&B from £35 to £75 single; £60 to £130 double

37 Mayfield Gardens, Edinburgh EH9 2BX • Tel: 0131 667 2511 • Fax: 0131 667 1112
e-mail: intergh1@yahoo.co.uk • www.accommodation-edinburgh.com

---

B&B   1/12

BLACKBURN. Cruachan B&B, 78 East Main Street, Blackburn EH47 7QS (01506 655221; Fax: 01506 652395).
A relaxed and friendly base is provided at Cruachan from which to explore central Scotland. The centre of Edinburgh can be reached by train in only 30 minutes from nearby Bathgate, and Glasgow is only 35 minutes by car. All rooms en suite/private facilities, full hospitality tray, fresh towels daily, colour TV and central heating. Hosts Kenneth and Jacqueline ensure you receive the utmost in quality of service, meticulously presented accommodation and of course a full Scottish breakfast. They look forward to having the pleasure of your company. SEE ALSO COLOUR ADVERT.
Rates: Bed and Breakfast from £29 per person per night.
STB ★★★ B&B, AA ★★★
e-mail: cruachan.bb@virgin.net   www.cruachan.co.uk

GUEST HOUSE   1/12

EDINBURGH. International Guest House, 37 Mayfield Gardens, Edinburgh EH9 2BX (0131-667 2511; Fax: 0131-667 1112).
Conveniently situated one-and-a-half miles south of Princes Street on the main A701, on the main bus route. Private parking. All bedrooms en suite, with direct-dial telephone, colour television and tea/coffee making facilities. Some rooms enjoy magnificent views across to the extinct volcano of Arthur's Seat. The full Scottish breakfasts served on the finest bone china are a delight. Contact Mrs Niven for details. SEE ALSO COLOUR ADVERT.
Rates: B&B from £35 to £75 single; £60 to £130 double.
AA ★★★★
e-mail: intergh1@yahoo.co.uk   www.accommodation-edinburgh.com

Fife

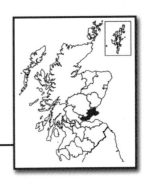

HOTEL

LUNDIN LINKS. The Lundin Links Hotel, Lundin Links KY8 6AP (01333 320207; Fax: 01333 320930)
Golfing Packages Are Our Speciality. The perfect location for a golfing break, only minutes from the famous 'Old Course' at St Andrews, and with over 40 top courses all within an hour's drive. Only 9 miles from St Andrews and 45 minutes from Edinburgh. 21 superb en suite bedrooms, with top cuisine and traditional bars. SEE ALSO COLOUR ADVERT IN GOLF SECTION.

e-mail: info@lundin-links-hotel.co.uk   www.lundin-links-hotel.co.uk

Glasgow & District

Stepps

Stepps village is situated north-east of Glasgow just off the A80. This self-built family home nestles down a quiet leafy lane offering the ideal location for an overnight stay or touring base with the main routes to Edinburgh, Stirling and the North on our doorstep. Easy commuting to Loch Lomond, the Trossachs or Clyde Valley. M8 exit 11 from the south, or A80 Cumbernauld Road from the north. Glasgow only ten minutes away, Glasgow Airport 12 miles. Ample parking.

All rooms offer colour TV, tea/coffee tray and en suite or private facilities. Generous Continental-style breakfast incl. Home from Home – warm welcome assured!

Self-catering also available.

From £25 to £35 per person per night.
Mrs P. Wells • 0141-779 1990 • Fax: 0141-779 1951
e-mail: phyl@avenueend.co.uk • www.avenueend.co.uk

"Avenue End" B&B
21 West Avenue, Stepps,
Glasgow G33 6ES

B&B   1/12

STEPPS. "Avenue End" B&B, Stepps, Glasgow G33 6ES (0141 779 1990; Fax: 0141 779 1951)
Stepps village is situated north-east of Glasgow just off the A80. This self-built family home nestles down a quiet leafy lane offering the ideal location for an overnight stay or touring base with the main routes to Edinburgh, Stirling and the North on our doorstep. Easy commuting to Loch Lomond, the Trossachs or Clyde Valley. M8 exit 11 from the south, or A80 Cumbernauld Road from the north. Glasgow only ten minutes away, Glasgow Airport 12 miles. Ample parking. All rooms offer colour TV, tea/coffee tray and en suite or private facilities. Generous Continental-style breakfast incl. Home from Home – warm welcome assured! Self-catering also available. SEE ALSO COLOUR ADVERT.

e-mail: phyl@avenueend.co.uk   www.avenueend.co.uk

Highlands

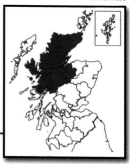

The Whins

114 Kenneth Street, Inverness IV3 5QG
Tel: 01463 236215

Comfortable, small, homely, non-smoking
accommodation awaits you here. Ten minutes bus
and railway stations, with easy access to many golf
courses, walking and cycling areas, and a great base
for touring North, East and West by car, rail or bus.
Two double/twin rooms with TV, tea making,
washbasins and heating off season. Bathroom,
shared toilet and shower; £17 per person.
Write or phone for full details.

HOTEL

INVERNESS. Dunain Park Hotel, Inverness IV3 8JN (01463 230512)
On the outskirts of Inverness and just five miles from Loch Ness, this attractive Georgian Country House stands
in six acres of secluded gardens and woodland. Six suites available, plus five generous sized bedrooms with
Italian marble bathrooms, comfortable lounges with open fires, and award-winning Chefs offering the finest
Highland produce. SEE ALSO COLOUR ADVERT.
e-mail: info@highlandescape.com   www.highlandescapehotels.com

B&B

1/12 🐈 🐕

INVERNESS. Mrs E. MacKenzie, The Whins, 114 Kenneth Street, Inverness IV3 5QG (01463 236215).
Comfortable, small, homely accommodation. 10 minutes bus and railway stations, with easy access to many golf
courses, walking and cycling areas, and a great base for touring North, East and West by car, rail or bus. Bedrooms
have TV, tea making, washbasins and heating off season. Bathroom, shared toilet and shower. Write or phone for
full details. SEE ALSO COLOUR ADVERT.
Rates: £17 per person.
• *Non-smoking.*

Please note

All the information in this book is given in good faith in the belief that it is correct. However, the
publishers cannot guarantee the facts given in these pages, neither are they responsible for
changes in policy, ownership or terms that may take place after the date of going to press.
Readers should always satisfy themselves that the facilities they require are available
and that the terms, if quoted, still apply.

Perth & Kinross

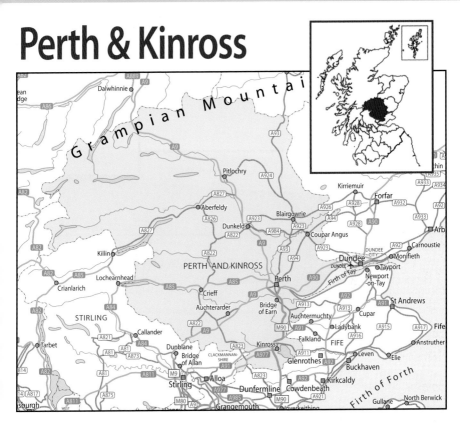

HOTEL

- Children welcome. • Pets welcome.
STB ★★★★ *SMALL HOTEL*
e-mail: hotel@fortingallhotel.com

ABERFELDY. Fortingall Hotel, Fortingall, Aberfeldy PH15 2NQ (Tel/Fax: 01887 830367).
The award-winning four star Fortingall Hotel is set in the heart of the enchanting thatched village of Fortingall, in stunning Highland Perthshire. From the graceful surroundings of the dining room, to the luxury and comfort of the eleven en suite bedrooms, the Hotel offers 21st century comfort and service, whilst retaining its Victorian style and heritage. Combined with the peace and tranquillity of the area, the friendliness of the staff, and the delicious food, the Fortingall Hotel offers first class facilities in a fabulous setting, ensuring you have a memorable stay.

www.fortingallhotel.com

ALYTH. Lands Of Loyal Hotel, Alyth PH11 8JQ (01828 633151; Fax: 01828 633313)
Set on hillside overlooking the Vale of Strathmore lies this impressive Victorian Mansion surrounded by 6 acres of tiered gardens. Our highly acclaimed restaurant makes full use of local fish and game in a style both traditional and imaginative. For the country sportsman fishing and shooting are available, with salmon and trout fishing in the loch and river. Pheasant and grouse shooting, wild fowling and deer stalking also available as the seasons permit. The hotel makes an ideal base for the ambitious golfer with 30 courses within an hour's drive. SEE COLOUR ADVERT IN GOLF SECTION.
STB ★★★★ *HOTEL*
e-mail: info@landsofloyal.com   **www.landsofloyal.com**

Scottish Islands

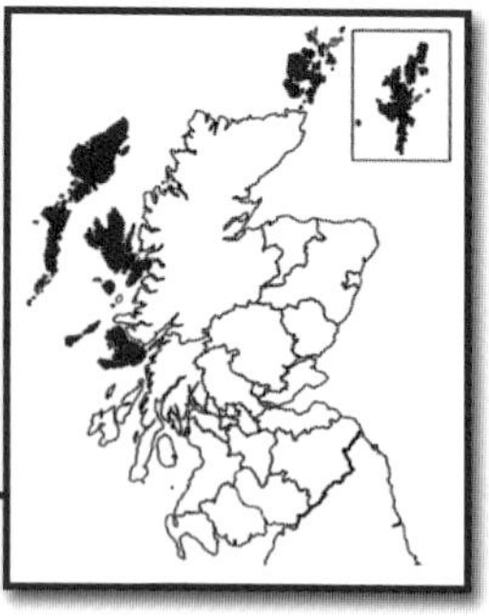

Isle of Islay

HOTEL

PORT ELLEN. Machrie Hotel & Golf Links, Port Ellen, Isle of Islay PA42 7AN (01496 302310; Fax: 01496 302404)
On the beautiful Hebridean island of Islay - a famous classic links course perched above the golden sands of Laggan Bay, and a hotel run with the warmth and informality that brings people back time and again. SEE ALSO COLOUR ADVERT IN GOLF SECTION.
e-mail: machrie@machrie.com **www.machrie.com**

Isle of Skye

Portree

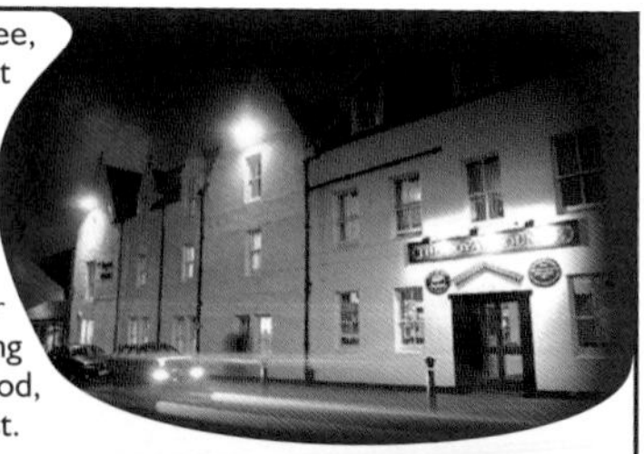

HOTEL 1/12

PORTREE. The Royal Hotel, Portree IV51 9BU (01478 612525; Fax: 01478 613198).
Set overlooking the picturesque harbour of Portree, The Royal Hotel offers you a quiet, relaxing retreat during your stay on Skye. Accommodation consists of 21 well appointed rooms, most overlooking the harbour and featuring private bathroom facilities and colour TV. Room service is available as well as a fitness centre and sauna for guests to use. The Royal Hotel offers a wide and varied menu serving sea food, lamb, venison and tender Highland beef. Vegetarians are also catered for. There is something for everyone, from walking, climbing and watersports to good food, great local arts & crafts, colourful museums and places of interest. SEE ALSO COLOUR ADVERT.
STB ★★★ *HOTEL*
e-mail: info@royal-hotel-skye.com **www.royal-hotel-skye.com**

Wales
Board

North Wales

HOTEL

LLANDUDNO. The Imperial Hotel, Llandudno LL30 1AP (01492 877466; Fax: 01492 878043)
Elegantly Victorian, The Imperial Hotel is situated on the promenade in the beautiful resort of Llandudno, with lovely views of the bay, making it an ideal base for touring North Wales. SEE ALSO COLOUR ADVERT.
e-mail: reception@theimperial.co.uk   www.theimperial.co.uk

HOTEL

LLANDUDNO. The Royal Hotel, Church Walks, Llandudno LL30 2HW(01492 876476; Fax: 01492 870210).
One hour from M6. Seven courses within 20 minutes of Hotel. Start times arranged. Summer and Winter golf breaks. All rooms TV, phone, beverage facilities, en suite. 5 course dinner, licensed. Large on-site car park. SEE ALSO COLOUR ADVERT IN GOLF SECTION.
e-mail: royalllandudno@aol.com   www.royalhotel-llandudno.com

Llanelli

Carmarthenshire

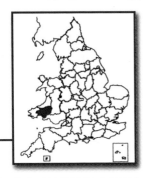

HOTEL   1/12 🐕 🎠 ♿   ♀

LLANELLI. The Diplomat Hotel, Felinfoel Road, Aelybryn, Llanelli SA15 3PJ (01554 756156; Fax: 01554 751649).
Privately owned and operated with warmth and generous hospitality. The Diplomat Hotel offers a rare combination of charm and character found only in old rural and country hotels, with excellent well appointed facilities to ensure your comfort and convenience, including Health and Leisure club. Explore the Gower Peninsula and the breathtaking West Wales coastline. Salmon and trout fishing, horse riding, championship golf courses or motor racing at Pembrey circuit are all within reach. SEE ALSO COLOUR ADVERT.
AA/WTB ★★★
e-mail: reservations@diplomat-hotel-wales.com   **www.diplomat-hotel-wales.com**

symbols

Months open (eg:4/10 means April to October)

🐕	Pets Welcome
🎠	Children Welcome
♿	Suitable for Disabled
🚭	Totally non-smoking
♀	Licensed

 board

Fishguard

Pembrokeshire

New Qu

Tre

A487

Strumble
Head

Cardigan
A484

Newcastle
Emlyn

A487

Fishguard

A484 · A485

A487

A40

CARMARTHENSHIRE

A40

St David's

Ramsey
Island

PEMBROKESHIRE

A478

Carmarthen

Llandei

St Brides
Bay

A487

Haverfordwest

A40

Narberth

A40 · St Clears

A48

A483

Amman

Skomer
Island

Milford
Haven

A4076

A477 · A4066

A484

A48

Neyland A4075

A478

Kidwelly

A476

SWANSEA

Skokholm
Island

Pembroke
Dock

A477

Tenby

Carmarthen
Bay

Burry
Port

Llanelli

M4

Pembroke

A4139

Caldey
Island

Swansea

A48

St Govan's
Head

SWANSEA

Port
Einon

A4118

Mumbles
Head

T

Heathfield Mansion
Letterston, Near Fishguard SA62 5EG
Tel: 01348 840263
e-mail: angelica.rees@virgin.net

★★★

A Georgian country house in 16 acres of pasture
and woodland, Heathfield is an ideal location for
the appreciation of Pembrokeshire's many natural
attractions. There is excellent golf, riding and fishing in the
vicinity and the coast is only a few minutes' drive away. The accommodation is very comfortable
and two of the three bedrooms have en suite bathrooms. The cuisine and wines are well above average.
This is a most refreshing venue for a tranquil and wholesome holiday. *Welcome Host Gold*

Pets welcome by prior arrangement only • Cyclists and Coastal Path walkers welcome
Bed & Breakfast from £30 per person • Dinner by arrangement • Discounts for weekly stays

---

B&B

FISHGUARD. Heathfield Mansion, Letterston, Near Fishguard SA62 5EG (01348 840263).
A Georgian country house in 16 acres of pasture and woodland, Heathfield is an ideal location for the appreciation
of Pembrokeshire's many natural attractions. There is excellent golf, riding and fishing in the vicinity and the coast
is only a few minutes' drive away. The accommodation is very comfortable and two of the three bedrooms have
en suite bathrooms. The cuisine and wines are well above average. This is a most refreshing venue for a tranquil
and wholesome holiday. Cyclists and Coastal Path walkers welcome. SEE ALSO COLOUR ADVERT.
Rates: Bed & Breakfast from £30 per person; Dinner by arrangement. Discounts for weekly stays
• Pets welcome by prior arrangement only
WTB ★★★, *WELCOME HOST GOLD*
e-mail: angelica.rees@virgin.net

Powys

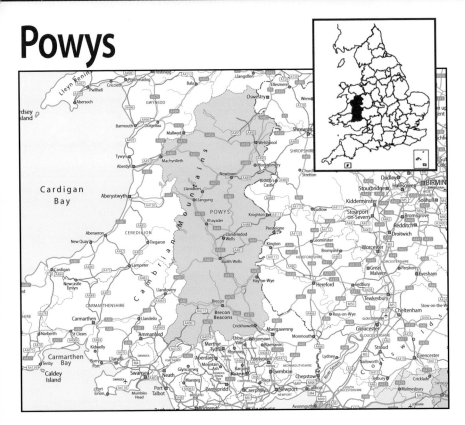

POWYS is situated right on England's doorstep and boasts some of the most spectacular scenery in Europe. Ideal for an action packed holiday with fishing, golfing, pony trekking, sailing and canal cruising readily available, and walkers have a choice of everything from riverside trails to mountain hikes. Offa's Dyke Path and Glyndwr's Way pass through the region. Offa's Dyke Path runs for 177 miles through Border country, often following the ancient earthworks, while Glyndwr's Way takes in some of the finest landscape features in Wales on its journey from Knighton to Machynlleth and back to the borders at Welshpool.

There are border towns with Georgian architecture and half-timbered black and white houses to visit, or wander round the wonderful shops in the book town of Hay, famous for its Literary Festival each May. There are Victorian spa towns too, with even the smallest of places holding festivals and events throughout the year.

Ratings & Awards

For the first time ever the AA, VisitBritain, VisitScotland, and the Wales Tourist Board will use a single method of assessing and rating serviced accommodation. Irrespective of which organisation inspects an establishment the rating awarded will be the same, using a common set of standards, giving a clear guide of what to expect. The RAC is no longer operating an Hotel inspection and accreditation business.

Accommodation Standards: Star Grading Scheme

Using a scale of 1-5 stars the objective quality ratings give a clear indication of accommodation standard, cleanliness, ambience, hospitality, service and food, This shows the full range of standards suitable for every budget and preference, and allows visitors to distinguish between the quality of accommodation and facilities on offer in different establishments. All types of board and self-catering accommodation are covered, including hotels, B&Bs, holiday parks, campus accommodation, hostels, caravans and camping, and boats.

VisitBritain and the regional tourist boards, enjoyEngland.com, VisitScotland and VisitWales, and the AA have full details of the grading system on their websites

The more stars, the higher level of quality

★★★★★
exceptional quality, with a degree of luxury

★★★★
excellent standard throughout

★★★
very good level of quality and comfort

★★
good quality, well presented and well run

★
acceptable quality; simple, practical, no frills

National Accessible Scheme

If you have particular mobility, visual or hearing needs, look out for the National Accessible Scheme. You can be confident of finding accommodation or attractions that meet your needs by looking for the following symbols.

 Typically suitable for a person with sufficient mobility to climb a flight of steps but would benefit from fixtures and fittings to aid balance

 Typically suitable for a person with restricted walking ability and for those that may need to use a wheelchair some of the time and can negotiate a maximum of three steps

 Typically suitable for a person who depends on the use of a wheelchair and transfers unaided to and from the wheelchair in a seated position. This person may be an independent traveller

 Typically suitable for a person who depends on the use of a wheelchair in a seated position. This person also requires personal or mechanical assistance (eg carer, hoist).

England
Self-Catering

Cornwall

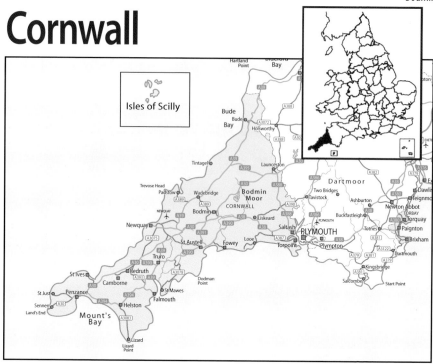

Penrose Burden Holiday Cottages

St Breward, Bodmin, Cornwall PL30 4LZ
Tel: 01208 850277 / 850617; Fax: 01208 850915
www.penroseburden.co.uk

Situated within easy reach of both coasts and Bodmin Moor on a large farm overlooking a wooded valley with own salmon and trout fishing. These stone cottages with exposed beams and quarry tiled floors have been featured on TV and are award-winners. Home-made meals can be delivered daily. All are suitable for wheelchair users and dogs are welcomed. Our cottages sleep from two to seven and are open all year.

Please write or telephone for a colour brochure.   Nancy Hall

Close to The Eden Project

Bude, Gorran Haven , Looe

LOWER KITLEIGH COTTAGE Week St Mary, Near Bude, Cornwall

Pretty, Listed farmhouse in unspoilt country near magnificent coast. Newly renovated with all conveniences, yet retaining its charm, it stands in a peaceful grassy garden with picnic table and own parking. The sitting room has period furniture, inglenook fireplace, free logs and colour TV. The fully equipped kitchen has fridge/freezer, double sink, electric cooker and washer/tumble dryer. Three bedrooms with panoramic views, cots, duvets. Well-controlled dogs allowed. Riding nearby, golf, safe beaches, surfing, Cornish Moors, markets, cliff walks. All electricity inclusive, and central heating ensures a cosy stay throughout the year. Prices from £275 to £650 weekly; reductions for part week. Sleeps seven plus cot.

Mr and Mrs T. Bruce-Dick, 114 Albert Street, London NW1 7NE
Tel: 0207-485 8976   www.tbdarchitects.co.uk

Two self-contained apartments situated in detached house surrounded by large garden, in quiet rural area with private parking. Both apartments have sea views, double glazing, central heating and are fully furnished. 600 yards from safe, clean, sandy beach, harbour and shops. Superb coastal walks. Gorran Haven is ideally located for exploring Cornwall with Mevagissey fishing village and the Lost Gardens of Heligan being only three miles distant.

Tregillan

Short breaks available • From £170 - £520 per week.

2 to 3 ★

- *Sleep 2-4 persons • Pets welcome*
- *Children welcome • Open all year*

e-mail: tregillanapartment@tiscali.co.uk
www.tregillanapartments.co.uk

Mrs S. Pike, Tregillan,
Trewollock Lane, Gorran Haven,
St Austell PL26 6NT
Tel: 01726 842452

Raven Rock and Spindrift
Contact: Mrs S. Gill, Bodrigy,
Plaidy, Looe PL13 1LF
Tel: 01503 263122

- *Two bungalows adjacent to Plaidy Beach. Spindrift has en suite bedroom, sleeps two; Raven Rock has two bedrooms and sleeps four. Own parking spaces, central heating, wheelchair accessible. Semi-detached bungalows are fully furnished, well equipped and have sea views. Set in peaceful surroundings at Plaidy. Open plan lounge-diner-kitchen. Colour TV. Patio garden. Electricity and gas included in rent. Pet by arrangement. Personally supervised.*
- *Looe is a fishing port with a variety of shops and restaurants and is only a few minutes by car or a 15 to 20 minute walk.*
- *Weekly terms: Spindrift from £210 to £350; Raven Rock from £280 to £435. Short breaks (three days minimum) before Easter and after middle of October.*
- *Apartment in centre of town also available (sleeps 6/8).*

Visit the FHG website

www.holidayguides.com

for details of the wide choice of accommodation

featured in the full range of FHG titles

Saltash

COTTAGES　　　　　　　　　　　　　　1/12 🐴　⛟　sleep 2/7

BODMIN. Nancy Hall, Penrose Burden Holiday Cottages, St Breward, Bodmin PL30 4LZ (01208 850277/850617; Fax: 01208 850915).
Situated within easy reach of both coasts and Bodmin Moor on a large farm overlooking a wooded valley with own salmon and trout fishing. Close to Eden Project. These stone cottages with exposed beams and quarry tiled floors have been featured on TV and are award-winners. Home-made meals can be delivered daily. Please write or telephone for a colour brochure. SEE ALSO COLOUR ADVERT.
- All are suitable for wheelchair users • Sleep from 2-7 • Dogs welcome • Open all year.
www.penroseburden.co.uk

SELF-CATERING　　　　　　　　　　　🐴　🐕　sleep 2/7

BUDE. Lower Kitleigh Cottage, Week St Mary, Near Bude.
Pretty, Listed farmhouse in unspoilt country near magnificent coast. Newly renovated with all conveniences, yet retaining its charm, it stands in a peaceful grassy garden with picnic table and own parking. The sitting room has period furniture, inglenook fireplace, free logs and colour TV. The fully equipped kitchen has fridge/freezer, double sink, electric cooker and washer/tumble dryer. Three bedrooms with panoramic views, cots, duvets. Well-controlled dogs allowed. Riding nearby, golf, safe beaches, surfing, Cornish Moors, markets, cliff walks. All electricity inclusive, and central heating ensures a cosy stay throughout the year. SEE ALSO COLOUR ADVERT.
- Sleeps seven plus cot.
Rates: from £275 to £650 weekly; reductions for part week.
For details contact: Mr and Mrs T. Bruce-Dick, 114 Albert Street, London NW1 7NE (0207-485 8976).
www.tbdarchitects.co.uk

FLATS　　　　　　　　　　　　　　1/12 🐴　🐕　📺 sleep 1/4

GORRAN HAVEN. Mrs S. Pike, Tregillan, Trewollock Lane, Gorran Haven, St Austell PL26 6NT (01726 842452).
Two self-contained apartments situated in detached house surrounded by large garden, in quiet rural area with private parking. Both apartments have sea views, double glazing, central heating and are fully furnished. 600 yards from safe, clean, sandy beach, harbour and shops. Superb coastal walks. Gorran Haven is ideally located for exploring Cornwall with Mevagissey fishing village and the Lost Gardens of Heligan being only three miles distant. Short breaks available. SEE ALSO COLOUR ADVERT.
Rates: From £170 - £520 per week.
- Sleep 2-4 persons • Pets welcome
- Children welcome • Open all year
ETC ★★/★★★
e-mail: tregillanapartment@tiscali.co.uk　　　**www.tregillanapartments.co.uk**

LOOE. Raven Rock and Spindrift.
Two bungalows adjacent to Plaidy Beach. Spindrift has en suite bedroom, sleeps two; Raven Rock has two bedrooms and sleeps four. Own parking spaces, central heating, wheelchair accessible. Semi-detached bungalows are fully furnished, well equipped and have sea views. Set in peaceful surroundings at Plaidy. Open plan lounge-diner-kitchen. Colour TV. Patio garden. Electricity and gas included in rent. Pet by arrangement. Personally supervised. Looe is a fishing port with a variety of shops and restaurants and is only a few minutes by car or a 15 to 20 minute walk. SEE ALSO COLOUR ADVERT.
Rates: weekly terms: Spindrift from £210 to £350; Raven Rock from £280 to £435. Short breaks (three days minimum) before Easter and after middle of October.
• Apartment in centre of town also available (sleeps 6/8).
Contact: Mrs S. Gill, Bodrigy, Plaidy, Looe PL13 1LF (01503 263122).

COTTAGES/HOUSES   1/12 🐕 🐎   🖼️
PADSTOW. Raintree House Holidays (01841 520228).
The Padstow area in North Cornwall - a superb setting offering sun, sea, sand, surfing, wonderful walks and a multitude of nearby attractions, from the historical to the modern. The properties we offer for your holiday home are just as varied but offer an excellent standard of self-catering retreats, with a level of service second to none! Visit our website or phone us to ask for a brochure. There is a 24-hour answering machine in case you phone outside office hours or we are busy when you call. SEE ALSO COLOUR ADVERT
e-mail: gill@raintreehouse.co.uk   www.raintreehouse.co.uk

SALTASH. St Mellion Golf Breaks (01579 383917)..
Self-catering golf breaks including free golf on St Mellion's fabulous courses. Luxury self-catering accommodation including the exclusive course-side Oakridge Estate. We cater from 2-22, and are open to golfers all year round. Free additional use of the superb leisure facilities at St Mellion. Free fishing and broadband internet at some cottages. SEE ALSO COLOUR ADVERT.
e-mail: info@stmelliongolfbreaks.co.uk   www.stmelliongolfbreaks.co.uk

The FHG Directory of Website Addresses
on pages 157-179 is a useful quick reference guide for
holiday accommodation with e-mail and/or website details

FREE or REDUCED RATE entry to Holiday Visits and Attractions – see our
READERS' OFFER VOUCHERS on pages 181-218

symbols

Months open (eg:4/10 means April to October)

   Pets Welcome

   Children Welcome

&   Suitable for Disabled

   Linen provided

self-catering

Min/Max no of persons in one unit (eg:2/6)

Dartmouth

Devon

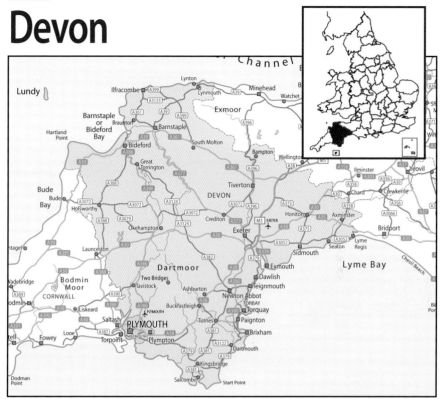

THE OLD BAKEHOUSE
7 Broadstone, Dartmouth TQ6 9NR
Tel & Fax: 01803 834585 • mobile: 07909 680884
ridallsleisure@aol.com • www.oldbakehousedartmouth.co.uk

NON-SMOKING

★★★
SELF CATERING

Four character cottages with free parking, one with garage.
Cottages are in the centre of Dartmouth, two minutes' walk
from River Dart, Royal Avenue Gardens, Coronation Park, shops
and restaurants. The beautiful Blackpool Sands is a 15 minute
drive away. The historic town of Dartmouth is a good centre for
boating, fishing, sailing and swimming. National Trust, coastal
and inland walks. Four cottages with beams and old stone
fireplaces, one with four-poster bed. Open all year. Central heating. Specialising in Autumn, Winter
and Spring Breaks. Pets welcome free. Green Tourism Bronze Award. Terms from £255 to £685.

Looking for holiday accommodation?
for details of hundreds of properties
throughout the UK visit:

www.holidayguides.com

Litle Torrington, Tavistock

COTTAGES   1/12 🐾 ⛱   📶 sleeps 2/6

DARTMOUTH. The Old Bakehouse, 7 Broadstone, Dartmouth TQ6 9NR (Tel & Fax: 01803 834585; mobile: 07909 680884).
Four character cottages with free parking, one with garage. Cottages are in the centre of Dartmouth, two minutes' walk from River Dart, Royal Avenue Gardens, Coronation Park, shops and restaurants. The beautiful Blackpool Sands is a 15 minute drive away. The historic town of Dartmouth is a good centre for boating, fishing, sailing and swimming. National Trust, coastal and inland walks. Four cottages with beams and old stone fireplaces, one with four-poster bed. Central heating. Specialising in Autumn, Winter and Spring Breaks. SEE ALSO COLOUR ADVERT.
Rates: from £255 to £685.
• Pets welcome free • Non-smoking • Open all year.
ETC ★★★, *GREEN TOURISM BRONZE AWARD*.
e-mail: ridallsleisure@aol.com   www.oldbakehousedartmouth.co.uk

LITTLE TORRINGTON. Torridge House Farm Cottages, Little Torrington EX38 8PS (01805 622542).
Join us on the farm, help feed the animals! Very child-friendly and highly recommended, Torridge House Farm Cottages is where young families can join in helping to feed the animals: lambs, hens, ducks, pigs and rabbits, as well as chicks and ducklings. The nine 3&4 star cottages are welcoming, comfortable and well appointed. The small, friendly, family-run farm has panoramic views of glorious Devon countryside. Lots of room to play in the gardens, a heated outdoor summer swimming pool, BBQs, pool, table tennis and play room. We have over 20 years' experience in offering relaxed, hands-on farm holidays. To find out more, please phone for a brochure or visit our website. SEE ALSO COLOUR ADVERT.
e-mail: holidays@torridgehouse.co.uk   www.torridgehouse.co.uk

TAVISTOCK. Mrs P.G.C. Quinton, Higher Quither, Milton Abbot, Tavistock PL19 0PZ (01822 860284).
Edge of Dartmoor. Comfortably furnished studio cottage five miles from the market town of Tavistock. Open-plan barn conversion, ideal for two, but with ample room for family of four. Private walled garden. Private parking. Free coal for open fire. All linen provided. Wonderful walking, riding, fishing country with excellent local pubs. Several golf courses in the area. Easy access to both coastlines of Devon and Cornwall.
• Terms £195 per week. • Pets welcome.

Weymouth

Dorset

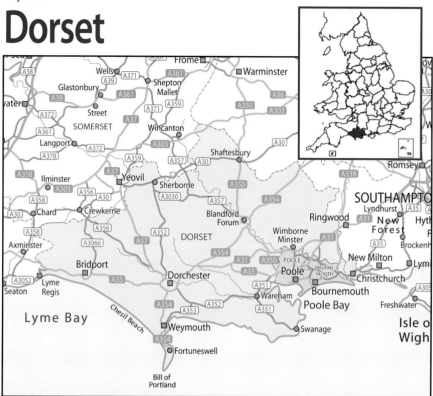

COTTAGES

WEYMOUTH. Grade II Listed Cottage with three bedrooms, two bathrooms, approximately one minute walk to beach, close to harbour. Other properties available weekly or short breaks. Weymouth has a lovely sandy beach and picturesque harbour with pavement cafes. There is plenty to do all year round. SEE ALSO COLOUR ADVERT.
VisitBritain ★★★
Phone: 01305 836495; Mobile: 0797 1256160
e-mail: postmaster@buckwells.plus.com

www.holidaycottageweymouth.co.uk
www.holidaycottagesweymouth.co.uk

Terms quoted in this publication may be subject to increase if rises in costs necessitate

Minehead

Somerset

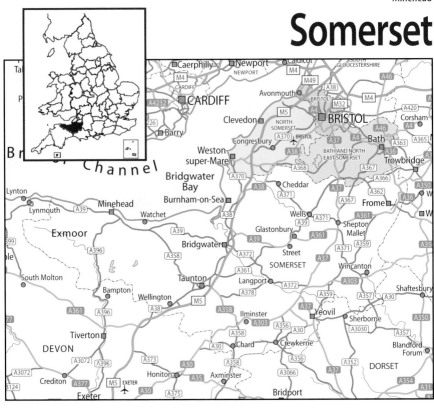

HOLIDAY CENTRE   4/10   🎠 ♿ ▦ sleep 2/8

MINEHEAD near. St Audries Bay Holiday Club, West Quantoxhead, near Minehead TA4 4DY (01984 632515; Fax: 01984 632785).

For over 70 years we have been providing relaxing holidays with a warm welcome at our family-owned and run Holiday Park situated in beautiful surroundings on the Somerset coast, with splendid views and access to the beach. St. Audries is at the foot of the rolling Quantock hills and near to Exmoor. Luxury caravans provide accommodation for self-catering guests, and comfortable chalets for those on half board, plus large level pitches for tents and tourers. With a licensed bar, restaurant, all day coffee bar, shop, entertainment and use of many leisure facilties, everything is on hand to make your stay enjoyable. SEE ALSO COLOUR ADVERT.

ETC ★★★★, *BH & HPA, DAVID BELLAMY GOLD AWARD.*

e-mail: info@staudriesbay.co.uk   www.staudriesbay.co.uk

Ryde

Isle of Wight

The Isle of Wight has several award-winning beaches, including Blue Flag winners, all of which are managed and maintained to the highest standard. Sandown, Shanklin and Ryde offer all the traditional delights; or head for Compton Bay where surfers brave the waves, fossil hunters admire the casts of dinosaur footprints at low tide, kitesurfers leap and soar across the sea and paragliders hurl themselves off the cliffs

Newport is the commercial centre of the Island with many famous high street stores and plenty of places to eat and drink. Ryde has a lovely Victorian Arcade lined with shops selling books and antiques. Cowes is great for sailing garb and Godshill is a treasure chest for the craft enthusiast. Lovers of fine food will enjoy the weekly farmers' markets selling home-grown produce and also the Garlic Festival held annually in August.

The Island's diverse terrain makes it an ideal landscape for walkers and cyclists of all ages and abilities. Pony trekking and beach rides are also popular holiday pursuits and the Island's superb golf courses, beautiful scenery and temperate climate combine to make it the perfect choice for a golfing break.

Creek Gardens

Nestled in a tranquil setting overlooking the picturesque Wootton Creek. These high quality, well equipped holiday apartments and cottages are ideally located for all of the Isle of Wight's many attractions and sandy beaches.

Close to Cowes, host to sailing regattas every summer weekend, or for just enjoying a wealth of outdoor activities including walking, riding, cycling, fishing, exploring, or relaxing and soaking in the wonderful scenery.

**Creek Gardens, New Road, Ryde,
Isle of Wight PO33 4JX
Tel: 01983 883100
enquiries@creekgardens.co.uk**

www.creekgardens.co.uk

RYDE. Creek Gardens, New Road, Ryde PO33 4JX (01983 883100).
Nestled in a tranquil setting overlooking the picturesque Wootton Creek. These high quality, well equipped holiday apartments and cottages are ideally located for all of the Isle of Wight's many attractions and sandy beaches. Close to Cowes, host to sailing regattas every summer weekend, or for just enjoying a wealth of outdoor activities including walking, riding, cycling, fishing, exploring, or relaxing and soaking in the wonderful scenery. SEE ALSO COLOUR ADVERT.
e-mail: enquiries@creekgardens.co.uk   www.creekgardens.co.uk

Ely

Cambridgeshire

COTTAGE   1/12   🛏 sleep 2/5
ELY. Cathedral House, 17 St Mary's Street, Ely CB7 4ER (01353 662124)
The Coach House has been imaginatively converted into a delightful abode full of character and charm, situated close to Ely Cathedral. Arranged on two floors, the accommodation downstairs comprises a sitting room and country-style kitchen. Upstairs there are two charming double rooms (one has a view of the Cathedral), and a cosy single room. All have an en suite bathroom, with a toilet, wash hand basin and a half-size bath with shower taps. Gas central heating. Linen, towels, toilet soap, cleaning materials and some basic provisions are provided. SEE ALSO COLOUR ADVERT.
Rates: Prices range from £200 to £750 depending on season and length of stay. Special rates for two people.
e-mail: farndale@cathedralhouse.co.uk   **www.cathedralhouse.co.uk**

symbols

Months open (eg:4/10 means April to October)

  Pets Welcome

  Children Welcome

♿ Suitable for Disabled

🛏 Linen provided

Min/Max no of persons in one unit (eg:2/6)

self-catering

Norfolk

GREAT YARMOUTH. Clippesby Hall, Clippesby NR29 3BL (01493 367800).
Lodges, cottages and touring park. Once visited, never forgotten, the award-winning Clippesby Hall is the ideal base for exploring the Broads National Park and the Norfolk coast (or even just putting your feet up). This unique wooded country setting offers swimming, tennis, mini golf, a family pub, and so much more. Winner of East of England Tourist Board Award "Best Holiday Park" 2007. Call now for a free brochure. SEE ALSO COLOUR ADVERT.
ETC ★★★★★
www.clippesby.com

Eye, Kessingland

Suffolk

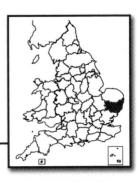

Countryside lodges situated in an idyllic location in North Suffolk. Very well appointed with fitted kitchen including microwave and fridge, en suite master bedroom, family bathroom and a twin bedded room. Open plan lounge with remote control colour TV and a sofa bed that can sleep two adults. Double-glazed, with full central heating. Open all year. Pets and children welcome. Credit cards accepted.

Terms
£285 to £595
Sleep 6

★★★★
SELF CATERING

Contact: **Peter Havers,**
Athelington Hall, Horham, Eye, Suffolk IP21 5EJ

Tel: 01728 628233 • Fax: 01379 384491 • mobile: 07850 989522
e-mail: peter@logcabinholidays.co.uk • www.logcabinholidays.co.uk

---

Kessingland Cottage Kessingland Beach

• Sleeps 6 • Children and disabled persons welcome • Available Ist March to 7th January •

An exciting three-bedroomed semi-detached cottage situated on the beach, three miles south of sandy beach at Lowestoft. Fully and attractively furnished with colour TV. Delightful sea and lawn views from floor-to-ceiling windows of lounge. Accommodation for up to six people. Well equipped kitchen with electric cooker, fridge, hot and cold water; electric immersion heater. Electricity by £1 coin meter. Bathroom with bath and shower. No linen or towels provided. Only a few yards to beach and sea fishing. One mile to wildlife country park with mini-train. Buses quarter-of-a-mile and shopping centre half-a-mile. Parking, but car not essential.

SAE to Mr. S. Mahmood, I56 Bromley Road, Beckenham, Kent BR3 6PG (Tel & Fax: 020 8650 0539) e-mail: jeeptrek@kjti.co.uk • www.k-cottage.co.uk

Weekly terms from £95 in early March and early December to £375 in high season.

The FHG Directory of Website Addresses
on pages 157-179 is a useful quick reference guide for holiday accommodation with e-mail and/or website details

Please note
All the information in this book is given in good faith in the belief that it is correct. However, the publishers cannot guarantee the facts given in these pages, neither are they responsible for changes in policy, ownership or terms that may take place after the date of going to press. Readers should always satisfy themselves that the facilities they require are available and that the terms, if quoted, still apply.

EYE. Athelington Hall Log Cabin Holidays.
Countryside lodges situated in an idyllic location in North Suffolk. Very well appointed with fitted kitchen including microwave and fridge, en suite master bedroom, family bathroom and a twin bedded room. Open plan lounge with remote control colour TV and a sofa bed that can sleep two adults. Double-glazed, with full central heating. Open all year. Credit cards accepted. SEE ALSO COLOUR ADVERT.
Rates: £285 to £595
• Sleep 6. • Pets and children welcome.
Contact: Peter Havers, Athelington Hall, Horham, Eye IP21 5EJ (01728 628233; Fax: 01379 384491; Mobile: 07850 989522)
e-mail: peter@logcabinholidays.co.uk   www.logcabinholidays.co.uk

COTTAGE   3/12 🐾 🐴 ♿   sleep 1/6
KESSINGLAND. Kessingland Cottage, Kessingland Beach.
An exciting three-bedroom, semi-detached cottage situated on the beach, three miles south of sandy beach at Lowestoft. Fully and attractively furnished with colour TV. Delightful sea and lawn views from floor-to-ceiling windows of lounge. Well equipped kitchen with electric cooker, fridge, hot and cold water; electric heater. Electricity by £1 coin meter. Bathroom with bath and shower. No linen or towels provided. Only a few yards to beach and sea fishing. One mile to wildlife country park with mini-train. Buses quarter-of-a-mile and shopping centre half-a-mile. Parking, but car is not essential.
Rates: Weekly terms from £95 in early March and early December to £375 in peak season.
• Accommodation for up to six people. • Children welcome. • Disabled persons welcome.
• Available 1st March to 7th January.
SAE to Mr. S. Mahmood, 156 Bromley Road, Beckenham, Kent BR3 6PG (Tel & Fax: 0208 650 0539)
e-mail: jeeptrek@kjti.co.uk   www.k-cottage.co.uk

Grosmont, Skipton

North Yorkshire

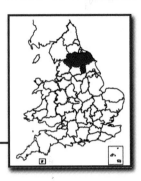

mallard cottage 25 Esk Valley, Grosmont, Whitby

A steam enthusiasts' dream! Beside the North Yorkshire Moors Railway, this tastefully refurbished cottage retains much of its original character with beams, inglenook fireplaces and views over open countryside. A haven for walkers; Whitby and York within easy reach. Shop, cafe, post office and pub nearby.

◆ Two bedrooms ◆ double sofa bed ◆ bathroom with shower ◆
◆ All fuel included ◆ electric cooking ◆
fridge/freezer ◆ microwave
◆ washing machine ◆ TV ◆ video ◆
storage heaters ◆ electric fire
◆ duvets and blankets ◆ garden &
furniture ◆ private parking ◆ no pets
◆ no smoking ◆ all linen provided

www.mallardcottageeskvalley.co.uk

Sleeps 4/6

Contact: **Mrs P. Robinson,
11 Scampton Close,
Thornaby,
Stockton-on-Tees,
Durham TS17 0LH**
Tel: 01642 761317

New Close Farm

FHG Diploma Award Winner

A supa dupa cottage on New Close Farm in the heart of Craven Dales with panoramic views over the Aire Valley. Excellent area for walking, cycling, fishing, golf and touring.

• Two double and one single bedrooms; bathroom.
• Colour TV and video.
• Full central heating and double glazing.
• Bed linen, towels and all amenities included in the price.
• Sorry, no young children, no pets.
• Non-smokers preferred.
• From £300-£350. Winter Short Breaks available.

The weather can't be guaranteed but your comfort can
Kirkby Malham, Skipton BD23 4DP
Tel: 01729 830240 • Fax: 01729 830179
e-mail: brendajones@newclosefarmyorkshire.co.uk
website: www.newclosefarmyorkshire.co.uk

Looking for holiday accommodation?

for details of hundreds of properties

throughout the UK including

comprehensive coverage of all areas of Scotland try:

www.holidayguides.com

knavesmire cottage, 52 tadcaster road, york

This early Victorian cottage is the ideal base for a holiday in York. Knavesmire Cottage is a charming, Grade II Listed period cottage which is situated close to York race course.

It offers cosy and comfortable accommodation which is tastefully decorated throughout; fully fitted, well equipped kitchen, separate dining room and sitting room. Courtyard garden and parking for one car.

The cottage sleeps four in one double room and one room with twin beds, plus a cot.

Prices from £250 to £390 per week.

Mr and Mrs Slater • Tel: 01904 798272

COTTAGE 1/12 sleep 2/6

GROSMONT. Mallard Cottage, 25 Esk Valley, Grosmont, Whitby.
A steam enthusiasts' dream! Beside the North Yorkshire Moors Railway, this tastefully refurbished cottage retains much of its original character with beams, inglenook fireplaces and views over open countryside. A haven for walkers; Whitby and York within easy reach. Shop, cafe, post office and pub nearby. Two bedrooms, double sofa bed, bathroom with shower. All fuel included. Electric cooking, fridge/freezer, microwave, washing machine, TV, video. Storage heaters, electric fire. Duvets and blankets. All linen provided. Garden and furniture. Private parking. SEE ALSO COLOUR ADVERT.
• No pets • No smoking • Sleeps 4/6
Contact: Mrs P. Robinson, 11 Scampton Close, Thornaby, Stockton-on-Tees, Durham TS17 0LH (01642 761317).

LODGES 1/12 sleep 2/10

HARROGATE. Rosemary Helme, Helme Pasture Lodges & Cottages, Old Spring Wood, Hartwith Bank, Summerbridge, Harrogate HG3 4DR (01423 780279; Fax: 01423 780994).
Country accommodation for owners and dogs and numerous walks in unspoilt Nidderdale. Central for Harrogate, York, Herriot and Bronte country. National Trust area.
ETC ★★★★, ETC Category 1 for Disabled Access.
e-mail: helmepasture@btinternet.com
www.helmepasture.co.uk

COTTAGE

SKIPTON. Mrs Brenda Jones, New Close Farm, Kirkby Malham, Skipton BD23 4DP (01729 830240; Fax: 01729 830179).
A supa dupa cottage on New Close Farm in the heart of Craven Dales with panoramic views over the Aire Valley. Excellent area for walking, cycling, fishing, golf and touring. Two double and one single bedrooms; bathroom. Colour TV and video. Full central heating and double glazing. Bed linen, towels and all amenities included in the price. The weather can't be guaranteed but your comfort can. SEE ALSO COLOUR ADVERT.
Rates: from £300-£350. Winter Short Breaks available.
• Sorry, no young children • No pets • Non-smokers preferred
FHG DIPLOMA AWARD WINNER
e-mail: brendajones@newclosefarmyorkshire.co.uk   www.newclosefarmyorkshire.co.uk

---

COTTAGE

YORK. Knavesmire Cottage, 52 Tadcaster Road, York.
This early Victorian cottage is the ideal base for a holiday in York. Knavesmire Cottage is a charming, Grade II Listed period cottage which is situated close to York race course. It offers cosy and comfortable accommodation which is tastefully decorated throughout; fully fitted, well equipped kitchen, separate dining room and sitting room. Courtyard garden and parking for one car. The cottage sleeps four in one double room and one room with twin beds, plus a cot. SEE ALSO COLOUR ADVERT.
Contact: Mr and Mrs Slater (01904 798272).
Rates: from £250 to £390 per week.
ETC ★★★

Northumberland

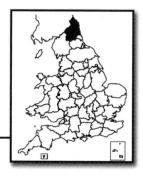

BAMBURGH. Waren Lea Hall, Waren Mill, Bamburgh.
Luxurious self-catering holiday accommodation for families, parties and friends, near Bamburgh on the beautiful coast of Northumberland. Standing on the shore of beautiful Budle Bay, an Area of Outstanding Natural Beauty and a Site of Special Scientific Interest for its birdlife, lies Waren Lea Hall (sleeps up to 14). This gracious Edwardian Gentleman's Residence, set in 2½ acres, enjoys spectacular views over the bay to Lindisfarne. In addition to the Hall there are two entirely self-contained apartments, Ghillie's View (sleeps up to 10) and Garden Cottage (sleeps up to 4). All accommodation is beautifully furnished and very well equipped. SEE ALSO COLOUR ADVERT.
ETC ★★★★★
For further information please contact the owners:
Carolynn and David Croisdale-Appleby, Abbotsholme, Hervines Road, Amersham, Bucks HP6 5HS (01494 725194; Fax: 01494 725474; Mobile: 07901 716136).
e-mail: croisdaleappleby@aol.com   www.selfcateringluxury.co.uk

MAISONETTE   1/12 🐕 🪀   🛏 sleep 2/12
BERWICK-UPON-TWEED. 2 The Courtyard, Church Street, Berwick-upon-Tweed TD15 1EE (01289 308737).
Artists, photographers, birders, walkers, cyclists, fishermen, golfers and especially families, find Berwick an architectural gem, an ideal centre for basing their holiday. On a clear day you can see no fewer than three magnificent castles, suggesting exciting days out, from the ramparts which surround the old part of the town and which form an excellent source for enjoyable walks. Our secluded quality maisonette and studio flat (first and second floors, sleeping up to 12) offer a comfortable choice of accommodation, amazingly within a few minutes' easy walk of shops, restaurants, golf course, beaches etc. See our website for more details and ideas. SEE ALSO COLOUR ADVERT IN GOLF SECTION.
www.berwickselfcatering.co.uk

FREE or REDUCED RATE entry to Holiday Visits and Attractions – see our
READERS' OFFER VOUCHERS on pages 181-218

symbols

Months open (eg:4/10 means April to October)
🐕   Pets Welcome
🪀   Children Welcome
♿   Suitable for Disabled
🛏   Linen provided
Min/Max no of persons in one unit (eg:2/6)

self-catering

WAREN LEA HALL

Waren Mill, Bamburgh

*Luxurious Self-Catering
Holiday Accommodation
for families, parties and friends.*

Near Bamburgh on the beautiful coast of Northumberland.

Standing on the shore of beautiful Budle Bay, an Area of Outstanding Natural Beauty and a Site of Special Scientific Interest for its birdlife, lies WAREN LEA HALL. This gracious Edwardian Gentleman's Residence, set in 2 ½ acres, enjoys spectacular views over the bay to Lindisfarne. In addition to the Hall there are two entirely self-contained apartments, GHILLIE'S VIEW and GARDEN COTTAGE.

THE HALL *(for up to 14 guests)*

Beautifully furnished to complement its Edwardian grandeur, with high ceilings, chandeliers, sash windows, fireplaces and polished wooden

floors. Breathtaking views from every room. Large drawing and dining rooms opening on to floodlit terrace; large, fully equipped kitchen/breakfast room. Ground floor twin bedroom and cloakroom/shower room; upstairs five further family/twin/double rooms including en suite master with four-poster; family bathroom. Own garden and use of secluded, walled garden and parkland.

GARDEN COTTAGE *(for up to 4 guests)*

The terrace wing of Waren Lea Hall, reached through its own entrance from the garden. All the light and sunny rooms are prettily furnished with high quality fabrics, pine furniture and polished wooden floors throughout, and face the secluded garden which guests can use. The well equipped kitchen/dining room, double and twin bedrooms, one en suite, and family shower room are all on one level.

GHILLIE'S VIEW *(for up to 10 guests)*

The former home of the estate ghillie, accommodation is all on one level, with luxurious furnishings throughout. Fully equipped kitchen/dining room, semi-circular drawing room and master bedroom with four-poster and en suite shower; all with fine views across the river and bay to Holy Island. Double and twin rooms, one en suite, and family shower room Guests have use of walled garden and parkland.

For further information please contact the owners:
Carolynn and David Croisdale-Appleby
Abbotsholme, Hervines Road
Amersham, Buckinghamshire HP6 5HS
Tel: 01494 725194
Fax: 01494 725474 • Mobile: 07901 716136
e-mail: croisdaleappleby@aol.com
www.selfcateringluxury.co.uk

English Tourism Council
★★★★★
SELF CATERING

Keswick, Kirkoswald, Wigton

Cumbria

KESWICK. Irton House Farm, Isel, Cockermouth, Near Keswick CA13 9ST (017687 76380).
Farm location with superb views of lake and mountains. Family accommodation (suitable for disabled guests – wheelchair accessible). Interesting walking area and comfortable motoring. Facilities for fishing, swimming and golf nearby. Ample parking. Also 6-berth static caravan for hire. Please telephone for colour brochure. SEE ALSO COLOUR ADVERT.
- Sleeps 2/6. • Children welcome. • Totally non-smoking.

www.irtonhousefarm.com

COTTAGES/FLAT   1/12 🐕 🎠   ▣ sleep 1/5

KIRKOSWALD. Crossfield Cottages & Leisure Fishing.
Accessible, tranquil, secluded quality cottages overlooking fishing lake amidst Lakeland's Eden Valley countryside. Centrally located only 30 minutes' drive from Ullswater, North Pennines, Hadrian's Wall and Scotland's Borderlands. Guaranteed clean. Well-equipped and maintained. Good coarse fishing for residents only; fly fishing nearby. Excellent walking. Laundry area. Relax and escape to your home in the country. 24 hour brochure line. Bookings and enquiries 6pm to 10pm. SEE ALSO COLOUR ADVERT.
- Pets VERY welcome.

ETC ★★★
Telephone or Fax: 01768 898711 or SAE to Crossfield Cottages, Kirkoswald, Penrith CA10 1EU.
e-mail: info@crossfieldcottages.co.uk   www.crossfieldcottages.co.uk

FARMHOUSE/HOUSE

LAKE DISTRICT.
Two luxury holiday houses available to rent in the Lake District. Routen House is a beautiful old farmhouse set in 4 acres in an outstanding position with fabulous views over Ennerdale Lake. Fully modernised while retaining the character of the old farmhouse, it has been furnished to a very high standard. Sleeps 12 plus cot. Little Parrock is an elegant Victorian Lakeland stone house a short walk from the centre of Grasmere with large rooms and a wealth of period features. Lovely private garden. Fully modernised to a very high standard; real log fires. Sleeps 10 plus cot. Both houses are non-smoking but pets are very welcome.
Please contact: **Mrs J. Green (Tel & Fax: 01604 626383)**
e-mail: joanne@routenhouse.co.uk
www.routenhouse.co.uk • www.littleparrock.co.uk

WIGTON. Foxgloves Cottage.
Spacious well-equipped, comfortable cottage on a working farm. Superlative setting and views, large kitchen/dining rooom. Aga, lounge, open fire, TV/video/DVD, three bedrooms, bathroom, separate shower room. Linen, towels, electricity, logs and coal inclusive. Extensive garden. Storage heaters, washing machine, dishwasher. Easy reach Lake District, Scottish Borders and Roman Wall. SEE ALSO COLOUR ADVERT.
Rates: from £205-£455. Short Breaks by arrangement.
- Sleeps 2/8. • Children and pets welcome.
Mr & Mrs E and J Kerr, Greenrigg Farm, Westward, Wigton CA7 8AH (016973 42676).

symbols

Months open (eg:4/10 means April to October)
🐕   Pets Welcome
🎠   Children Welcome
♿   Suitable for Disabled
▣   Linen provided
Min/Max no of persons in one unit (eg:2/6)

self-catering

Scotland
Self-Catering

Dalmally

Argyll & Bute

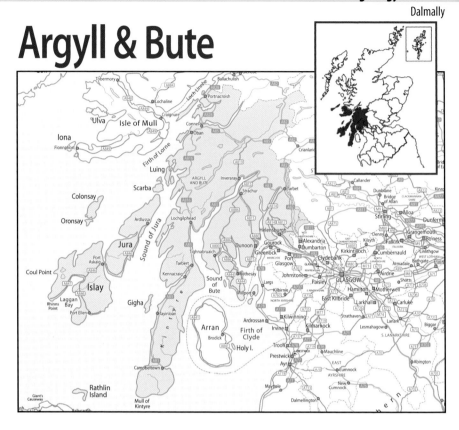

Looking for holiday accommodation?

for details of hundreds of properties
throughout the UK including
comprehensive coverage of all areas of Scotland try:

www.holidayguides.com

ROSNEATH CASTLE PARK
SO NEAR... YET SO FAR AWAY

Rosneath Castle Park has everything to offer if you are looking for a relaxing holiday. No more than an hour's drive from Glasgow, the 57 acres that the park occupies along the shore of Gareloch offer the perfect opportunity to relax and discover another world, and another you.

Thistle Awarded Luxury Self-Catering Holiday Homes with superb views. In a beautiful setting with first class facilities including an adventure playground, boat house, fun club, restaurant and bar, there's no end to the reasons why you would 'wish you were here'.

Rosneath Castle Park, Rosneath,
Near Helensburgh, Argyll G84 0QS
Tel: (01436) 831208
Fax: (01436) 831978
enquiries@rosneathcastle.demon.co.uk
www.rosneathcastle.demon.co.uk

COLOGIN – a haven in the hills

If you've just got married or just retired, have toddlers in tow or dogs you can't bear to leave at home, or you just want to get away for a break with all the freedom of a self-catering holiday, then we may have just what you are looking for. Our cosy chalets and well appointed lodges offer everything you need for a relaxing country holiday.

One of the most appealing features of Cologin is its peace and tranquillity. With 14 lodges, 4 chalets, Cologin Farmhouse and Cruachan Cottage at Cologin we have plenty of different accommodation options. Choose from a cosy one-bedroom chalet or the larger two-bedroomed lodges, or sleep up to 10 adults and 4 children in our traditional Scottish farmhouse.

Our award-winning family-friendly pub and restaurant, *The Barn,* is within easy reach of all our properties. It's a perfect place to unwind and relax. With its unique atmosphere and friendly staff it is the reason why many of Cologin's guests return year after year.

If you love the great outdoors come rain or shine and want to escape from the routine of city life, Cologin is for you. With 17,000 acres of waymarked forest trails above the farm you can enjoy nature at its finest, with glorious scenery and breathtaking views from the summit over Oban Bay to the islands beyond.

Contact us for colour brochure:
Jim and Linda Battison – resident owners
Cologin, Lerags Glen, Oban, Argyll PA34 4SE
Telephone: 01631 564501 • Fax: 01631 566925
e-mail: info@cologin.co.uk
www.cologin.co.uk

COLOGIN
a haven in the hills
STB ★★★–★★★★
Self Catering

COTTAGES

1/12   sleep 2/6

DALMALLY. Mrs I. Crawford, Blarghour Farm, Lochaweside, By Dalmally PA33 1BW (01866 833246; Fax: 01866 833338).

At Blarghour, a working hill farm on the shores of lovely Loch Awe, the holiday guest has a choice of high quality, well appointed, centrally heated, double glazed accommodation of individual character, each enjoying its own splendid view over loch and mountain in this highly scenic area. Barn House accommodates four, Stable House accommodates four, Barr-beithe Lower sleeps five and Barr-beithe Upper sleeps six. All have fitted kitchens with fridge/freezer, washing machine, microwave and electric cooker; telephone and TV. The cottages at Barr-beithe also include a dishwasher, and a cot and highchair are also available. Linen and towels are supplied. Parking beside each house. Barn and Stable Houses are unsuitable for children under five years. No pets allowed. Non-Smoking. Open all year. The area, centrally situated for touring, offers opportunities for walking, bird-watching, boating and fishing. Golf is available at Dalmally and Inveraray. Wheelchair access. Colour brochure sent on request. SEE ALSO COLOUR ADVERT.
• One cottage suitable for disabled visitors.
STB ★★★★ SELF-CATERING, ASSC MEMBER
e-mail: blarghour@btconnect.com   website: www.self-catering-argyll.co.uk

HOLIDAY PARK

HELENSBURGH. Rosneath Castle Park, Rosneath, Near Helensburgh G84 0QS (01436 831208; Fax: 01436 831978).

Rosneath Castle Park has everything to offer if you are looking for a relaxing holiday. No more than an hour's drive from Glasgow, the 57 acres that the park occupies along the shore of Gareloch offers the perfect opportunity to relax and discover another world, and another you. Thistle Awarded Luxury Self-Catering Holiday Homes with superb views. In a beautiful setting with first class facilities including an adventure playground, boat house, fun club, restaurant and bar, there's no end to the reasons why you would 'wish you were here'.
STB ★★★★★ HOLIDAY PARK.
e-mail: enquiries@rosneathcastle.demon.co.uk   www.rosneathcastle.demon.co.uk

CHALETS/LODGES/COTTAGE

OBAN. Jim and Linda Battison, Cologin, Lerags Glen, Oban PA34 4SE (01631 564501; Fax: 01631 566925).

Our cosy chalets and well appointed lodges offer everything you need for a relaxing country holiday. Choose from a cosy one-bedroom chalet, or the larger two-bedroom lodges, or our traditional Scottish farmhouse (sleeps up to 10 adults and 4 children). Our award-winning family-friendly pub and restaurant is the perfect place to relax and unwind. With 17,000 acres of waymarked forest trails you can enjoy nature at its finest, with glorious scenery and breathtaking views. SEE ALSO COLOUR ADVERT.
• Sleep 2/14
STB ★★★–★★★★ SELF-CATERING
e-mail:info@cologin.co.uk   www.cologin.co.uk.

VARIED ACCOMMODATION   1/12 🐎 🐴   ▣ sleep 1/6
sleep 2/9
ROTHESAY. Jacqueline's Property Services.
Bute's No. 1 self-catering company with the widest choice of luxury properties in various locations to suit all budgets and tastes. Pets welcome in selected properties. Make yourself at home! Contact us for details. SEE ALSO COLOUR ADVERT.
Jacqueline's Property Services, Ian Villa, Academy Road, Rothesay PA20 0BG (01700 503906)
e-mail: holidays@jpsbute.com   www.jpsbute.com

Dumfries & Galloway

DUMFRIES & GALLOWAY is a mixture of high moorland and sheltered glens, and presents abundant opportunities for hill walking, rambling, fishing for salmon and sea trout, cycling, bird watching and field sports. There are at least 32 golf courses, ranging from the challenging Stranraer course at Creachmore to the scenic, clifftop course at Port Patrick. The Stranraer course has the distinction of being the last course designed by James Braid. The warming influence of the Gulf Stream ensures a mild climate which makes touring a pleasure, and many visitors come here to visit the dozens of interesting castles, gardens, museums and historic sites. In addition, pony trekking and riding plus a never-ending succession of ceilidhs, village fairs, country dances, classical music concerts and children's entertainment guarantee plenty of scope for enjoyment. Discover the many hidden secrets of this lovely and unspoilt landscape such as the pretty little villages along the coast or visit some of the interesting towns in the area including Stranraer, the principal town and ferry port with its busy shopping streets, park and leisure centre. Those who love 'the written word' must surely visit the book town of Wigtown, and the gourmet amongst us will love the new concept of Castle Douglas, the recently designated 'Food Town'.

COTTAGES   🐕 🐴 ▣   sleep 2/9
PORTPATRICK. G & S Cottages.
Once you have experienced the magic of Portpatrick, you will be sure to return. Situated on the beautiful Gallowaycoast, this friendly place has something for everyone. Many superb golf courses including Portpatrick Dunskey. Our three cottages form a most elegant and private complex, a few minutes' walk from the sea. With modern fittings and decor, plus extensive decked terracing and barbecue facilities, the accommodation is a must for the discerning visitor. All properties have TV, video, washer, dryer, dishwasher, fridge, freezer, CD player, microwave. Cots/highchairs available; linen provided. SEE ALSO COLOUR ADVERT IN GOLF SECTION.
• Sleep 4/6 and 7/9
STB ★★★★ *SELF-CATERING.*
For details contact **Graham and Sue Fletcher, 468 Otley Road, Leeds LS16 8AE (0113 230 1391 or 07976 671926).**
e-mail: info@gscottages.co.uk www.gscottages.co.uk

Edinburgh

Edinburgh & Lothians

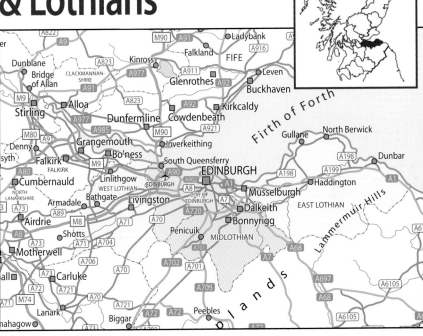

FLATS
EDINBURGH. Festival Flats.
Short City Breaks - please also get in touch for short stays throughout the year. Anything from two-night stay considered. All properties in the heart of Edinburgh City Centre. SEE ALSO COLOUR ADVERT. Solve your accommodation problems by calling
Carole Smith/Anne Goring, Festival Flats, 3 Linkylea Cottages, Gifford, East Lothian EH41 4PE (01620 810620)
e-mail: festflats@aol.com   www.festivalflats.net

Highlands

SPEYSIDE LEISURE PARK

Self-Catering Holidays in the Heart of the Highlands

The park is situated in a quiet riverside setting with mountain views, only a short walk from Aviemore centre and shops. We offer a range of warm, well equipped chalets, cabins and caravans, including a caravan for the disabled. Prices include electricity, gas, linen, towels and use of our heated indoor pool and sauna. There are swings, a climbing frame and low level balance beams for the children. Permit fishing is available on the river. Discounts are given on some local attractions.

Families, couples or groups will find this an ideal location for a wide range of activities including:

- *Horse riding • Golf • Fishing • Hillwalking*
- *RSPB Reserves • Mountain and Watersports • Reindeer herd*
  - *Steam railway and the Whisky Trail*

Only slightly further afield you will find Culloden Moor, the Moray Firth dolphins and of course, the not to be missed, Loch Ness.
Accommodation sleeps from 4-8, but we offer a reduced rate for a couple.
Short Breaks are available. Sorry, no pets, except guide and hearing dogs.

Speyside Leisure Park
Dalfaber Road, Aviemore, Inverness-shire PH22 1PX
Tel: 01479 810236 • Fax: 01479 811688
e-mail: fhg@speysideleisure.com • www.speysideleisure.com

CHALETS/CARAVANS   1/12   sleep 1/8

AVIEMORE. Speyside Leisure Park, Dalfaber Road, Aviemore PH22 1PX (01479 810236; Fax: 01479 811688).
The park is situated in a quiet riverside setting with mountain views, only a short walk from Aviemore centre and shops. We offer a range of warm, well equipped chalets, cabins and caravans, including a caravan for the disabled. Prices include electricity, gas, linen, towels and use of our heated indoor pool and sauna. There are swings, a climbing frame and low level balance beams for the children. Permit fishing is available on the river. Discounts are given on some local attractions. Families, couples or groups will find this an ideal location for a wide range of activities including horse riding, golf, fishing, hillwalking, RSPB Reserves, mountain and watersports. Also reindeer herd, steam railway and the Whisky Trail. Only slightly further afield you will find Culloden Moor, Moray Firth Dolphins and of course, the not to be missed, Loch Ness. SEE ALSO COLOUR ADVERT.
• Sleeps 4-8, reduced rate for a couple. • Short Breaks available. • Sorry, no pets, except guide and hearing dogs
STB ★★★ *HOLIDAY PARK*
e-mail: fhg@speysideleisure.com   www.speysideleisure.com

BEAULY. Mr & Mrs G.G. MacDonald, Glen Affric Chalet Park, Cannich, Beauly, Inverness-shire IV4 7LT (01456 415369; Fax: 01456 415429).
Great value summer holidays and autumn-winter/spring breaks. Set beside the River Glass and surrounded by spectacular mountain scenery, 15 minutes from Loch Ness, our accommodation provides three-bedroom bungalow chalets, fully equipped and comfortably furnished with central heating and bed linen. An ideal base for walking, climbing, cycling, fishing and stalking, or a central base for touring and viewing the scenery. We have a laundry, games room, children's play area and barbecue area on site; shop, pub and hotel within five minutes' walk. SEE ALSO COLOUR ADVERT.
STB ★★★. ASSC.
e-mail: info@glenaffricchaletpark.com   www.glenaffricchaletpark.com

APARTMENTS

BRORA. Highland Escape Apartments, The Royal Marine Hotel, Golf Road, Brora, Sutherland KW9 6QS (01408 621252; Fax: 01408 621181)
Luxury two bedroom en suite apartments with fully appointed kitchens, lounge and dining areas, enjoying magnificent views over James Braid's golf links, the Dornoch Firth and Sutherland hills. At the neighbouring Royal Marine Hotel, apartment residents enjoy complimentary membership of the leisure club, plus access to the restaurants and bars. SEE ALSO COLOUR ADVERT.
e-mail: info@highlandescape.com   www.highlandescapehotels.com

Looking for holiday accommodation?
for details of hundreds of properties
throughout the UK visit:
www.holidayguides.com

Biggar

Lanarkshire

COTTAGES   1/12 🐕 🐄 🛏 sleep 2/6
BIGGAR (Clyde Valley) Carmichael Country Cottages, Carmichael Estate Office, Westmains, Carmichael, Biggar ML12 6PG (01899 308336; Fax: 01899 308481). Working farm, join in.
These 200-year-old stone cottages nestle among the woods and fields of our 700-year-old family estate. Still managed by the descendants of the original Chief of Carmichael. We guarantee comfort, warmth and a friendly welcome in an accessible, unique, rural and historic time capsule. We farm deer, cattle and sheep and sell meats and tartan – Carmichael of course! Children and pets welcome. Open all year. Terms from £225 to £595. 15 cottages with a total of 32 bedrooms. We have the ideal cottage for you. Private tennis court and fishing loch; cafe, farm shop and visitor centre.SEE ALSO COLOUR ADVERT.
STB ★★/★★★★ *SELF-CATERING*. *ASSC MEMBER. FARM STAY UK MEMBER.*
e-mail: chiefcarm@aol.com   www.carmichael.co.uk/cottages

Perth & Kinross

Aberfeldy

LODGES 1/12 🐕 🐎 📖 sleep 2/8

ABERFELDY. Loch Tay Lodges, Acharn, By Aberfeldy PH15 2HR (01887 830209; Fax: 01887 830802). Escape the rat race. Enjoy the tranquillity, the grandeur, the beauty and the comfort of Highland Perthshire. Walk around the farm in the woods or up the mountains, play golf, fish, tour or sail. Fully modernised stone building Listed for its architectural interest. There are six self-catering lodges. Log fires. Linen provided. Highland Perthshire has half a dozen golf courses. 18-hole Taymouth Castle and Kenmore courses on the doorstep; Gleneagles and Rosemount one hour's drive. SEE ALSO COLOUR ADVERT.
• Well behaved dogs welcome • One lodge suitable for disabled guests.
STB ★★★ *SELF-CATERING*
e-mail: remony@btinternet.com   **www.lochtaylodges.co.uk**

LODGES 1/12 🐎 📖 sleep 2/8

DUNKELD. Laighwood Holidays, Butterstone, By Dunkeld PH8 0HB (01350 724241; Fax: 01350 724212).
A de luxe detached house, comfortably accommodating eight, created from the West Wing of a 19th century shooting lodge with panoramic views. Two popular cottages sleeping four to six, situated on our hill farm, with beautiful views. Two well-equipped apartments adjoining Butterglen House near Butterstone Loch. Butterstone lies in magnificent countryside (especially Spring/ Autumn), adjacent to Nature Reserve (ospreys). Central for walking, touring, historic houses, golf and fishing. Private squash court and hill loch (wild brown trout) on the farm. SEE ALSO COLOUR ADVERT
Rates: House £480 to £688; Cottages and Apartments £172 to £500per week.
• Sorry, no pets.
STB ★★★ to ★★★★ *SELF-CATERING. ASSC MEMBER.*
e-mail: holidays@laighwood.co.uk   **www.laighwood.co.uk**

symbols

Months open (eg:4/10 means April to October)

🐕   Pets Welcome

🐎   Children Welcome

♿   Suitable for Disabled

📖   Linen provided

self-catering

Min/Max no of persons in one unit (eg:2/6)

Wales
Self-Catering

Ratings & Awards

For the first time ever the AA, VisitBritain, VisitScotland, and the Wales Tourist Board will use a single method of assessing and rating serviced accommodation. Irrespective of which organisation inspects an establishment the rating awarded will be the same, using a common set of standards, giving a clear guide of what to expect. The RAC is no longer operating an Hotel inspection and accreditation business.

Accommodation Standards: Star Grading Scheme

Using a scale of 1-5 stars the objective quality ratings give a clear indication of accommodation standard, cleanliness, ambience, hospitality, service and food, This shows the full range of standards suitable for every budget and preference, and allows visitors to distinguish between the quality of accommodation and facilities on offer in different establishments. All types of board and self-catering accommodation are covered, including hotels, B&Bs, holiday parks, campus accommodation, hostels, caravans and camping, and boats.

The more stars, the higher level of quality

★★★★★
exceptional quality, with a degree of luxury

★★★★
excellent standard throughout

★★★
very good level of quality and comfort

★★
good quality, well presented and well run

★
acceptable quality; simple, practical, no frills

VisitBritain and the regional tourist boards, **enjoyEngland.com**, **VisitScotland** and **VisitWales**, and **the AA** have full details of the grading system on their websites

National Accessible Scheme

If you have particular mobility, visual or hearing needs, look out for the National Accessible Scheme. You can be confident of finding accommodation or attractions that meet your needs by looking for the following symbols.

 Typically suitable for a person with sufficient mobility to climb a flight of steps but would benefit from fixtures and fittings to aid balance

 Typically suitable for a person with restricted walking ability and for those that may need to use a wheelchair some of the time and can negotiate a maximum of three steps

 Typically suitable for a person who depends on the use of a wheelchair and transfers unaided to and from the wheelchair in a seated position. This person may be an independent traveller

 Typically suitable for a person who depends on the use of a wheelchair in a seated position. This person also requires personal or mechanical assistance (eg carer, hoist).

Haverfordwest

Pembrokeshire

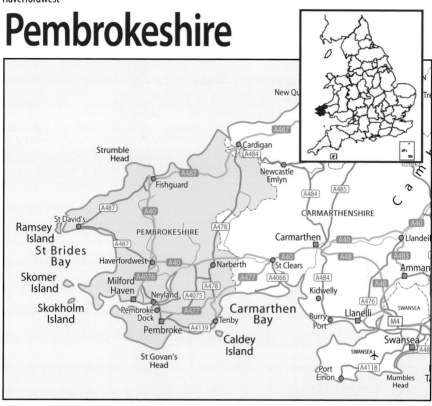

PEMBROKESHIRE'S entire coastline is a designated National Park, with its sheltered coves and wooded estuaries, fine sandy beaches and some of the most dramatic cliffs in Britain. The islands of Skomer, Stokholm and Grasholm are home to thousands of seabirds, and Ramsey Island, as well as being an RSPB Reserve boasts the second largest grey seal colony in Britain. Pembrokeshire's mild climate and the many delightful towns and villages, family attractions and outdoor facilities such as surfing, water skiing, diving, pony trekking and fishing make this a favourite holiday destination.

Whitland

COTTAGES   1/12 🐴 🐎   sleep 2/6
HAVERFORDWEST. Nolton Haven Farm Cottages, Nolton Haven, Haverfordwest SA62 3NH (01437 710200).
In an Area of Outstanding Natural Beauty, with excellent bathing, boating and surfing. Golf and fishing locally; ideal
for walking. Sympathetically converted cottages situated on a grass bank overlooking Nolton Haven's sandy
beach. Primrose Cottage sleeps 5, Bluebell Cottage sleeps 6, Thrift Cottage sleeps 2+2, Honeysuckle and Buttercup
Cottages sleep 5, Rose Cottage sleeps 6. All are fully equipped, with colour TV, fridge/freezer, microwave etc. Duvets
supplied, but no linen. Coin meters for cooking and hot water. SEE ALSO COLOUR ADVERT.
* Children welcome * Pets welcome * Sleep 2/6
e-mail:info@havencottages.co.uk   www.havencottages.co.uk

COTTAGES   1/12 🐴 🐎 🖳   sleep 2/6
WHITLAND. Farm Holidays at Gwarmacwydd.
A country estate of over 450 acres, including two miles of riverbank. See a real farm in action, the hustle and bustle
of harvest, newborn calves and lambs. Choose from six character stone cottages, lovingly converted tradtional farm
buildings, some over 200 years old. Each cottage is fully furnished and equipped, electricity and linen included,
with all year round heating. Brochure available. SEE ALSO COLOUR ADVERT.
* Children welcome.
WTB ★★★★ *COTTAGES*
Contact Mrs Angela Colledge, Llanfallteg, Whitland SA34 0XH (01437 563260; Fax: 01437 563839).
www.davidsfarm.com

FREE or REDUCED RATE entry to Holiday Visits and Attractions – see our
READERS' OFFER VOUCHERS on pages 181-218

Visit the FHG website
www.holidayguides.com
for details of the wide choice of accommodation
featured in the full range of FHG titles

Garthmyl

Powys

A Superb Holiday Setting for all Seasons

Set in a 30-acre woodland, all our lodges are individually designed and fully fitted throughout, including colour TV, microwave, full kitchen, bath/shower room, and include all bedding. 19 lodges sleeping 2 – 8 people and one cottage which sleeps six. Fishing on the Montgomery canal, River Severn and our own private lake. Quad trekking and pony trekking nearby.
Pets welcome in certain cabins.
From £175 to £692 per cabin per week inc. VAT • Short Breaks • Open all year round

Tel/Fax 01686 640269 for a colour brochure
Penllwyn Lodges, Garthmyl, Powys SY15 6SB
e-mail: daphne.jones@onetel.net
www.penllwynlodges.co.uk

GARTHMYL. Penllwyn Lodges, Garthmyl SY15 6SB (Tel/Fax 01686 640269).
A. superb holiday setting for all seasons. Set in a 30-acre woodland, all our lodges are individually designed and fully fitted throughout, including colour TV, microwave, full kitchen, bath/shower room, and include all bedding. 19 lodges sleeping 2 – 8 people and one cottage which sleeps six. Fishing on the Montgomery canal, River Severn and our own private lake. Quad trekking and pony trekking nearby. Colour brochure available. Pets welcome in certain cabins. SEE ALSO COLOUR ADVERT.
Rates: from £175 to £692 per cabin per week inc. VAT. Short Breaks available.
• Open all year round
e-mail: daphne.jones@onetel.net   **www.penllwynlodges.co.uk**

The FHG Directory of Website Addresses
on pages 157-179 is a useful quick reference guide for
holiday accommodation with e-mail and/or website details

IRELAND
Self-Catering

Wexford

1/12   ♿   🛏   sleep 1/4

FERRYCARRIG. Fit4All Wexford, Knockahone, Barntown Wexford (00 353 (0)53 9172313)
Fit4All Wexford is located in a tranquil waterside setting by the River Slaney in Ferrycarrig, Wexford. This purpose-built facility features a modern, customised Training Studio and a lodge for individuals on overnight programmes or fitness breaks. The Holiday Lodge is the perfect relaxation sanctuary for holiday breaks, overnight packages and fitness and spa breaks. The modern decor and high standard of comfort are designed to provide perfect relaxation as a stand-alone break or as part of a fitness and spa break. The studio complex has been designed to the highest specifications with modern décor throughout. There is a wide range of equipment and facilities, carefully designed for fitness purposes but with privacy, relaxation and luxury. SEE ALSO COLOUR ADVERT IN ACTIVITY SECTION.
• No pets or children under 14.
e-mail: info@fit4all.ie   **www.fit4all.ie**

symbols

Months open (eg:4/10 means April to October)
🐕   Pets Welcome
🐎   Children Welcome
♿   Suitable for Disabled
🛏   Linen provided
Min/Max no of persons in one unit (eg:2/6)

self-catering

Caravans & Camping

England
Caravans & Camping

Cornwall

FHG Guides
publish a large range of well-known accommodation guides.
We will be happy to send you details or you can use the order form
at the back of this book.

CORNWALL. St Ives Bay Holiday Park, Upton Towans, Hayle TR27 5BH (0800 317713).
The park on the beach. St Ives Bay Holiday Park is set in sand dunes which run down to its own sandy beach. Many units have superb sea views. There is a large indoor pool and 2 clubs with FREE entertainment on the Park.
www.stivesbay.co.uk

NEWQUAY. Treloy Touring Park, Newquay TR8 4JN (01637 872063/876279).
A friendly family site for touring caravans, tents and motor homes, just off the A3059 Newquay Road. A central location for touring the whole of Cornwall. Facilities include heated swimming pool, licensed bar/family room, entertainment, cafe/takeaway, shop, laundry, FREE showers, private washing cubicles, baby bathrooms, indoor dishwashing sinks, TV and games rooms, adventure playground. Facilities for the disabled. Electric hook-ups. Coarse fishing nearby. Own superb 9-hole Par 32 golf course with concessionary green fees for our guests. Please write or telephone for free colour brochure.
ETC ★★★★ *TOURING PARK,* **AA** *THREE PENNANTS.*
Rates: £8 to £15 per night for two adults, car and caravan.
www.treloy.co.uk

WADEBRIDGE. Mrs E. Hodge, Pengelly Farm, Burlawn, Wadebridge PL27 7LA (01208 814217)
One only, fully serviced and equipped, self-contained, two-bedroom static caravan in quiet location on working dairy farm overlooking wooded valleys. Large garden with patio table and chairs plus own barbecue. An ideal walking, touring and cycling base, only six miles from the coast, with sailing, surfing, golf, riding and coastal walks; Camel Trail, Saints' Way and Pencarrow House nearby. The Eden Project 35 minutes' drive, Padstow 20 minutes, Wadebridge one and a half miles, with shopping, pubs, restaurants and leisure facilities. B&B also available from £26 pppn. SEE ALSO COLOUR ADVERT.
ETC Inspected.
e-mail: hodgepete@hotmail.com   **www.pengellyfarm.co.uk**

symbols

Months open (eg:4/10 means April to October)

🐴   Pets Welcome
🏠   Shop on site
🍽   Restaurant/Takeaway on site
🚿   Showers/hot water
🍷   Licensed Bar

caravans & camping

Cumbria

LODGES/CARAVANS
3/11   🐕   ⊞   ♣   sleep up to 11

AMBLESIDE. Greenhowe Caravan Park, Great Langdale, Ambleside LA22 9JU (015394) 37231; Fax: (015394) 37464). Greenhowe is a permanent caravan park with self-contained holiday accommodation. Subject to availabilty holiday homes may be rented for long or short periods from 1st March until mid-November. The park is situated in the Lake District half-a-mile from Dungeon Ghyll at the foot of the Langdale Pikes. It is an ideal centre for climbing, fell walking, riding, swimming. Please ask about short breaks. New for 2008 - self-catering lodges available, please telephone for details. SEE ALSO COLOUR ADVERT.
ETC ★★★★, *DAVID BELLAMY SILVER AWARD, ROSE AWARD PARK, WELCOME HOST.*
www.greenhowe.com

CARAVANS FOR HIRE/TOURING
3/1   🐕   ♣ ♀

SILLOTH-ON-SOLWAY. Tanglewood Caravan Park, Causeway Head, Silloth-on-Solway CA7 4PE (016973 31253).
Tanglewood is a family-run park on the fringes of the Lake District National Park. It is tree-sheltered and situated one mile inland from the small port of Silloth on the Solway Firth, with a beautiful view of the Galloway Hills. Large modern holiday homes are available from March to January, with car parking beside each home. Fully equipped except for bed linen, with end bedroom, panel heaters in bedrooms and bathroom, electric lighting, hot and cold water, toilet, shower, gas fire, fridge and colour TV, all of which are included in the tariff. Touring pitches also available with electric hook-ups and water/drainage facilities, etc. Play area. Licensed lounge with adjoining children's play room. Full colour brochure available. Downloadable brochure with tariff and booking form available on website. SEE ALSO COLOUR ADVERT.
• Pets welcome free but must be kept under control at all times.
★★★, AA *THREE PENNANTS.*
e-mail: tanglewoodcaravanpark@hotmail.com   www.tanglewoodcaravanpark.co.uk

Taunton, Cheddar

Somerset

HOLIDAY PARK   3/11

CHEDDAR Broadway House Holiday Touring, Caravan and Camping Park, Cheddar BS27 3DB (01934 742610; Fax: 01934 744950).
Just steps, not miles, from Cheddar Gorge. A totally unique four star caravan and camping family experience. One of the most interesting inland parks in the West Country. A family business specialising in family holidays. Visit our llama and parrot. Prices include the use of the heated outdoor swimming pool, entrance to the Bar/Family Room, skateboard park and BMX track. Activities from the park include fishing, archery, shooting; bike hire, table tennis, crazy golf, boules, croquet etc. Log Cabins for sale. SEE ALSO COLOUR ADVERT, INSIDE BACK COVER.
ETC ★★★★, **AA** *5 PENNANTS, DAVID BELLAMY GOLD AWARD.*
e-mail: info@broadwayhouse.uk.com   www.broadwayhouse.uk.com

TOURING PARK   1/12

TAUNTON. Michael & Sarah Barrett, Quantock Orchard Caravan Park, Flaxpool, Crowcombe, Near Taunton TA4 4AW (01984 618618).
A small, family-run touring park set in the beautiful Quantock Hills close to Exmoor and the coast in a designated Area of Outstanding Natural Beauty - we look forward to welcoming you to our five star park at any time of the year. Please phone or write for colour brochure and tariff. Static caravans for hire. SEE ALSO COLOUR ADVERT.
ETC ★★★★★, **AA** *FOUR PENNANTS, DE LUXE PARK*
e-mail: qocp@flaxpool.freeserve.co.uk   www.quantockorchard.co.uk

Just **1.1 miles** (1770metres) *Steps*

"NOT MILES" from
Cheddar Gorge & Village

BROADWAY HOUSE

Holiday Touring Caravan Camping Park CHEDDA

LOG CABINS FOR SALE
HOLIDAY CARAVANS FOR HIRE
PREMIER TOURING AND CAMPING
PITCHES
FREE HEATED SWIMMING POOL
& PIXIE PLAYGROUND
FREE ADVENTURE PLAYGROUND
DISABLED AND BABIES ROOM
CORNER SHOP WITH FRIENDLY
SERVICE
COME AND SEE OUR PET LLAMA
AND PARROT
FREE ENTRANCE TO THE BAR-
CAFÉ & FAMILY ROOM
LAUNDERETTE, AMUSEMENTS,
CRAZY GOLF,
SKATEBOARD PARK, INDOOR
TABLE TENNIS
BMX TRACK+ BMX HIRE

ACTIVITY PROGRAM
ARCHERY, CANOEING,
RIFLE SHOOTING,
ABSEILING, CAVING,
NATURE TRAILS.

SOMERSET LAND OF THE SUMMER PEOPL

AA

BROADWAY HOUSE CHEDDAR, SOMERSET. BS27
TEL:01934 742610 FAX:01934 7449
email: info@broadwayhouse.uk.com www.broadwayhouse.uk

DIRECTORY OF WEBSITE AND E-MAIL ADDRESSES

A quick-reference guide to holiday accommodation with an e-mail address and/or website, conveniently arranged by country and county, with full contact details.

Self-Catering Apartments
Mary & Simon Ette, The Independent Traveller, 8 The Glebe, Thorverton, Exeter EX5 5LS
Tel: 01392 860807
• e-mail: help@gowithit.co.uk
• website: www.gowithit.co.uk

•LONDON

Hotel
Athena Hotel, 110-114 Sussex Gardens, Hyde Park, LONDON W2 1UA
Tel: 020 7706 3866
• e-mail: athena@stavrouhotels.co.uk
• website: www.stavrouhotels.co.uk

Hotel
Elizabeth Hotel, 37 Eccleston Square, LONDON SW1V 1PB Tel: 020 7828 6812
• e-mail: info@elizabethhotel.com
• website: www.elizabethhotel.com

Hotel
Gower Hotel, 129 Sussex Gardens, Hyde Park, LONDON W2 2RX
Tel: 020 7262 2262
• e-mail: gower@stavrouhotels.co.uk
• website: www.stavrouhotels.co.uk

B & B
Manor Court Hotel, 7 Clanricarde Gardens, LONDON W2 4JJ Tel: 020 7792 3361 or 020 7727 5407
• e-mail: enquiries@manorcourthotel.com
• website: www.abc-london.com
        www.123europe-londonhotels.com

Hotel
Queens Hotel, 33 Anson Road, Tufnell Park, LONDON N7 Tel: 020 7607 4725
• e-mail: queens@stavrouhotels.co.uk
• website: www.stavrouhotels.co.uk

•BERKSHIRE

Guest House
Clarence Hotel, 9 Clarence Road, WINDSOR, Berkshire SL4 5AE
Tel: 01753 864436
• e-mail: clarence.hotel@btconnect.com
• website: www.clarence-hotel.co.uk

•BUCKINGHAMSHIRE

B & B / Self-Catering Cottages
Poletrees Farm, Ludgershall Road, Brill, AYLESBURY, Buckinghamshire HP18 9TZ
Tel: 01844 238276
• e-mail: poletrees.farm@virgin.net
• web:
www.country-accom.co.uk/poletrees-farm

•CAMBRIDGESHIRE

Self-Catering
Hilary's Cottage, CAMBRIDGE.
Contact: Mrs H. Marsh, The Meadow House, 2A High Street, BURWELL, Cambridgeshire CB25 0HB
Tel: 01638 741926
• e-mail: hilary@themeadowhouse.co.uk
• website: www.themeadowhouse.co.uk

B & B
Mrs Hatley, Manor Farm, Landbeach, CAMBRIDGE, Cambridgeshire CB4 8ED
Tel: 01223 860165
• e-mail: vhatley@btinternet.com
• website:
www.smoothhound.co.uk/hotels/manorfarm4

www.holidayguides.com

•CHESHIRE

Guest House / Self-Catering
Mrs Joanne Hollins, Balterley Green Farm,
Deans Lane, BALTERLEY, near Crewe
Cheshire CW2 5QJ Tel: 01270 820 214
• e-mail: greenfarm@balterley.fsnet.co.uk
• website: www.greenfarm.freeserve.co.uk

B & B
Needhams Farm, Uplands Road, Werneth
Low, Gee Cross, HYDE (near Manchester),
Cheshire SK14 3AG Tel: 0161 3684610
• e-mail: charlotte@needhamsfarm.co.uk

•CORNWALL

Self-Catering
Cornish Traditional Cottages, Blisland,
BODMIN, Cornwall PL30 4HS
Tel: 01208 821666
• e-mail: info@corncott.com
• website: www.corncott.com

Self-Catering
Penrose Burden Holiday Cottages,
St Breward, BODMIN, Cornwall PL30 4LZ
Tel: 01208 850277 or 01208 850617
• website: www.penroseburden.co.uk

Self-Catering
Henwood Barns, Henwood, BODMIN
MOOR, Cornwall PL14 5BP
Tel: 01579 363 576
• e-mail: henwoodbarns@tiscali.co.uk
• website: www.henwoodbarns.co.uk

Hotel
Stratton Gardens Hotel, Cot Hill, Stratton,
BUDE, Cornwall EX23 9DN Tel: 01288
352500
• e-mail: moira@stratton-gardens.co.uk
• website: www.stratton-gardens.co.uk

Self-Catering
Mineshop Holiday Cottages,
CRACKINGTON HAVEN, Bude,
Cornwall EX23 0NR Tel: 01840 230338
• e-mail: tippett@mineshop.freeserve.co.uk
• website: www.mineshop.co.uk

Self-Catering
Mr M. Watson, Creekside Cottages,
Restronguet, Near FALMOUTH, Cornwall
Tel: 01326 375972
• e-mail: martin@creeksidecottages.co.uk
• website: www.creeksidecottages.co.uk

Self-Catering
Mr P. Watson, Creekside Holiday Houses,
Restronguet, FALMOUTH, Cornwall
Tel: 01326 372722
• website: www.creeksideholidayhouses.co.uk

Hotel
Rosemullion Hotel, Gyllyngvase Hill,
FALMOUTH, Cornwall TR11 4DF
Tel: 01326 314 690
• e-mail: gail@rosemullionhotel.demon.co.uk
• www.SmoothHound.co.uk/hotels/rosemullion.

Self-Catering
Mrs K Terry, "Shasta", Carwinion Road,
Mawnan Smith, FALMOUTH, Cornwall
TR11 5JD Tel: 01326 250775
• e-mail: katerry@btopenworld.com

Guest House
Jenny Lake, Wickham Guest House,
21 Gyllyngvase Terrace, FALMOUTH,
Cornwall TR11 4DL Tel: 01326 311140
• e-mail:
enquiries@wickhamhotel.freeserve.co.uk
• website: www.wickham-hotel.co.uk

Caravan Park
St Ives Bay Holiday Park, Upton Towans,
HAYLE, Cornwall TR27 5BH
Tel: 0800 317713
• website: www.stivesbay.co.uk

Self-Catering / Campsite
Franchis Holidays, Cury Cross Lanes,
Mullion, HELSTON, Cornwall TR12 7AZ
Tel: 01326 240301
• e-mail: enquiries@franchis.co.uk
• website: www.franchis.co.uk

Static Caravan & Camping
Little Trevothan Caravan Park, Coverack,
NEAR HELSTON, Cornwall TR12 6SD
Tel: 01326 280260
• e-mail: sales@littletrevothan.co.uk
• website: www.littletrevothan.co.uk

Readers are requested to mention this FHG
guidebook when seeking accommodation

Self-Catering
Celia Hutchinson,
Caradon Country Cottages, East Taphouse,
LISKEARD, Cornwall PL14 4NH
Tel: 01579 320355
- e-mail: celia@caradoncottages.co.uk
- website: www.caradoncottages.co.uk

Self-Catering
Tracy Dennett, Talehay Holiday Cottages,
Pelynt, Near LOOE, Cornwall PL13 2LT
Tel: 01503 220252
- e-mail: infobookings@talehay.co.uk
- website: www.talehay.co.uk

Holiday Park
Tregoad Park, St Martins, LOOE, Cornwall
PL13 1PB Tel: 01503 262718
- e-mail: info@tregoadpark.co.uk
- website: www.tregoadpark.co.uk

Self-Catering
Mr & Mrs Holder, Valleybrook Holidays,
Peakswater, Lansallos, LOOE,
Cornwall PL13 2QE Tel: 01503 220493
- website: www.valleybrookholidays.com

Self-Catering Cottages
Wringworthy Cottages, LOOE, Cornwall
PL13 1PR Tel: 01503 240 685
- e-mail: pets@wringworthy.co.uk
- website: www.wringworthy.co.uk

Self-catering Lodges
Blue Bay Lodge, Trenance, MAWGAN
PORTH, Cornwall TR8 4DA
Tel: 01637 860324
- e-mail: hotel@bluebaycornwall.co.uk
- website: www.bluebaycornwall.co.uk

B & B
Mrs Dawn Rundle, Lancallan Farm,
MEVAGISSEY, St Austell,Cornwall PL26
6EW Tel: 01726 842 284
- e-mail: dawn@lancallan.fsnet.co.uk
- website: www.lancallanfarm.co.uk

Guest House
Mrs Dewolfreys, Dewolf Guest House, 100
Henver Road, NEWQUAY, Cornwall TR7 3BL
Tel: 01637 874746
- e-mail: holidays@dewolfguesthouse.com
- website: www.dewolfguesthouse.com

Guest House
Pensalda Guest House, 98 Henver Road,
NEWQUAY, Cornwall TR7 3BL
Tel: 01637 874 601
- e-mail: karen_pensalda@yahoo.co.uk
- website: www.pensalda-guesthouse.co.uk

Caravan & Camping / Self-Catering
Quarryfield Caravan & Camping Park,
Crantock, NEWQUAY, Cornwall
Contact: Mrs A. Winn, Tretherras, Newquay,
Cornwall TR7 2RE
Tel: 01637 872 792
- website: www.quarryfield.co.uk

Hotel
St George's Hotel, 71 Mount Wise,
NEWQUAY, Cornwall TR7 2BP
Tel: 01637 873010
- e-mail:
enquiries@stgeorgeshotel.free-online.co.uk
- website: www.st-georges-newquay.co.uk

Self-Catering
Raintree House Holidays, Whistlers,
Treyarnon Bay, PADSTOW, Cornwall PL28
8JR Tel: 01841 520228
- e-mail: gill@raintreehouse.co.uk
- website: www.raintreehouse.co.uk

Hotel
Tregea Hotel, 16-18 High Street, PADSTOW,
Cornwall PL28 8BB Tel: 01841 532 455
- e-mail: enquiries@tregea.co.uk
- website: www.tregea.co.uk

Guest House
Lynda Sowerby, Torwood House, Alexandra
Road, PENZANCE, Cornwall TR18 4LZ
Tel: 01736 360063
- e-mail: lyndasowerby@aol.com
- website: www.torwoodhousehotel.co.uk

Hotel
Rosevine Hotel, Porthcurnick Beach,
PORTSCATHO, Near St Mawes,
Cornwall TR2 5EW Tel: 01872 580206
- e-mail: info@rosevine.co.uk
- website: www.rosevine.co.uk

Caravan & Camping / Holiday Park
Chiverton Park, Blackwater, ST AGNES,
Cornwall TR4 8HS Tel: 01872 560667
- e-mail: info@chivertonpark.co.uk
- website: www.chivertonpark.co.uk

Hotel / Inn
Driftwood Spars Hotel, Trevaunance Cove,
ST AGNES, Cornwall TR5 0RT
Tel: 01872 552428
- website: www.driftwoodspars.com

Hotel / B & B
Penkerris, Penwinnick Road, ST AGNES,
Cornwall TR5 0PA Tel: 01872 552262
- e-mail: info@penkerris.co.uk
- website: www.penkerris.co.uk

Guest House

Mr Gardener, The Elms, 14 Penwinnick Road, ST AUSTELL, Cornwall PL25 5DW
Tel: 01726 74981
• e-mail: pete@edenbb.co.uk
• website: www.edenbb.co.uk

Self-Catering

Mr & Mrs C.W. Pestell, Hockadays, Tregenna, Near Blisland, ST TUDY, Cornwall PL30 4QJ Tel: 01208 850146
• website: www.hockadays.co.uk

Self-Catering

Mrs R. Reeves, Polstraul, Trewalder, Delabole, ST TUDY, Cornwall PL33 9ET
Tel: 01840 213 120
• e-mail: ruth.reeves@hotmail.co.uk
• website: www.maymear.co.uk

Self-Catering

Mrs Sandy Wilson, Salutations, Atlantic Road, TINTAGEL, Cornwall PL34 0DE
Tel: 01840 770287
• e-mail: sandyanddave@tinyworld.co.uk
• website: www.salutationstintagel.co.uk

Farm B & B

Mrs E. Hodge, Pengelly Farmhouse, Pengelly Farm, Burlawn, WADEBRIDGE, Cornwall PL27 7LA
Tel: 01208 814 217
• e-mail: hodgepete@hotmail.com
• website: www.pengellyfarm.co.uk

Self- catering

Great Bodieve Farm Barns, WADEBRIDGE, Cornwall.
Contact: Mrs T Riddle, Molesworth House, Wadebridge, Cornwall PL27 7SE
Tel: 01208 814916
• e-mail: enquiries@great-bodieve.co.uk
• website: www.great-bodieve.co.uk

•CUMBRIA

Caravan Park

Greenhowe Caravan Park, Great Langdale, AMBLESIDE, Cumbria LA22 9JU
Tel: 015394 37231
• e-mail: enquiries@greenhowe.com
• website: www.greenhowe.com

Hotel / Guest House

Ian & Helen Burt, The Old Vicarage, Vicarage Road, AMBLESIDE, Cumbria LA22 9DH. Tel: 015394 33364
• e-mail: info@oldvicarageambleside.co.uk
• website: www.oldvicarageambleside.co.uk

Hotel

Rothay Manor Hotel, Rothay Bridge, AMBLESIDE, Cumbria LL22 OEH
Tel: 01539 433605
• e-mail: hotel@rothaymanor.co.uk
• website: www.rothaymanor.co.uk

Self-Catering

43A Quarry Rigg, BOWNESS-ON-WINDERMERE, Cumbria.
Contact: Mrs E. Jones, 45 West Oakhill Park, Liverpool L13 4BN Tel: 0151 228 5799
• e-mail: eejay@btinternet.com

B & B

Amanda Vickers, Mosser Heights, Mosser, COCKERMOUTH, Cumbria CA13 0SS
Tel: 01900 822644
• e-mail: amandavickers1@aol.com
• website: www.stayonacumbrianfarm.co.uk

Guest House

Rose Cottage Guest House, Lorton Road, COCKERMOUTH, Cumbria CA13 9DX
Tel: 01900 822189
• website: www.rosecottageguest.co.uk

Self-Catering

Hodyoad Cottage, Cumbria.
Contact: Mrs J. A. Cook, Hodyoad House, Lamplugh, Near COCKERMOUTH, Cumbria CA14 4TT Tel: 01946 861338
• e-mail: hodyoad@tiscali.co.uk
• website: www.hodyoad.com

Self-Catering

Mr P. Johnston, The Coppermines & Lakes Cottages, The Estate Office, The Bridge, CONISTON, Cumbria LA21 8HJ
Tel: 01539 441765
• e-mail: info@coppermines.co.uk
• website: www.coppermines.co.uk

Self-Catering

Fisherground Farm Holidays, ESKDALE, Cumbria.
Contact: Ian & Jennifer Hall, Orchard House, Applethwaite, Keswick, Cumbria CA12 4PN
Tel: 017687 73175
• e-mail: holidays@fisherground.co.uk
• website: www.fisherground.co.uk

Hotel

Hampsfell House Hotel, Hampsfell Road, GRANGE-OVER-SANDS, Cumbria LA11 6BG
Tel: 015395 32567
• e-mail: enquiries@hampsfellhouse.co.uk
• website: www.hampsfellhouse.co.uk

Self-Catering
Routen House & Little Parrock,
Ennerdale, GRASMERE, Cumbria
Contact: Mrs J. Green Tel: 01604 626383
- e-mail: joanne@routenhouse.co.uk
- website: www.routenhouse.co.uk

Farm / Self-Catering
Mr P. Brown, High Dale Park Farm, High Dale
Park, Satterthwaite, Ulverston, GRIZEDALE
FOREST, Cumbria LA12 8LJ
Tel: 01229 860226
- e-mail: peter@lakesweddingmusic.com
- www.lakesweddingmusic.com/accomm

Self-Catering Cottages
Hideaways, The Square, HAWKSHEAD,
Cumbria LA22 0NZ Tel: 015394 42435
- e-mail: bookings@lakeland-hideaways.co.uk
- website: www.lakeland-hideaways.co.uk

Self-Catering
Derwent Water Marina, Portinscale,
KESWICK, Cumbria CA12 5RF
Tel: 017687 72912
- e-mail: info@derwentwatermarina.co.uk
- website: www.derwentwatermarina.co.uk

Guest House
Mr Taylorson, Rickerby Grange, Portinscale,
KESWICK, Cumbria CA12 5RH
Tel: 017687 72344
- e-mail: stay@rickerbygrange.co.uk
- website: www.rickerbygrange.co.uk

Self-Catering / Farm
Mrs J. M. Almond, Irton House Farm,
Isel, Near KESWICK, Cumbria CA13 9ST
Tel: 017687 76380
- e-mail: joan@irtonhousefarm.co.uk
- website: www.irtonhousefarm.com

Self-Catering
Mrs S.J. Bottom, Crossfield Cottages,
KIRKOSWALD, Penrith, Cumbria CA10 1EU
Tel: 01768 898711
- e-mail: info@crossfieldcottages.co.uk
- website: www.crossfieldcottages.co.uk

Inn
The Britannia Inn, Elterwater, LANGDALE,
Cumbria LA22 9HP Tel: 015394 37210
- e-mail: info@britinn.co.uk
- website: www.britinn.co.uk

Self-Catering
Mr & Mrs Iredale, Carrock Cottages,
Carrock House, Hutton Roof, PENRITH,
Cumbria CA11 0XY Tel: 01768 484111
- e-mail: info@carrockcottages.co.uk
- website: www.carrockcottages.co.uk

Guest House / Inn
Troutbeck Inn, Troutbeck, PENRITH,
Cumbria CA11 0SJ
Tel: 01768 483635
- website: www.thetroutbeckinn.co.uk

Golf Club
Seascale Golf Club, The Banks, SEASCALE,
Cumbria CA20 1QL Tel: 01946 728202
- e-mail: seascalegolfclub@googlemail.com
- website: www.seascalegolfclub.co.uk

Self-Catering / Caravan & Camping
Tanglewood Caravan Park, Causeway Head,
SILLOTH-ON-SOLWAY, Cumbria CA7 4PE
Tel: 016973 31253
- e-mail: tanglewoodcaravanpark@hotmail.com
- website: www.tanglewoodcaravanpark.co.uk

B & B / Self-Catering
Barbara Murphy, Land Ends Country Lodge,
Watermillock, ULLSWATER, Near Penrith,
Cumbria CA11 0NB Tel: 01768 486438
- e-mail: infolandends@btinternet.com
- website: www.landends.co.uk

•DERBYSHIRE

Self-Catering
Patti Cust, The Old Laundry, Sturston Hall,
ASHBOURNE, Derbyshire DE6 1LN
Tel: 01335 346711
- e-mail: p.cust@virgin.net
- website: www.sturston.com

Self-Catering Holiday Cottages
Mark Redfern, Paddock House Farm Holiday
Cottages, Alstonefield, ASHBOURNE,
Derbyshire DE6 2FT Tel: 01335 310282
- e-mail: info@paddockhousefarm.co.uk
- website: www.paddockhousefarm.co.uk

B&B
Mrs J. Salisbury, Turlow Bank, Hognaston,
ASHBOURNE, Derbyshire DE6 1PW
Tel: 01335 370299
- e-mail: turlowbank@w3z.co.uk
- website: www.turlowbank.co.uk

Self-Catering
P. Skemp, Cotterill Farm,
BIGGIN-BY-HARTINGTON, Buxton,
Derbyshire SK17 0DJ Tel: 01298 84447
- e-mail: enquiries@cotterillfarm.co.uk
- website: www.cotterillfarm.co.uk

Hotel
Biggin Hall, Biggin-by-Hartington,
BUXTON, Derbyshire SK17 0DH
Tel: 01298 84451
- e-mail: enquiries@bigginhall.co.uk
- website: www.bigginhall.co.uk

Self-Catering
Mrs Gillian Taylor, Priory Lea Holiday Flats,
50 White Knowle Road, BUXTON,
Derbyshire SK17 9NH Tel: 01298 23737
- e-mail: priorylea@tiscali.co.uk
- website:
www.cressbrook.co.uk/buxton/priorylea

Caravan & Camping Park
Newhaven Caravan & Camping Park,
Newhaven, NEAR BUXTON,
Derbyshire SK17 0DT Tel: 01298 84300
- e-mail: bobmacara@ntlworld.com
- website: www.newhavencaravanpark.co.uk

Guest House
Ivy House Farm Guest House,
STANTON-BY-BRIDGE, Derby,
Derbyshire DE73 7HT Tel: 01332 863152
- e-mail: mary@guesthouse.fsbusiness.co.uk
- website: www.ivy-house-farm.com

•DEVON

Self-Catering
Toad Hall Cottages, DEVON
Tel: 01548 853089 (24 Hours)
- e-mail: thc@toadhallcottages.com
- website: www.toadhallcottages.co.uk

Self-Catering
Farm & Cottage Holidays, DEVON
Tel: 01237 479698
- website: www.holidaycottages.co.uk

B & B
Lynda Richards, Gages Mill, Buckfastleigh
Road, ASHBURTON, Devon TQ13 7JW
Tel: 01364 652391
- e-mail: gagesmill@aol.com
- website: www.gagesmill.co.uk

Self-Catering / Caravan Park
Parkers Farm Holiday Park, Higher Mead
Farm, ASHBURTON, Devon TQ13 7LJ
Tel: 01364 654869
- e-mail: parkersfarm@btconnect.com
- website: www.parkersfarm.co.uk

Self-Catering
Braddon Cottages, ASHWATER, Beaworthy,
Holsworthy, Devon EX21 5EP
Tel: 01409 211350
- e-mail: holidays@braddoncottages.co.uk
- website: www.braddoncottages.co.uk

Self-Catering
North Devon Holiday Homes,
19 Cross Street, BARNSTAPLE,
Devon EX31 1BD Tel: 01271 376322
- e-mail: info@northdevonholidays.co.uk
- website: www.northdevonholidays.co.uk

Hotel
Sandy Cove Hotel, Combe Martin Bay,
BERRYNARBOR, Devon EX34 9SR
Tel: 01271 882243/882888
- website: www.sandycove-hotel.co.uk

Hotel
Yeoldon House Hotel, Durrant Lane,
Northam, BIDEFORD, Devon EX39 2RL
Tel: 01237 474400
- e-mail: yeoldonhouse@aol.com
- website: www.yeoldonhousehotel.co.uk

B & B / Self-Catering
Mr & Mrs Lewin, Lake House Cottages
and B&B, Lake Villa, BRADWORTHY,
Devon EX22 7SQ Tel: 01409 241962
- e-mail: info@lakevilla.co.uk
- website: www.lakevilla.co.uk

Self-Catering / Organic Farm
Little Comfort Farm Cottages,
Little Comfort Farm, BRAUNTON,
North Devon EX33 2NJ Tel: 01271 812414
- e-mail: info@littlecomfortfarm.co.uk
- website: www.littlecomfortfarm.co.uk

Guest House
Woodlands Guest House, Parkham Road,
BRIXHAM, South Devon TQ5 9BU
Tel: 01803 852040
- e-mail: woodlandsbrixham@btinternet.com
- website: www.woodlandsdevon.co.uk

Self-Catering
Amanda Williams, West Banbury Farm
Cottages, BROADWOODWIDGER, NEAR
LIFTON, Devon PL16 0JJ
Tel: 01566 784946
- e-mail: amanda@westbanbury.co.uk
- website: www.westbanbury.co.uk

Self-Catering / B & B / Caravans
Mrs Gould, Bonehayne Farm, COLYTON,
Devon EX24 6SG
Tel: 01404 871416/871396
- e-mail: gould@bonehayne.co.uk
- website: www.bonehayne.co.uk

Self-Catering
Mrs Lee, Church Approach Holidays,
Farway, COLYTON, Devon EX24 6EQ
Tel: 01404 871383/871202
- e-mail: lizlee@eclipse.co.uk
- website: www.churchapproach.co.uk

Self-Catering
Karen Jackson, Boathouse Cottage, Torcross,
DARTMOUTH, Devon TQ7 2TQ
Tel: 01548 580206
- e-mail: enquiries@torcross.com
- website: www.torcross.com

Self-Catering
Mrs S.R. Ridalls, The Old Bakehouse,
7 Broadstone, DARTMOUTH, Devon TQ6 9NR
Tel: 01803 834585
- e-mail: ridallsleisure@aol.com
- website: www.oldbakehousedartmouth.co.uk

Self-Catering
Watermill Cottages, Higher North Mill,
Hansel, DARTMOUTH, Devon TQ6 0LN
Tel: 01803 770219
- e-mail: graham@hanselpg.freeserve.co.uk
- website: www.watermillcottages.co.uk

Self-Catering
Ian West, Station House,
Doddiscombsleigh, EXETER, Devon
EX6 7PW Tel: 01647 253104
- e-mail: enquiries@station-lodge.co.uk
- website: www.station-lodge.co.uk

Self-Catering
Beach Haven, INSTOW, Devon
Contact: Mrs P. I. Barnes, 140 Bay View
Road, Northam, Bideford, Devon EX39 1BJ
Tel: 01237 473801
- website: www.seabirdcottages.co.uk

Self-Catering
Doone Valley Holidays
Contact: Mr C. Harman, Cloud Farm, Oare,
LYNTON, Devon EX35 6NU
Tel: 01598 714234
- e-mail: doonevalleyholidays@hotmail.com
- website: www.doonevalleyholidays.co.uk

Guest House
Mrs T. Williams, Cookshayes, 33 Court
Street, MORETONHAMPSTEAD, Devon
TQ13 8LG Tel: 01647 440374
- e-mail: cookshayes@aol.com
- website: www.cookshayes.co.uk

Farm B & B
Mrs T.M. Merchant, Great Sloncombe Farm,
MORETONHAMPSTEAD, Newton Abbot,
Devon TQ13 8QF Tel: 01647 440595
- e-mail: hmerchant@sloncombe.freeserve.co.uk
- website: www.greatsloncombefarm.co.uk

Self-Catering
Crab Cottage, NOSS MAYO, South Devon
Tel: 01425 471 372
- website: www.crab-cottage.co.uk

Hotel
Christine Clark, Amber House Hotel, 6
Roundham Road, PAIGNTON, Devon TQ4
6EZ Tel: 01803 558372
- e-mail: enquiries@amberhousehotel.co.uk
- website: www.amberhousehotel.co.uk

Guest House
Jane Hill, Beaumont, Castle Hill, SEATON,
Devon EX12 2QW Tel: 01297 20832
- e-mail: jane@lymebay.demon.co.uk
- website:
www.smoothhound.co.uk/beaumon1.html

Camping & Caravan Park
Salcombe Regis Camping & Caravan Park,
Salcombe Regis, SIDMOUTH, Devon
EX10 0JH Tel: 01395 514303
- e-mail: contact@salcombe-regis.co.uk
- website: www.salcombe-regis.co.uk

Self-Catering Lodges
Dartmoor Country Holidays, Magpie Leisure
Park, Horrabridge, Yelverton, TAVISTOCK,
Devon PL20 7RY Tel: 01822 852651
- website: www.dartmoorcountryholidays.co.uk

Caravan & Camping
Harford Bridge Holiday Park, Peter Tavy,
TAVISTOCK, Devon PL19 9LS
Tel: 01822 810349
- e-mail: enquiry@harfordbridge.co.uk
- website: www.harfordbridge.co.uk

Guest House
Mrs Arnold, The Mill, Lower Washfield,
TIVERTON, Devon EX16 9PD
Tel: 01884 255297
- e-mail: themillwashfield@hotmail.co.uk
- website: www.washfield.freeserve.co.uk

Guest House
Mr Butler, Lanscombe House Hotel,
Cockington, TORQUAY, Devon
TQ2 6XA Tel: 01803 606938
• e-mail: stay@lanscombehouse.co.uk
• website: www.lanscombehouse.co.uk

Self-Catering
West Pusehill Farm Cottages,
West Pusehill Farm, Pusehill,
WESTWARD HO!, Devon EX39 5AH
Tel: 01237 475638 or 01237 474622
• e-mail: info@wpfcottages.co.uk
• website: www.wpfcottages.co.uk

Self-Catering
Marsdens Cottage Holidays, 2 The Square,
Braunton, WOOLACOMBE, Devon
EX33 2JB Tel: 01271 813777
• e-mail: holidays@marsdens.co.uk
• website: www.marsdens.co.uk

Holiday Park
Woolacombe Bay Holiday Parcs,
WOOLACOMBE, North Devon
Tel: 01271 870343
• website: www.woolacombe.com/fcw

Caravan & Camping
North Morte Farm Caravan & Camping Park,
Mortehoe, WOOLACOMBE, Devon
EX34 7EG. Tel: 01271 870381
• e-mail: info@northmortefarm.co.uk
• website: www.northmortefarm.co.uk

Farmhouse / B & B
Mrs Linda Landick, Eggworthy Farm,
Sampford Spiney, YELVERTON, Devon
PL20 6LJ Tel: 01822 852142
• e-mail: eggworthyfarm@aol.com
• website: www.eggworthyfarm.co.uk

•DORSET

Self-catering
Dorset Coastal Cottages, The Manor House,
Winfrith Newburgh, Dorchester,
Dorset DT2 8JR Tel: 0800 980 4070
• e-mail: hols@dorsetcoastalcottages.com
• website: www.dorsetcoastalcottages.com

Inn
The Anvil Inn, Salisbury Road, Pimperne,
BLANDFORD, Dorset DT11 8UQ
Tel: 01258 453431
• e-mail: theanvil.inn@btconnect.com
• website: www.anvilinn.co.uk

Hotel
Southbourne Grove Hotel, 96 Southbourne
Road, BOURNEMOUTH, Dorset BH6 3QQ
Tel: 01202 420 503
• e-mail: neil@pack1462.freeserve.co.uk

Self-Catering
C Hammond, Stourcliff Court, 56 Stourcliffe
Avenue, Southbourne, BOURNEMOUTH,
Dorset BH6 3PX Tel: 01202 420698
• website: www.stourcliffecourt.co.uk

Self-Catering
Lancombes House, West Milton, BRIDPORT,
Dorset DT6 3TN Tel: 01308 485375
• e-mail: info@lancombes-house.co.uk
• website: www.lancombes-house.co.uk

Caravan Park
Giants Head Caravan & Camping Park,
Old Sherborne Road, Cerne Abbas,
DORCHESTER, Dorset DT2 7TR
Tel: 01300 341242
• e-mail: holidays@giantshead.co.uk
• website: www.giantshead.co.uk

Farm / Self-Catering
Tamarisk Farm, West Bexington,
DORCHESTER, Dorset DT2 9DF
Tel: 01308 897784
• e-mail: holidays@tamariskfarm.com
• website: www.tamariskfarm.com

Hotel
Cromwell House Hotel, LULWORTH COVE,
Dorset BH20 5RJ
Tel: 01929 400253
• e-mail: catriona@lulworthcove.co.uk
• website: www.lulworthcove.co.uk

Self-Catering
Westover Farm Cottages, Wootton Fitzpaine,
Near LYME REGIS, Dorset DT6 6NE
Tel: 01297 560451/561395
• e-mail: wfcottages@aol.com
• website: www.westoverfarmcottages.co.uk

Farm / Self-Catering
White Horse Farm, Middlemarsh,
SHERBORNE, Dorset DT9 5QN
Tel: 01963 210222
• e-mail: enquiries@whitehorsefarm.co.uk
• website: www.whitehorsefarm.co.uk

Hotel
The Knoll House, STUDLAND BAY,
Dorset BH19 3AW Tel: 01929 450450
• e-mail: info@knollhouse.co.uk
• website: www.knollhouse.co.uk

Hotel
The Limes, 48 Park Road, SWANAGE,
Dorset BH19 2AE Tel: 01929 422664
• e-mail: info@limeshotel.net
• website: www.limeshotel.net

Farm/ Guest House/ Caravan & Camping
Luckford Wood House, East Stoke, Near
Lulworth, WAREHAM, Dorset BH20 6AW
Tel: 01929 463098/07888 719002
• e-mail: info@luckfordleisure.co.uk
• website: www.luckfordleisure.co.uk

Guest House/ Self-Catering
Glenthorne, Castle Cove, 15 Old Castle
Road, WEYMOUTH, Dorset DT4 8QB
Tel: 01305 777281
• e-mail: info@glenthorne-holidays.co.uk
• website: www.glenthorne-holidays.co.uk

•DURHAM

Self-Catering Cottages
Low Lands Farm, Lowlands, Cockfield,
BISHOP AUCKLAND, Durham DL13 5AW
Tel: 01388 718251
• e-mail: info@farmholidaysuk.com
• website: www.farmholidaysuk.com

Hotel
The Teesdale Hotel, MIDDLETON-IN-
TEESDALE, Durham DL12 0QG
Tel: 01833 640264
• e-mail: john@teesdalehotel.co.uk
• website: www.teesdalehotel.co.uk

•GLOUCESTERSHIRE

Hotel
Chester House Hotel, Victoria Street,
BOURTON-ON-THE-WATER,
Gloucs GL54 2BU Tel: 01451 820286
• e-mail: info@chesterhousehotel.com
• website: www.chesterhousehotel.com

Hotel
The Bowl Inn & Lilies Restaurant, 16 Church
Road, Lower Almondsbury, BRISTOL,
Gloucs BS32 4DT Tel: 01454 612757
• e-mail: reception@thebowlinn.co.uk
• website: www.thebowlinn.co.uk

Farmhouse B & B
Box Hedge Farm B & B, Box Hedge Farm
Lane, Coalpit Heath, BRISTOL,
Gloucs BS36 2UW Tel: 01454 250786
• e-mail: marilyn@bed-breakfast-bristol.com
• website: www.bed-breakfast-bristol.com

Hotel
Thornbury Golf Lodge, Bristol Road,
Thornbury, BRISTOL, Gloucs BS35 3XL
Tel: 01454 281144
• e-mail: info@thornburygc.co.uk
• website: www.thornburygc.co.uk

Self-Catering
Rose's Cottage, BROADWELL
Tel: 01451 830007
• e-mail: richard.drinkwater@ukonline.co.uk

B & B
Mrs C. Hutsby, Holly House, Ebrington,
CHIPPING CAMPDEN, Gloucs GL55 6NL
Tel: 01386 593213
• e-mail: hutsbybandb@aol.com
• website: www.hollyhousebandb.co.uk

Hotel
Tudor Farmhouse Hotel, CLEARWELL,
Forest of Dean, Gloucs GL16 8JS
Tel: 0800 7835935
• e-mail: info@tudorfarmhousehotel.co.uk
• website: www.tudorhousehotel.co.uk

Self-Catering
Wharton Lodge Cottages, FOREST OF
DEAN, Gloucs
Contact: Nicky Cross, Wharton Lodge
Cottages, Weston-Under-Penyard,
Herefordshire HR9 7JX Tel: 01989 750140
• e-mail: ncross@whartonlodge.co.uk
• website: www.whartonlodge.co.uk

B & B
Anthea & Bill Rhoton, Hyde Crest, Cirencester Road, MINCHINHAMPTON, Gloucs GL6 8PE.
Tel: 01453 731631
• e-mail: **stay@hydecrest.co.uk**
• website: **www.hydecrest.co.uk**

•HAMPSHIRE

B & B
Mr & Mrs Farrell, Honeysuckle House, 24 Clinton Road, LYMINGTON, Hampshire SO41 9EA Tel: 01590 676635
• e-mail: **skyblue@beeb.net**
• website:
http://explorethenewforest.co.uk/honeysuckle.htm

Hotel
Crown Hotel, High Street, LYNDHURST, Hampshire SO43 7NF Tel: 023 8028 2922
• e-mail: **reception@crownhotel-lyndhurst.co.uk**
• website: **www.crownhotel-lyndhurst.co.uk**

Hotel
Bramble Hill Hotel, Bramshaw, Near LYNDHURST, New Forest, Hampshire SO43 7JG Tel: 02380 813165
• website: **www.bramblehill.co.uk**

Caravan Park
Downton Holiday Park, Shorefield Road, Milford-on-Sea, NEW FOREST, Hampshire SO41 0LH
Tel: 01425 476131/01590 642515
• e-mail: **info@downtonholidaypark.co.uk**
• website: **www.downtonholidaypark.co.uk**

•HEREFORDSHIRE

Hotel
David & June Slade, Baskerville Arms Hotel, Clyro, Near HAYE-ON-WYE, Herefordshire HR3 5RZ Tel: 01497 820670
• e-mail: **bookings@baskervillearms.co.uk**
• website: **www.baskervillearms.co.uk**

Self-catering
The Rock Cottage, Huntington, KINGTON.
Contact: Mrs Williams, Radnor's End, Huntington, KINGTON, Herefordshire HR5 3NZ Tel: 01544 370289
• e-mail: **enquires@the-rock-cottage.co.uk**
• website: **www.the-rock-cottage.co.uk**

Farmhouse / B & B
Mrs M. E. Drzymalski, Thatch Close, Llangrove, ROSS-ON-WYE, Herefordshire HR9 6EL Tel: 01989 770300
• e-mail: **info@thatchclose.co.uk**
• website: **www.thatchclose.co.uk**

•KENT

Guest House
S. Twort, Heron Cottage, Biddenden, ASHFORD, Kent TN27 8HH. Tel: 01580 291358
• e-mail: **susantwort@hotmail.com**
• website: **www.heroncottage.info**

Hotel
Collina House Hotel, 5 East Hill, TENTERDEN, Kent TN30 6RL Tel: 01580 764852/764004
• e-mail: **enquiries@collinahousehotel.co.uk**
• website: **www.collinahousehotel.co.uk**

•LEICESTERSHIRE & RUTLAND

Golf Club
Birstall Golf Club, Station Road, Birstall, LEICESTER, Leicestershire LE4 3BB
Tel: 0116 267 4322
• e-mail: **sue@birstallgolfclub.co.uk**
• website: **www.birstallgolfclub.co.uk**

•LINCOLNSHIRE

Farm B & B / Self-catering cottage
Mrs C.E. Harrison, Baumber Park, Baumber, HORNCASTLE, Lincolnshire LN9 5NE
Tel: 01507 578235/07977 722776
• e-mail: **baumberpark@amserve.com**
• website: **www.baumberpark.com**
         www.gathmanscottage.co.uk

Farmhouse B & B
S Evans, Willow Farm, Thorpe Fendykes, SKEGNESS, Lincolnshire PE24 4QH
Tel: 01754 830316
• e-mail: **willowfarmhols@aol.com**
• website: **www.willowfarmholidays.co.uk**

Hotel
Petwood Hotel, Stixwood Road, WOODHALL SPA, Lincolnshire LN10 6QF
Tel: 01526 352411
• e-mail: **reception@petwood.co.uk**
• website: **www.petwood.co.uk**

• MERSEYSIDE

Guest House
Holme Leigh Guest House, 93 Woodcroft
Road, Wavertree, LIVERPOOL,
Merseyside L15 2HG Tel: 0151 734 2216
• e-mail: info@holmeleigh.com
• website: www.holmeleigh.com

• NORFOLK

Self-Catering
Sand Dune Cottages, Tan Lane,
CAISTER-ON-SEA, Great Yarmouth,
Norfolk NR30 5DT Tel: 01493 720352
• e-mail: sand.dune.cottages@amserve.net
• website:
www.eastcoastlive.co.uk/sites/sanddunecottages.php

Self-catering
Scarning Dale, Dale Road, Scarning,
DEREHAM, Norfolk NR1 2QN
Tel: 01362 687269
• e-mail: jean@scarningdale.co.uk
• website: www.scarningdale.co.uk

Self-Catering
Idyllic Cottages at Vere Lodge,
South Raynham, FAKENHAM,
Norfolk NR21 7HE Tel: 01328 838261
• e-mail: major@verelodge.co.uk
• website: www.idylliccottages.co.uk

Self-Catering
Carefree Holidays, Chapel Briars, Yarmouth
Road, GREAT YARMOUTH, Norfolk NR29
4NJ Tel: 01493 732176
• e-mail: tony@carefree-holidays.co.uk
• website: www.carefree-holidays.co.uk

Self-Catering
Blue Riband Holidays, HEMSBY,
Great Yarmouth, Norfolk NR29 4HA
Tel: 01493 730445
• website: www.BlueRibandHolidays.co.uk

Hotel
The Stuart House Hotel, 35 Goodwins Road,
KING'S LYNN, Norfolk PE30 5QX
Tel: 01553 772169
• e-mail: reception@stuarthousehotel.co.uk
• website: www.stuarthousehotel.co.uk

B & B
Mrs J. Douglas, Greenacres Farm, Wood
Green, LONG STRATTON, Norwich, Norfolk
NR15 2RR Tel: 01508 530261
• website: www.abreakwithtradition.co.uk

B & B
Dolphin Lodge, 3 Knapton Road, Trunch,
NORTH WALSHAM, Norfolk NR28 0QE
Tel: 01263 720961
• e-mail: dolphin.lodge@btopenworld.com
• website: www.dolphinlodges.net

Self-Catering
Mr & Mrs Castleton, Poppyland Holiday
Cottages, The Green, THORPE MARKET,
Norfolk NR11 8AJ Tel: 01263 833219
• e-mail: poppylandjc@netscape.net
• website: www.poppyland.com

Self-Catering
Winterton Valley Holidays, WINTERTON-
ON-SEA/CALIFORNIA, Norfolk
Contact: 15 Kingston Avenue,Caister-on-
Sea NR30 5ET Tel: 01493 377175
• e-mail: info@wintertonvalleyholidays.co.uk
• website: www.wintertonvalleyholidays.co.uk

• NORTHUMBERLAND

Self-Catering
Buston Farm Holiday Cottages, ALNWICK,
Northumberland
Contact: Bygate, Black Heddon, Newcastle
Upon Tyne NE20 0JJ Tel: 01665 714805
• e-mail: stay@buston.co.uk
• website: www.buston.co.uk

Self-Catering
Heritage Coast Holidays, 6G Greensfield
Court, ALNWICK, Northumberland NE66
2DE
Tel: 01665 604935
• e-mail: info@heritagecoastholidays.com
• website: www.heritagecoastholidays.com

Self-Catering
Swinhoe Farm Cottages & Riding Centre,
Swinhoe Farmhouse, BELFORD,
Northumberland NE70 7LJ
Tel: 016682 13370
• e-mail: valerie@swinhoecottages.co.uk or
           valerie.nixon@farming.co.uk
• website: www.swinhoecottages.co.uk

Hotel / Self-Catering
Riverdale Hall Hotel, BELLINGHAM,
Northumberland NE48 2JT
Tel: 01434 220254
- e-mail: reservations@riverdalehallhotel.co.uk
- website: www.riverdalehallhotel.co.uk

Hotel
The Cobbled Yard Hotel, 40 Walkergate,
BERWICK-UPON-TWEED, Northumberland
TD15 1DJ Tel: 01289 308407
- e-mail:
cobbledyardhotel@berwick35.fsnet.co.uk
- website: www.cobbledyardhotel.com

B & B / Farm / Camping
Mrs S. Maughan, Greencarts Farm, Near
Humshaugh, HEXHAM, Northumberland
NE46 4BW Tel: 01434 681320
- e-mail: sandra@greencarts.co.uk
- website: www.greencarts.co.uk

Self-Catering
Burradon Farm Cottages & Houses,
Burradon Farm, Cramlington, NEWCASTLE-
UPON-TYNE, Northumberland NE23 7ND
Tel: 0191 2683203
- e-mail: judy@burradonfarm.co.uk
- website: www.burradonfarm.co.uk

Golf Club
Seahouses Golf Club, Beadnell Road,
SEAHOUSES, Northumberland NE67 7XT
Tel: 01665 720794
- e-mail: secretary@seahousesgolf.co.uk
- website: www.seahousesgolf.co.uk

Guest House / B & B
Mrs M. Halliday, Beck'n'Call, Birling West
Cottage, WARKWORTH, Northumberland
NE65 0XS Tel: 01665 711653
- e-mail: beck-n-call@lineone.net
- website: www.beck-n-call.co.uk

•OXFORDSHIRE

Leisure Park
Cotswold Wildlife Park, BURFORD,
Oxfordshire OX18 4JN Tel: 01993 823006
- website: www.cotswoldwildlifepark.co.uk

B & B
The Old Bakery, Skirmett, Near HENLEY-ON-
THAMES, Oxfordshire RG9 6TD
Tel: 01491 410716
- e-mail: lizzroach@aol.com

Guest House
The Bungalow, Cherwell Farm, Mill Lane,
Old Marston, OXFORD,
Oxfordshire OX3 0QF Tel: 01865 557171
- e-mail: ros.bungalowbb@btinternet.com
- www.cherwellfarm-oxford-accomm.co.uk

Guest House
Nanford Guest House, 137 Iffley Road,
OXFORD, Oxfordshire, OX4 1EJ
Tel: 01865 244743
- e-mail: b.cronin@btinternet.com
- website: www.nanfordguesthouse.com

B & B / Self-Catering
Katharine Brown, Hill Grove Farm, Crawley
Dry Lane, Minster Lovell, WITNEY,
Oxfordshire OX29 0NA Tel: 01993 703120
- e-mail: katharinemcbrown@btinternet.com
- website:
www.countryaccom.co.uk/hill-grove-farm

•SHROPSHIRE

Farm / B & B
Mrs Mary Jones, Acton Scott Farm, Acton
Scott, CHURCH STRETTON, Shropshire
SY6 6QN Tel: 01694 781260
- e-mail: fhg@actonscottfarm.co.uk
- website: www.actonscottfarm.co.uk

Self-Catering
Clive & Cynthia Prior, Mocktree Barns
Holiday Cottages, Leintwardine, LUDLOW,
Shropshire SY7 0LY Tel: 01547 540441
- e-mail: mocktreebarns@care4free.net
- website: www.mocktreeholidays.co.uk

Inn / Hotel

The Four Alls Inn, Woodseaves,
MARKET DRAYTON, Shropshire TF9 2AG
Tel: 01630 652995
• e-mail: inn@thefouralls.com
• website: www.thefouralls.com

Hotel

M. Hunter, Pen-Y-Dyffryn Hotel,
Rhydycroseau, OSWESTRY, Shropshire
SY10 7JD Tel: 01691 653700
• e-mail: stay@peny.co.uk
• website: www.peny.co.uk

• SOMERSET

B&B

Mrs C. Bryson, Walton Villa, 3 Newbridge
Hill, BATH, Somerset BA1 3PW
Tel: 01225 482792
• e-mail: walton.villa@virgin.net
• website: www.waltonvilla.com

Inn

The Talbot 15th Century Coaching Inn,
Selwood Street, Mells, Near BATH,
Somerset BA11 3PN Tel: 01373 812254
• e-mail: roger@talbotinn.com
• website: www.talbotinn.com

Farm Guest House / Self-Catering

Jackie & David Bishop, Toghill House Farm,
Freezing Hill, Wick, Near BATH,
Somerset BS30 5RT. Tel: 01225 891261
• e-mail:
accommodation@toghillhousefarm.co.uk
• website: www.toghillhousefarm.co.uk

Self-Catering

Westward Rise Holiday Park, South Road,
BREAN, Burnham-on-Sea, Somerset
TA8 2RD Tel: 01278 751310
• e-mail: info@westwardrise.com
• website: www.westwardrise.com

Farm / B & B

Mrs M. Hasell, The Model Farm, Norton
Hawkfield, Pensford, BRISTOL, Somerset
BS39 4HA Tel: 01275 832144
• e-mail: margarethasell@hotmail.com
• website: www.themodelfarm.co.uk

Farmhouse / Self-Catering

Josephine Smart, Leigh Farm, Old Road,
Pensford, NEAR BRISTOL, Somerset
BS39 4BA Tel: 01761 490281
• website: www.leighfarm.co.uk

Self-Catering Cottages

Mrs E. M. Neville, Wood Dairy, Wood Lane,
North Perrott, Near CREWKERNE, Somerset
TA18 7TA Tel: 01935 891532
• e-mail: liz@acountryretreat.co.uk
• website: www.acountryretreat.co.uk

Self-Catering

The Pack Horse, Allerford, Near Porlock,
EXMOOR, Somerset TA24 8HW
Tel: 01643 862475
• e-mail: holidays@thepackhorse.net
• website: www.thepackhorse.net

Farm Self-Catering & Camping

Westermill Farm, Exford, EXMOOR,
Somerset TA24 7NJ
Tel: 01643 831238
• e-mail: fhg@westermill.com
• website: www.westermill.com

Farm Self-Catering

Jane Styles, Wintershead Farm,
Simonsbath, EXMOOR, Somerset TA24 7LF
Tel: 01643 831222
• e-mail: wintershead@yahoo.co.uk
• website: www.wintershead.co.uk

B & B / Half-Board / Self-Catering / Towing Pitches

St Audries Bay Holiday Club, West
Quantoxhead, MINEHEAD, Somerset
TA4 4DY Tel: 01984 632515
• e-mail: info@staudriesbay.co.uk
• website: www.staudriesbay.co.uk

Guest House

The Old Mill, Netherclay, Bishop's Hull,
TAUNTON, Somerset TA1 5AB
Tel: 01823 289732
• website: www.theoldmillbandb.co.uk

B & B

North Down Farm, Pyncombe Lane,
Wiveliscombe, TAUNTON, Somerset TA4
2BL Tel: 01984 623730
• e-mail: jennycope@btinternet.com
• website: north-down-farm.co.uk

B & B

G. Clark, Yew Tree Farm, THEALE,
Near Wedmore, Somerset BS28 4SN
Tel: 01934 712475
• e-mail: enquiries@yewtreefarmbandb.co.uk
• website: www.yewtreefarmbandb.co.uk

Self-Catering

Croft Holiday Cottages, 2 The Croft, Anchor
Street, WATCHET, Somerset TA23 0BY
Tel: 01984 631121
• e-mail: croftcottages@talk21.com
• website: www.cottagessomerset.com

Guest House
Infield House, 36 Portway, WELLS,
Somerset BA5 2BN Tel: 01749 670989
• e-mail: infield@talk21.com
• website: www.infieldhouse.co.uk

B & B
Susan Crane, Birdwood House, Bath Road,
WELLS, Somerset BA5 3EW
Tel: 01749 679250
• e-mail: susancrane@mb2online.net
• website: www.birdwood-bandb.co.uk

Self-Catering / B & B
Mrs C. Glass, Islington Farm, WELLS,
Somerset BA5 1US Tel: 01749 673445
• e-mail: islingtonfarm2004@yahoo.co.uk
• website: www.islingtonfarmatwells.co.uk

Caravan Park
Ardnave Holiday Park, Kewstoke, WESTON-
SUPER-MARE, Somerset BS22 9XJ
Tel: 01934 622319
• website: www.ardnaveholidaypark.co.uk

Guest House
Julie Bridgeman, Sunset Bay Hotel, 53
Beach Road, WESTON-SUPER-MARE,
Somerset BS23 1BH Tel: 01934 623519
• e-mail: relax@sunsetbayhotel.co.uk
• website: www.sunsetbayhotel.co.uk

•STAFFORDSHIRE

Farm B & B / Self-Catering
Mrs M. Hiscoe-James, Offley Grove Farm,
Adbaston, ECCLESHALL, Staffordshire
ST20 0QB. Tel: 01785 280205
• e-mail: enquiries@offleygrovefarm.co.uk
• website: www.offleygrovefarm.co.uk

•SUFFOLK

Guest House
Dunston Guest House, 8 Springfield Road,
BURY ST EDMUNDS, Suffolk IP33 3AN
Tel: 01284 764574
• website: www.dunstonguesthouse.co.uk

B & B
Kay Dewsbury, Manorhouse, The Green,
Beyton, BURY ST EDMUNDS, Suffolk IP30 9AF
Tel: 01359 270960
• e-mail: manorhouse@beyton.com
• website: www.beyton.com

Hotel
Ravenwood Hall Country House Hotel &
Restaurant, Rougham,
BURY ST EDMUNDS, Suffolk IP30 9JA
Tel: 01359 270345
• e-mail: enquiries@ravenwoodhall.co.uk
• website: www.ravenwoodhall.co.uk

Guest House
The Grafton Guest House, 13 Sea Road,
FELIXSTOWE, Suffolk IP11 2BB
Tel: 01394 284881
• e-mail: info@grafton-house.com
• website: www.grafton-house.com

B & B / Self-Catering
Mrs Sarah Kindred, High House Farm,
Cransford, Woodbridge, FRAMLINGHAM,
Suffolk IP13 9PD Tel: 01728 663461
• e-mail: b&b@highhousefarm.co.uk
• website: www.highhousefarm.co.uk

Self-Catering
Kessingland Cottages, Rider Haggard Lane,
KESSINGLAND, Suffolk.
Contact: S. Mahmood,
156 Bromley Road, Beckenham,
Kent BR3 6PG Tel: 020 8650 0539
• e-mail: jeeptrek@kjti.co.uk
• website: www.k-cottage.co.uk

Hotel
The Black Lion Hotel & Restaurant,
The Green, LONG MELFORD, Suffolk
CO10 9DN Tel: 01787 312356
• e-mail: enquiries@blacklionhotel.net
• website: www.blacklionhotel.net

Self-Catering
Southwold/Walberswick Self-Catering
Properties.
Durrants incorporating, H.A. Adnams, 98
High Street, SOUTHWOLD, Suffolk
IP18 6DP Tel: 01502 723292
• website: www.durrants.com

Self-Catering
Windmill Lodges Ltd, Redhouse Farm,
Saxtead, WOODBRIDGE, Suffolk IP13 9RD
Tel: 01728 685338
• e-mail: holidays@windmilllodges.co.uk
• website: www.windmilllodges.co.uk

Readers are requested to mention this FHG
guidebook when seeking accommodation

•EAST SUSSEX

Self-Catering

Crowhurst Park, Telham Lane, BATTLE, East Sussex TN33 0SL Tel: 01424 773344
- **e-mail: enquiries@crowhurstpark.co.uk**
- **website: www.crowhurstpark.co.uk**

Hotel / B & B

Maon Hotel, 26 Upper Rock Gardens, BRIGHTON, East Sussex BN2 1QE
Tel: 01273 694400
- **e-mail: maonhotel@aol.com**
- **website: www.maonhotel.co.uk**

Self- Catering

Kilcolgan Premier Bungalows, Rottingdean Seaside Village, BRIGHTON, East Sussex BN2 7DL
Contact: J. C. St George, 22 Baches Street, London N1 6DL Tel: 020 7250 3678
- **e-mail: jc.stgeorge@virgin.net**
- **website:**
www.holidaybungalowsbrightonuk.com

Self-Catering

"Pekes", CHIDDINGLY, East Sussex
Contact: Eva Morris, 124 Elm Park Mansions, Park Walk, London SW10 0AR
Tel: 020 7352 8088
- **e-mail: pekes.afa@virgin.net**
- **website: www.pekesmanor.com**

Guest House / Self-Catering

Longleys Farm Cottage, Harebeating Lane, HAILSHAM, East Sussex BN27 1ER
Tel: 01323 841227
- **e-mail: longleysfarmcottagebb@dsl.pipex.com**
- **website: www.longleysfarmcottage.co.uk**

Hotel

Grand Hotel, Grand Parade, St. Leonards, HASTINGS, East Sussex TN38 0DD
Tel: 01424 428510
- **e-mail: info@grandhotelhastings.co.uk**
- **website: www.grandhotelhastings.co.uk**

Hotel

Jeake's House, Mermaid Street, RYE, East Sussex TN31 7ET
Tel: 01797 222828
- **e-mail: stay@jeakeshouse.com**
- **website: www.jeakeshouse.com**

Hotel

Flackley Ash Hotel & Restaurant, Peasmarsh, Near RYE, East Sussex TN31 6YH. Tel: 01797 230651
- **e-mail: enquiries@flackleyashhotel.co.uk**
- **website: www.flackleyashhotel.co.uk**

Self-Catering Cottage

4 Beach Cottages, Claremont Road, SEAFORD, East Sussex BN25 2QQ
Contact: Julia Lewis, 47 Wandle Bank, London SW19 1DW Tel: 020 8542 5073
- **e-mail: cottage@beachcottages.info**
- **website: www.beachcottages.info**

• WEST SUSSEX

B & B

Mrs Vicki Richards, Woodacre, Arundel Road, Fontwell, ARUNDEL, West Sussex BN18 0QP Tel: 01243 814301
- **e-mail: wacrebb@aol.com**
- **website: www.woodacre.co.uk**

Self-Catering

Honeybridge Park, Honeybridge Lane, DIAL POST, Horsham, West Sussex RH13 8NX
Tel: 01403 710923
- **e-mail: enquiries@honeybridgepark.co.uk**
- **website: www.honeybridgepark.co.uk**

B & B

Broxmead Paddock, Broxmead Lane, Bolney, HAYWARDS HEATH, West Sussex RH17 5RG
Tel: 01444 881458
- **e-mail: broxmeadpaddock@hotmail.com**
- **website: www.broxmeadpaddock.eclipse.co.uk**

Self-Catering

Mrs M. W. Carreck, New Hall Holiday Flat and Cottage, New Hall Lane, Small Dole, HENFIELD, West Sussex BN5 9YJ
Tel: 01273 492546
- **website: www.newhallcottage.co.uk**

•WARWICKSHIRE

Guest House / B & B

Julia & John Downie, Holly Tree Cottage, Pathlow, STRATFORD-UPON-AVON, Warwickshire CV37 0ES Tel: 01789 204461
- **e-mail: john@hollytree-cottage.co.uk**
- **website: www.hollytree-cottage.co.uk**

Caravan Park

Riverside Caravan Park, Tiddington Road, STRATFORD-UPON-AVON, Warwickshire CV37 7AB Tel: 01789 292312
- **website: www.stratfordcaravans.co.uk**

•WEST MIDLANDS

Hotel / Self-catering
Featherstone Farm Hotel, New Road,
Featherstone, WOLVERHAMPTON, West
Midlands WV10 7NW Tel: 01902 725371
• e-mail: info@featherstonefarm.co.uk
• website: www.featherstonefarm.co.uk

•WILTSHIRE

Guest House
Alan & Dawn Curnow, Hayburn Wyke
Guest House, 72 Castle Road, SALISBURY,
Wiltshire SP1 3RL Tel:01722 412627
• e-mail: hayburn.wyke@tinyonline.co.uk
• website: www.hayburnwykeguesthouse.co.uk

Golf Club
High Post Golf Club, High Post, SALISBURY,
Wiltshire SP4 6AT Tel: 01722 782219
• e-mail: secretary@highpostgolfclub.co.uk
• website: www.highpostgolfclub.co.uk

Self-Catering Cottage
Manor Farm Cottages, Manor Farm, Sutton
Mandeville, SALISBURY, Wiltshire SP3 5NL
Tel: 01722 714226
• e-mail: strangf@aol.com
• website: www.strangcottages.com

Golf Club
Wrag Barn Golf & Country Club, Shrivenham
Road, High Worth, SWINDON, Wiltshire
SN6 7QQ Tel: 01793 861327
• e-mail: manager@wragbarn.com
• website: www.wragbarn.co.uk

Golf Club
West Wilts Golf Club, Elm Hill,
WARMINSTER, Wiltshire BA12 0AU
Tel: 01985 213133
• e-mail: sec@westwiltsgolfclub.co.uk
• website: www.westwiltsgolfclub.co.uk

•WORCESTERSHIRE

B & B / Self-Catering
Mrs Tricia Havard, Phepson Farm,
Himbleton, DROITWICH, Worcestershire
WR9 7J2 Tel: 01905 391205
• e-mail: havard@globalnet.co.uk
• website: www.phepsonfarm.co.uk

Guest House
Ann & Brian Porter, Croft Guest House,
Bransford, GREAT MALVERN, Worcester,
Worcestershire WR6 5JD Tel: 01886 832227
• e-mail: hols@crofthousewr6.fsnet.co.uk
• website: www.croftguesthouse.com

Self-Catering Cottages
Rochford Park, TENBURY WELLS,
Worcestershire WR15 8SP
Tel: 01584 781 372
• e-mail: cottages@rochfordpark.co.uk
• website: www.rochfordpark.co.uk

Inn
The Manor Arms At Abberley, The Village,
Abberley, WORCESTER, Worcestershire
WR6 6BH Tel: 01299 896507
• e-mail: info@themanorarms.co.uk
• website: www.themanorarms.co.uk

•EAST YORKSHIRE

Self-Catering
Chris Wade, Waterfront Cottages, 2 Star
Row, NORTH DALTON, Driffield, East
Yorkshire YO25 9UX Tel: 01377 217662
• e-mail: chris.wade@adastra-music.co.uk
• www.waterfrontcottages.co.uk

Guest House / Camping
Mrs Jeanne Wilson, Robeanne House,
Driffield Lane, Shiptonthorpe, YORK, East
Yorkshire YO43 3PW Tel: 01430 873312
• e-mail: enquiries@robeannehouse.co.uk
• website: www.robeannehouse.co.uk

•NORTH YORKSHIRE

Self-Catering
Recommended Cottage Holidays, Eastgate
House, Pickering, NORTH YORKSHIRE
Tel: 01751 475547
• website: www.recommended-cottages.co.uk

Farmhouse B & B
Mrs Julie Clarke, Middle Farm, Woodale,
COVERDALE, Leyburn,
North Yorkshire DL8 4TY Tel: 01969 640271
• e-mail: j-a-clarke@hotmail.co.uk
• www.yorkshirenet.co.uk/stayat/middlefarm

Farm
Mrs Linda Tindall, Rowantree Farm, Fryup
Road, Ainthorpe, DANBY, Whitby,
North Yorkshire YO21 2LE
Tel: 01723 515155
• e-mail: krbsatindall@aol.com
• website: www.rowantreefarm.co.uk

Farmhouse B&B
Mr & Mrs Richardson, Egton Banks
Farmhouse, GLAISDALE, Whitby, North
Yorkshire YO21 2QP Tel: 01947 897289
• e-mail: egtonbanksfarm@agriplus.net
• website: www.egtonbanksfarm.agriplus.net

Caravan & Camping
Bainbridge Ings Caravan & Camping Site,
HAWES, North Yorkshire DL8 3NU
Tel: 01969 667354
• e-mail: janet@bainbridge-ings.co.uk
• website: www.bainbridge-ings.co.uk

Guest House
The New Inn Motel, Main Street, HUBY,
York, North Yorkshire YO61 1HQ
Tel: 01347 810219
• enquiries@newinnmotel.freeserve.co.uk
• website: www.newinnmotel.co.uk

Hotel
Anne Wood, Golden Lion Hotel, Market
Square, LEYBURN, North Yorkshire DL8 5AS
Tel: 01969 622161
• e-mail: info@goldenlionleyburn.co.uk
• website: www.goldenlionleyburn.co.uk

Self-Catering
Mrs L. J. Story, Holmes Farm Cottage,
Holmes Farm, LOW BENTHAM, Lancaster
LA2 7DE Tel: 01524 261198
• e-mail: lucy@holmesfarmcottage.co.uk
• website: www.holmesfarmcottage.co.uk

Self-Catering
Abbey Holiday Cottages, MIDDLESMOOR.
12 Panorama Close, Pateley Bridge,
Harrogate, North Yorkshire HG3 5NY
Tel: 01423 712062
• e-mail: info@abbeyhall.cottages.co.uk
• website: www.abbeyholidaycottages.co.uk

B & B
Banavie, Roxby Road, Thornton-Le-Dale,
PICKERING, North Yorkshire YO18 7SX
Tel: 01751 474616
• e-mail: info@banavie.co.uk
• website: www.banavie.uk.com

Guest House / Self-Catering
Sue & Tony Hewitt, Harmony Country Lodge,
80 Limestone Road, Burniston,
SCARBOROUGH, North Yorkshire
YO13 0DG Tel: 0800 2985840
• e-mail: mail@harmonylodge.net
• website: www.harmonylodge.net

B & B
Beck Hall, Malham, SKIPTON, North
Yorkshire BD23 4DJ Tel: 01729 830332
• e-mail: simon@beckhallmalham.com
• website: www.beckhallmalham.com

Inn
Gamekeepers Inn, Long Ashes Park,
Threshfield, NEAR SKIPTON, North
Yorkshire BD23 5PN Tel: 01756 752434
• e-mail: info@gamekeeperinn.co.uk
• website: www.gamekeeperinn.co.uk

Self-Catering
Mrs Jones, New Close Farm, Kirkby Malham,
SKIPTON, North Yorkshire BD23 4DP
Tel: 01729 830240
• brendajones@newclosefarmyorkshire.co.uk
• website: www.newclosefarmyorkshire.co.uk

Self-Catering
Pennystell Cottage, 3 Boathouse Yard,
STAITHES, North Yorkshire TS13 5BN
Contact: Chris Wade, 2 Star Row, Driffield,
East Yorkshire YO25 9UX Tel: 01377 217662
• e-mail: chris.wade@adastra-music.co.uk
• www.waterfrontcottages.co.uk

Guest House
Ashford Guest House, 8 Royal Crescent,
WHITBY, North Yorkshire YO21 3EJ
Tel: 01947 602138
• e-mail: info@ashfordguesthouse.co.uk
• website: www.ashfordguesthouse.co.uk

Self-Catering
Greenhouses Farm Cottages, Near WHITBY.
Contact: Mr J.N. Eddleston, Thistledown
Cottage. Greenhouses Farm, Lealholm,
North Yorkshire YO21 2AD
Tel: 01947 897486
• e-mail: n_eddleston@yahoo.com
• www.greenhouses-farm-cottages.co.uk

Hotel
Blossoms Hotel York, 28 Clifden, YORK,
North Yorkshire YO3 6AE Tel: 01904 652391
• e-mail: fhg@blossomsyork.co.uk
• website: www.blossomsyork.co.uk

B & B
Mrs Butterworth, Wellgarth House,
Wetherby Road, Rufforth, YORK, North
Yorkshire YO23 3QB Tel: 01904 738592
• e-mail: enquiries@wellgarthhouse.co.uk
• website: wellgarthhouse.co.uk

• WEST YORKSHIRE

B & B / Self-Catering Cottages
Currer Laithe Farm, Moss Carr Road, Long
Lee, KEIGHLEY, West Yorkshire BD21 4SL
Tel: 01535 604387
• website: www.currerlaithe.co.uk

•SCOTLAND

Self-Catering Cottages
Islands & Highlands Cottages, Bridge Road, Portree, Isle of Skye, SCOTLAND IV51 9ER
Tel: 01478 612123
• website: www.islands-and-highlands.co.uk

•ABERDEEN, BANFF & MORAY

Hotel
P. A. McKechnie, Cambus O' May Hotel, BALLATER, Aberdeenshire AB35 5SE
Tel: 013397 55428
• e-mail: mckechnie@cambusomay.freeserve.co.uk
• website: www.cambusomayhotel.co.uk

B & B
Davaar B & B, Church Street, DUFFTOWN, Moray, AB55 4AR Tel: 01340 820464
• e-mail: davaar@cluniecameron.co.uk
• website: www.davaardufftown.co.uk

Self-catering
Newseat & Kirklea, FRASERBURGH, Aberdeenshire.
Contact: Mrs E.M. Pittendrigh, Kirktown, Tyrie, Fraserburgh, Aberdeenshire AB43 7DQ.
Tel: 01346 541231
•e-mail: pittendrigh@supanet.com

Self-Catering
The Greenknowe, INVERURIE.
Contact: Kingsfield House, Kingsfield Road, Kintore, Inverurie, Aberdeenshire AB51 0UD
Tel: 01467 632366
• e-mail: info@holidayhomesaberdeen.com
• website: www.holidayhomesaberdeen.com

Golf Club
Moray Golf Club, Stotfield Road, LOSSIEMOUTH, Moray IV31 6QS
Tel: 01343 812018
• e-mail: secretary@moraygolf.co.uk
• website: www.moraygolf.co.uk

•ANGUS & DUNDEE

Golf Club
Edzell Golf Club, High Street, EDZELL, Brechin, Angus DD9 7TF
Tel: 01356 648462
• e-mail: secretary@edzellgolfclub.net
• website: www.edzellgolfclub.net

Golf Club
Forfar Golf Club, Cunninghill, Arbroath Road, FORFAR, Angus DD8 2RL
Tel: 01307 463773
• e-mail: info@forfargolfclub.com
• website: www.forfargolfclub.com

•ARGYLL & BUTE

Self-Catering / Touring Park
Resipole Farm Camping & Caravan Park, Loch Sunart, ACHARACLE, Argyll PH36 4HX
Tel: 01967 431235
• e-mail: info@resipole.co.uk
• website: www.resipole.co.uk

Self-Catering
Ardtur Cottages, APPIN, Argyll PA38 4DD
Tel: 01631 730223
• e-mail: pery@btinternet.com
• website: www.selfcatering-appin-scotland.com

Inn
Mr D. Fraser, Cairndow Stagecoach Inn, CAIRNDOW, Argyll PA26 8BN
Tel: 01499 600286
• e-mail: cairndowinn@aol.com
• website: www.cairndow.com

Golf Club
The Machrihanish Golf Club, Machrihanish, CAMPBELTOWN, Argyll PA28 6PT
Tel: 01586 810213
• e-mail: secretary@machgolf.com
• website: www.machgolf.com

Guest House / Self-Catering
Rockhill Waterside Country House, DALMALLY, Argyll PA33 1BH
Tel: 01866 833218
• website: www.rockhillfarmguesthouse.co.uk

Self-Catering
Mrs I. Crawford, Blarghour Farm Cottages, Blarghour Farm, By DALMALLY, Argyll PA33 1BW Tel: 01866 833246
• e-mail: blarghour@btconnect.com
• website: www.self-catering-argyll.co.uk

Self-catering
Kilbride Croft, Balvicar, ISLE OF SEIL, Argyll PA34 4RD Tel: 01852 300475
• e-mail: kilbridecroft@aol.com
• website: www.kilbridecroft.co.uk

Caravans
Caolasnacon Caravan Park, KINLOCHLEVEN, Argyll PH50 4RJ Tel: 01855 831279
• website: www.kinlochlevencaravans.com

Self-Catering
Inchmurrin Island Self-Catering Holidays,
Inchmurrin Island, LOCH LOMOND
G63 0JY Tel: 01389 850245
• e-mail: scotts@inchmurrin-lochlomond.com
• website: www.inchmurrin-lochlomond.com

Self-Catering
Linda Battison,
Cologin Country Chalets & Lodges,
Lerags Glen, OBAN, Argyll PA34 4SE
Tel: 01631 564501
• e-mail: info@cologin.co.uk
• website: www.west-highland-holidays.co.uk

Self-Catering
Colin Mossman, Lagnakeil Lodges,
Lerags, OBAN, Argyll PA34 4SE
Tel: 01631 562746
• e-mail: info@lagnakeil.co.uk
• website: www.lagnakeil.co.uk

Self-Catering
Mrs Barker, Barfad Farm, TARBERT,
Loch Fyne, Argyll PA29 6YH
Tel: 01880 820549
• e-mail: vbarker@hotmail.com
• website: www.tarbertlochfyne.com

•AYRSHIRE & ARRAN

B & B
Mrs J Clark, Eglinton Guest House,
23 Eglinton Terrace, AYR, Ayrshire KA7 1JJ
Tel: 01292 264623
• e-mail: eglintonguesthouse@yahoo.co.uk
• website: www.eglinton-guesthouse-ayr.com

Hotel
Catacol Bay Hotel, CATACOL, Lochranza,
Isle of Arran KA27 8HN
Tel: 01770 830231
• e-mail: catbay@tiscali.co.uk
• website: www.catacol.co.uk

Farmhouse / B & B
Mrs Nancy Cuthbertson, West Tannacrieff,
Fenwick, KILMARNOCK, Ayrshire KA3 6AZ
Tel: 01560 600258
• e-mail: westtannacrieff@btopenworld.com
• website: www.smoothhound.co.uk/hotels/
westtannacrieff.html

Farmhouse / B & B / Caravan & Camping
Mrs M Watson, South Whittlieburn Farm,
Brisbane Glen, LARGS, Ayrshire KA30 8SN
Tel: 01475 675881
• e-mail:
largsbandb@southwhittlieburnfarm.freeserve.co.uk
• website: www.ukcampsite.co.uk
www.smoothhound.co.uk/hotels/whittlie.html

•BORDERS

Guest House
Ferniehirst Mill Lodge, JEDBURGH,
Borders TD8 6PQ Tel: 01835 863279
• e-mail: ferniehirstmill@aol.com
• website: www.ferniehirstmill.co.uk

Self-Catering
Mill House, JEDBURGH.
Contact: Mrs A. Fraser, Overwells,
Jedburgh, Borders TD8 6LT
Tel: 01835 863020
• e-mail: abfraser@btinternet.com
• website: www.overwells.co.uk

Self-Catering
Mrs C. M. Kilpatrick, Slipperfield House,
WEST LINTON, Peeblesshire EH46 7AA
Tel: 01968 660401
• e-mail: cottages@slipperfield.com
• website: www.slipperfield.com

•DUMFRIES & GALLOWAY

Self-Catering
Cloud Cuckoo Lodge, CASTLE DOUGLAS,
Dumfries & Galloway
Contact: Mrs Lesley Wykes, Cuckoostone
Cottage, St John's Town Of Dalry, Castle
Douglas DG7 3UA Tel: 01644 430375
• e-mail: enquiries@cloudcuckoolodge.co.uk
• website: www.cloudcuckoolodge.co.uk

Guest House
Celia Pickup, Craigadam,
CASTLE DOUGLAS, Kirkcudbrightshire
DG7 3HU Tel: 01556 650233
• website: www.craigadam.com

Self-Catering
Ae Farm Cottages, Gubhill Farm,
DUMFRIES, Dumfriesshire DG1 1RL
Tel: 01387 860648
• e-mail: gill@gubhill.co.uk
• website: www.aefarmcottages.co.uk

B & B
Langlands Bed & Breakfast, 8 Edinburgh
Road, DUMFRIES, Dumfries & Galloway
DG1 1JQ Tel: 01387 266549
• e-mail: langlands@tiscali.co.uk
• website: www.langlands.info

Farm / Camping & Caravans / Self-Catering
Barnsoul Farm Holidays, Barnsoul Farm,
Shawhead, DUMFRIES, Dumfriesshire
Tel: 01387 730249
• e-mail: barnsouldg@aol.com
• website: www.barnsoulfarm.co.uk

Self-Catering
Rusko Holidays, GATEHOUSE OF FLEET,
Castle Douglas, Kirkcudbrightshire
DG7 2BS Tel: 01557 814215
• e-mail: info@ruskoholidays.co.uk
• website: www.ruskoholidays.co.uk

Self-Catering
G & S Cottages, PORTPATRICK,
Dumfries & Galloway
Contact: Graham & Sue Fletcher, 468 Otley
Road, Leeds, Yorkshire LS16 8AE
Tel: 0113 2301391
• e-mail: info@gscottages.co.uk
• website: www.gscottages.co.uk

•EDINBURGH & LOTHIANS

Guest House
Kenvie Guest House, 16 Kilmaurs Road,
EDINBURGH EH16 5DA Tel: 0131 6681964
•e-mail: dorothy@kenvie.co.uk
• website: www.kenvie.co.uk

Guest House
International Guest House, 37 Mayfield
Gardens, EDINBURGH EH9 2BX
Tel: 0131 667 2511
• e-mail: intergh1@yahoo.co.uk
• website: www.accommodation-edinburgh.com

•HIGHLANDS

Self-Catering
Mr M W MacLeod, Dornie House Chalets,
Dornie House, ACHILTIBUIE, By Ullapool,
Ross-shire IV26 2YP Tel: 01854 622271
• e-mail: dorniehousebandb@aol.com

Self-Catering
Cairngorm Highland Bungalows,
AVIEMORE.
Contact: Linda Murray, 29 Grampian View,
Aviemore, Inverness-shire PH22 1TF
Tel: 01479 810653
• e-mail: linda.murray@virgin.net
• website: www.cairngorm-bungalows.co.uk

Self Catering / Caravans
Speyside Leisure Park, Dalfaber Road,
AVIEMORE, Inverness-shire PH22 1PX
Tel: 01479 810236
• e-mail: fhg@speysideleisure.com
• website: www.speysideleisure.com

Luxury Self-Catering
Crubenbeg Highland Holiday Cottages,
Near AVIEMORE, Highlands PH20 1BE
Tel: 01540 673566
• e-mail: enquiry@highlandholidaycottages.com
• website: www.highlandholidaycottages.com

Hotel / Self-Catering
Royal Marine Hotel & Leisure Club, Golf
Road, BRORA, Sutherland KW9 6QS
Tel: 01408 621252
• e-mail: info@highlandescape.com
• website: www.highlandescapehotels.com

Guest House
Mrs Lynn Benge, The Pines Country House,
Duthil, CARRBRIDGE, Inverness-shire
PH23 3ND Tel: 01479 841220
• e-mail: lynn@thepines-duthil.co.uk
• website: www.thepines-duthil.co.uk

Golf Club
The Royal Dornoch Golf Club, Golf Road,
DORNOCH, Sutherland IV25 3LW
Tel: 01862 810219 Ext 185
• e-mail: bookings@royaldornoch.com
• website: www.royaldornoch.com

Self-Catering
Carol Hughes, Glenurquhart Lodges,
Balnain, DRUMNADROCHIT, Inverness-shire
IV63 6TJ Tel: 01456 476234
• e-mail: info@glenurquhart-lodges.co.uk
• website: www.glenurquhart-lodges.co.uk

Hotel
The Clan MacDuff Hotel, Achintore Road,
FORT WILLIAM, Inverness-shire PH33 6RW
Tel: 01397 702341
• e-mail: reception@clanmacduff.co.uk
• website: www.clanmacduff.co.uk

Caravan & Camping
Auchnahillin Caravan & Camping Park,
Daviot East, INVERNESS, Inverness-shire
IV2 5XQ Tel: 01463 772286
• e-mail: info@auchnahillin.co.uk
• website: www.auchnahillin.co.uk

Self-Catering
Wildside Highland Lodges, Whitebridge,
By LOCH NESS, Inverness-shire IV2 6UN
Tel: 01456 486373
• e-mail: info@wildsidelodges.com
• website: www.wildsidelodges.com

B & B / Self-Catering Chalets
D.J. Mordaunt, Mondhuie, NETHY BRIDGE,
Inverness-shire PH25 3DF Tel: 01479 821062
• e-mail: david@mondhuie.com
• website: www.mondhuie.com

Hotel
Kintail Lodge Hotel, SHIEL BRIDGE,
Glenshiel, Ross-shire IV40 8HL
Tel: 01599 511275
• e-mail: kintaillodgehotel@btinternet.com
• website: www.kintaillodgehotel.co.uk

Hotel / Sporting Lodge
Borgie Lodge Hotel, SKERRAY, Sutherland
KW14 7TH Tel: 01641 521332
- e-mail: **info@borgielodgehotel.co.uk**
- website: **www.borgielodgehotel.co.uk**

Hotel
Whitebridge Hotel, WHITEBRIDGE,
Inverness IV2 6UN Tel: 01456 486226
- e-mail: **info@whitebridgehotel.co.uk**
- website: **www.whitebridgehotel.co.uk**

•LANARKSHIRE

Caravan & Holiday Home Park
Mount View Caravan Park, Station Road,
ABINGTON, South Lanarkshire ML12 6RW
Tel: 01864 502808
- e-mail: **info@mountviewcaravanpark.co.uk**
- website: **www.mountviewcaravanpark.co.uk**

Self-Catering
Carmichael Country Cottages,
Carmichael Estate Office, Westmains,
Carmichael, BIGGAR, Lanarkshire ML12 6PG
Tel: 01899 308336
- e-mail: **chiefcarm@aol.com**
- website: **www.carmichael.co.uk/cottages**

•PERTH & KINROSS

Hotel
Fortingall Hotel, Fortingall, ABERFELDY,
Perthshire PH15 2NQ Tel: 01887 830367
- e-mail: **hotel@fortingallhotel.com**
- website: **www.fortingallhotel.com**

Self-Catering
Loch Tay Lodges, Remony, Acharn,
ABERFELDY, Perthshire PH15 2HS
Tel: 01887 830209
- e-mail: **remony@btinternet.com**
- website: **www.lochtaylodges.co.uk**

Hotel
Lands of Loyal Hotel, ALYTH, Perthshire
PH11 8JQ Tel: 01828 633151
- e-mail: **info@landsofloyal.com**
- website: **www.landsofloyal.com**

Self-Catering
Laighwood Holidays, Laighwood,
Butterstone, BY DUNKELD,
Perthshire PH8 0HB Tel: 01350 724241
- e-mail: **holidays@laighwood.co.uk**
- website: **www.laighwood.co.uk**

•STIRLING & TROSSACHS

Guest House
Croftburn Bed & Breakfast, Croftamie,
DRYMEN, Loch Lomond G63 0HA
Tel: 01360 660796
- e-mail: **johnreid@croftburn.fsnet.co.uk**
- website: **www.croftburn.co.uk**

•SCOTTISH ISLANDS
•SKYE

Hotel & Restaurant
Royal Hotel, Bank Street, PORTREE, Isle of
Skye IV51 9BU Tel: 01478 612525
- e-mail: **info@royal-hotel-skye.com**
- website: **www.royal-hotel-skye.com**

•WALES

Self-Catering
Quality Cottages, Cerbid, Solva,
HAVERFORDWEST, Pembrokeshire
SA62 6YE Tel: 01348 837871
- website: **www.qualitycottages.co.uk**

•ANGLESEY & GWYNEDD

Caravan & Camping
Mr John Billingham, Islawrffordd Caravan
Park, Tal-y-Bont, Near BARMOUTH,
Gwynedd LL43 2BQ Tel: 01341 247269
- e-mail: **info@islawrffordd.co.uk**
- website: **www.islawrffordd.co.uk**

Country House
Sygun Fawr Country House, BEDDGELERT,
Gwynedd LL55 4NE Tel: 01766 890258
- e-mail: **sygunfawr@aol.com**
- website: **www.sygunfawr.co.uk**

Self-Catering / Caravans
Plas-y-Bryn Chalet Park, Bontnewydd,
CAERNARFON, Gwynedd LL54 7YE
Tel: 01286 672811
- **www.plasybrynholidayscaernarfon.co.uk**

Self-Catering within a Castle
BrynBras Castle, Llanrug,
Near CAERNARFON, Gwynedd LL55 4RE
Tel: 01286 870210
- e-mail: **holidays@brynbrascastle.co.uk**
- website: **www.brynbrascastle.co.uk**

Golf Club
Porthmadog Golf Club, Morfa Bychan,
PORTHMADOG, Gwynedd LL49 9UU
Tel: 01766 514124
- e-mail: secretary@porthmadog-golf-club.co.uk
- website: www.porthmadog-golf-club.co.uk

Golf Club
Anglesey Golf Club Ltd, Station Road,
RHOSNEIGR, Anglesey LL64 5QX
Tel: 01407 811202
- e-mail: info@theangleseygolfclub.com
- website: www.angleseygolfclub.co.uk

•NORTH WALES

Hotel
Fairy Glen Hotel, Beaver Bridge,
BETWS-Y-COED, Conwy, North Wales
LL24 0SH Tel: 01690 710269
- e-mail: fairyglen@youe.fsworld.co.uk
- website: www.fairyglenhotel.co.uk

Hotel
Sychnant Pass House, Sychnant Pass Road
CONWY LL32 8BJ Tel: 01492 596868
- e-mail: bre@sychnant-pass-house.co.uk
- website: www.sychnant-pass-house.co.uk

Golf Club
Denbigh Golf Club, Henllan Road, DENBIGH,
North Wales LL16 5AA Tel: 01745 816669
- e-mail: denbighgolfclub@aol.com
- website: www.denbighgolfclub.co.uk

Self-Catering Cottages
Glyn Uchaf, Conwy Old Road,
PENMAENMAWR, North Wales
LL34 6YS Tel: 01492 623737
- e-mail: john@baxter6055.freeserve.co.uk
- website: www.glyn-uchaf.co.uk

Golf Club
Rhuddlan Golf Club, Meliden Road,
RHUDDLAN, Denbighshire LL18 6LB
Tel: 01745 590217
- e-mail: secretary@rhuddlangolfclub.co.uk
- website: www.rhuddlangolfclub.co.uk

•CARMARTHENSHIRE

Faerm / B & B
Margaret Thomas, Plas Farm, Llangynog,
CARMARTHEN, Carmarthenshire SA33 5DB
Tel: 01267 211492
- website: www.plasfarm.co.uk

•CEREDIGION

Hotel
Queensbridge Hotel, Victoria Terrace,
ABERYSTWYTH, Ceredigion SY23 2DH
Tel: 01970 612343
- e-mail: queensbridgehotel@btinternet.com
- website: www.queensbridgehotel.com
www.queensbridgehotelaberystwyth.co.uk

• PEMBROKESHIRE

Hotel / Guest House
Ivybridge, Drim Mill, Dyffryn, Goodwick,
FISHGUARD, Pembrokeshire SA64 0JT
Tel: 01348 875366
- e-mail: ivybridge5366@aol.com
- website: www.ivybridgeleisure.co.uk

Country House
Angelica Rees, Heathfield House, Letterston,
NEAR FISHGUARD, Pembrokeshire
SA62 5EG Tel: 01348 840263
- e-mail: angelica.rees@virgin.net
- website: www.heathfieldaccommodation.co.uk

Hotel
Trewern Arms Hotel, Nevern, NEWPORT,
Pembrokeshire SA42 0NB
Tel: 01239 820395
- e-mail:
info@trewern-arms-pembrokeshire.co.uk
- www.trewern-arms-pembrokeshire.co.uk

Self-catering
Ffynnon Ddofn, ST DAVIDS, Pembrokeshire.
Contact: Mrs B. Rees White, Brick House
Farm, Burnham Road, Woodham Mortimer,
Maldon, Essex CM9 6SR
Tel: 01245 224611
- e-mail: daisypops@madasafish.com
- website: www.ffynnonddofn.co.uk

Farm Guest House
Mrs Morfydd Jones,
Lochmeyler Farm Guest House, Llandeloy,
Pen-y-Cwm, Near Solva, ST DAVIDS,
Pembrokeshire SA62 6LL
Tel: 01348 837724
- e-mail: stay@lochmeyler.co.uk
- website: www.lochmeyler.co.uk

Golf Club
Tenby Golf Club, The Burrows, TENBY,
Pembrokeshire SA70 7NP
Tel: 01834 842978
- e-mail: tenbygolfclub@uku.co.uk
- website: www.tenbygolf.co.uk

Self-catering

Mrs A Colledge, Gwarmacwydd, Llanfallteg, WHITLAND, Pembrokeshire SA34 0XH
Tel: 01437 563260
• website: www.davidsfarm.com

•POWYS

Farm

Caebetran Farm, Felinfach, BRECON, Powys LD3 0UL Tel: 01874 754460
• e-mail: hazelcaebetran@aol.com
• website: caebetranfarmhousebedandbreakfastwales.com

Self-Catering

Tyn-Y-Castell, ELAN VALLEY, Powys
Contact: Joan Morgan, Old Bedw Farmhouse, Near Erwood, Builth Wells, Powys LD2 3LQ Tel: 01982 560402
• e-mail: oldbedw@lineone.net
• website: www.rhayader.co.uk/tynycastell

Self-Catering

Mrs Jones, Penllwyn Lodges, GARTHMYL, Powys SY15 6SB
Tel: 01686 640269
• e-mail: daphne.jones@onetel.net
• website: www.penllwynlodges.co.uk

Self-Catering

Old Stables Cottage & Old Dairy, Lane Farm, Paincastle, Builth Wells, HAY-ON-WYE, Powys LD2 3JS Tel: 01497 851 605
• e-mail: lanefarm@onetel.com
• website: www.lane-farm.co.uk

Self-Catering

Ann Reed, Madog's Wells, Llanfair Caereinion, WELSHPOOL, Powys SY21 0DE
Tel: 01938 810446
• e-mail: info@madogswells.co.uk
• website: www.madogswells.co.uk

•SOUTH WALES

Narrowboat Hire

Castle Narrowboats, Church Road Wharf, Gilwern, Monmouthshire NP7 0EP
Tel: 01873 830001
• e-mail: info@castlenarrowboats.co.uk
• website: www.castlenarrowboats.co.uk

B & B

George Lawrence, Half Moon Inn, Llanthony, ABERGAVENNY, Monmouthshire NP7 7NN
Tel: 01873 890611
• e-mail: halfmoon@llanthony.wanadoo.co.uk
• website: www.halfmoon-llanthony.co.uk

B & B / Self-Catering Cottages

Mrs Norma James, Wyrloed Lodge, Manmoel, BLACKWOOD, Caerphilly, South Wales NP12 0RN Tel: 01495 371198
• e-mail: norma.james@btinternet.com
• website: www.btinternet.com/~norma.james/

Guest House

Rosemary & Derek Ringer, Church Farm Guest House, Mitchel Troy, MONMOUTH, South Wales NP25 4HZ Tel: 01600 712176
• e-mail: info@churchfarmguesthouse.eclipse.co.uk
• website: www.churchfarmmitcheltroy.co.uk

•IRELAND

CO. CLARE

Self-Catering

Ballyvaughan Village & Country Holiday Homes, BALLYVAUGHAN.
Contact: George Quinn, Frances Street, Kilrush, Co. Clare Tel: 00 353 65 9051977
• e-mail: vchh@iol.ie
• website: www.ballyvaughan-cottages.com

• CHANNEL ISLANDS

GUERNSEY

Self-Catering Apartments

Swallow Apartments, La Cloture, L'Ancresse, GUERNSEY Tel: 01481 249633
• e-mail: swallowapt@aol.com
• website: www.swallowapartments.com

Looking for Holiday Accommodation?

for details of hundreds of properties throughout the UK, visit our website

www.holidayguides.com

LEIGHTON BUZZARD RAILWAY

Page's Park Station, Billington Road,
Leighton Buzzard, Bedfordshire LU7 4TN
Tel: 01525 373888
e-mail: info@buzzrail.co.uk
www.buzzrail.co.uk

FHG
·K·U·P·E·R·A·R·D·
READERS'
OFFER
2008

One FREE adult/child with full-fare adult ticket
Valid 11/3/2008 - 28/10/2008

NOT TO BE USED IN CONJUNCTION WITH ANY OTHER OFFER

THE LIVING RAINFOREST

Hampstead Norreys,
Berkshire RG18 0TN
Tel: 01635 202444 • Fax: 01635 202440
e-mail: enquiries@livingrainforest.org
www.livingrainforest.org

FHG
·K·U·P·E·R·A·R·D·
READERS'
OFFER
2008

One FREE child with each full paying adult.
Valid during 2008.

NOT TO BE USED IN CONJUNCTION WITH ANY OTHER OFFER

BEKONSCOT MODEL VILLAGE & RAILWAY

Warwick Road, Beaconsfield,
Buckinghamshire HP9 2PL
Tel: 01494 672919
e-mail: info@bekonscot.co.uk
www.bekonscot.com

FHG
·K·U·P·E·R·A·R·D·
READERS'
OFFER
2008

One child FREE when accompanied by full-paying adult
Valid February to October 2008

NOT TO BE USED IN CONJUNCTION WITH ANY OTHER OFFER

BUCKINGHAMSHIRE RAILWAY CENTRE

Quainton Road Station, Quainton,
Aylesbury HP22 4BY
Tel & Fax: 01296 655720
e-mail: bucksrailcentre@btopenworld.com
www.bucksrailcentre.org

FHG
·K·U·P·E·R·A·R·D·
READERS'
OFFER
2008

One child FREE with each full-paying adult
Not valid for Special Events

NOT TO BE USED IN CONJUNCTION WITH ANY OTHER OFFER

A 70-minute journey into the lost world of the English narrow gauge light railway. Features historic steam locomotives from many countries.

PETS MUST BE KEPT UNDER CONTROL AND NOT ALLOWED ON TRACKS

Open: Sundays and Bank Holiday weekends 11 March to 28 October. Additional days in summer.

Directions: on A4146 towards Hemel Hempstead, close to roundabout junction with A505.

Discover the exotic collection of tropical plants and animals inhabiting this living re-creation of the rainforest under glass.
Explore your impact on the world's ecosystems using interactive displays.
All-weather attraction.
Children's play area.

Open: daily 10am to 5.15pm. Closed over Christmas period.

Directions: clearly signposted from J13 of M4. From Oxford take A34, exit at East Ilsley and follow signs. Nearest mainline station Newbury (8 miles). £1 'green discount' for visitors arriving by bus or bike.

Be a giant in a magical miniature world of make-believe depicting rural England in the 1930s.
"A little piece of history that is forever England."

Open: 10am-5pm daily mid February to end October.

Directions: Junction 16 M25, Junction 2 M40.

A working steam railway centre. Steam train rides, miniature railway rides, large collection of historic preserved steam locomotives, carriages and wagons.

Open: Sundays and Bank Holidays April to October, plus Wednesdays in school holidays 10.30am to 4.30pm.

Directions: off A41 Aylesbury to Bicester Road, 6 miles north west of Aylesbury.

THE RAPTOR FOUNDATION

The Heath, St Ives Road,
Woodhurst, Huntingdon, Cambs PE28 3BT
Tel: 01487 741140 • Fax: 01487 841140
e-mail: heleowl@aol.com
www.raptorfoundation.org.uk

READERS'
OFFER
2008

TWO for the price of ONE
Valid until end 2008 (not Bank Holidays)

NOT TO BE USED IN CONJUNCTION WITH ANY OTHER OFFER

SACREWELL FARM & COUNTRY CENTRE

Sacrewell, Thornhaugh,
Peterborough PE8 6HJ
Tel: 01780 782254
e-mail: info@sacrewell.fsnet.co.uk
www.sacrewell.org.uk

READERS'
OFFER
2008

One child FREE with one full paying adult
Valid from March 1st to October 1st 2008

NOT TO BE USED IN CONJUNCTION WITH ANY OTHER OFFER

THE NATIONAL WATERWAYS MUSEUM

South Pier Road, Ellesmere Port,
Cheshire CH65 4FW
Tel: 0151-355 5017 • Fax: 0151-355 4079
ellesmereport@thewaterwaystrust.org.uk
www.nwm.org.uk/ellesmere

READERS'
OFFER
2008

20% discount on standard admissions.
Valid during 2008.

NOT TO BE USED IN CONJUNCTION WITH ANY OTHER OFFER

CHINA CLAY COUNTRY PARK

Wheal Martyn, Carthew, St Austell,
Cornwall PL26 8XG
Tel & Fax: 01726 850362
e-mail: info@chinaclaycountry.co.uk
www.chinaclaycountry.co.uk

READERS'
OFFER
2008

TWO for ONE adult entry, saving £7.50.
One voucher per person. Valid until July 2008.

NOT TO BE USED IN CONJUNCTION WITH ANY OTHER OFFER

Birds of Prey Centre offering audience participation in flying displays which are held 3 times daily. Tours, picnic area, gift shop, tearoom, craft shop.

Open: 10am-5pm all year except Christmas and New Year.

Directions: follow brown tourist signs from B1040.

Farm animals, Shire Horse Centre, 18th century watermill and farmhouse, farm artifacts, caravan and camping, children's play areas. Cafe and farm & gift shop.

Open: all year.
9.30am to 5pm 1st March -30th Sept
10am-4pm 1st Oct to 28th Feb

Directions: signposted off both A47 and A1.

Can you imagine your family living in a space measuring 6' x 8'? Clamber aboard our collection of narrowboats. New interactive galleries, shop, cafe. Large free car park. Daily boat trips.

Open: 10am to 5pm daily

Directions: Junction 9 off the M53, signposted.

The Country Park covers 26 acres and includes woodland and historic trails, picnic sites, children's adventure trail and award-winning cycle trail. Remains of a Victorian clay works complete with the largest working water wheel in Cornwall. Shop, cafe, exhibitions, museum.

Open: 10am-6pm daily (closed Christmas Day)

Directions: two miles north of St Austell on the B3274. Follow brown tourist signs. 5 minutes from Eden Project.

Geevor is the largest mining history site in the UK in a spectacular setting on Cornwall's Atlantic coast. Guided underground tour, many surface buildings, museum, cafe, gift shop. Free parking.

Open: daily except Saturdays 10am to 4pm

Directions: 7 miles from Penzance beside the B3306 Land's End to St Ives coast road

FHG GUIDES, ABBEY MILL BUSINESS CENTRE, PAISLEY PA1 1TJ • www.holidayguides.com

---

Britain's leading grey seal rescue centre

Open: daily (except Christmas Day) from 10am

Directions: from A30 follow signs to Helston, then brown tourist signs to Seal Sanctuary.

FHG GUIDES, ABBEY MILL BUSINESS CENTRE, PAISLEY PA1 1TJ • www.holidayguides.com

---

Cornwall's only Donkey Sanctuary set in 14 acres overlooking the beautiful Tamar Valley. Donkey rides, rabbit warren, goat hill, children's playgrounds, cafe and picnic area. New all-weather play barn.

Open: Easter to end Oct: daily 10am to 5.30pm. Nov to March: weekends and all school holidays 10.30am to 4.30pm

Directions: just off A390 between Callington and Gunnislake at St Ann's Chapel.

FHG GUIDES, ABBEY MILL BUSINESS CENTRE, PAISLEY PA1 1TJ • www.holidayguides.com

---

Children's open farm animal interaction centre. Large indoor soft play, bouncy castle, go-karts, driving school, playground, cafe. Full disabled facilities, wheelchair-friendly.

Open: March to October 10.30am to 4pm

Directions: M6 J36. Follow A590 through Grange-over-Sands on the B5277. From Barrow-in-Furness turn right at Haverthwaite on to the B278 and follow signs to Flookburgh.

FHG GUIDES, ABBEY MILL BUSINESS CENTRE, PAISLEY PA1 1TJ • www.holidayguides.com

CARS OF THE STARS MOTOR MUSEUM

**Standish Street, Keswick,
Cumbria CA12 5HH
Tel: 017687 73757
e-mail: cotsmm@aol.com
www.carsofthestars.com**

**READERS'
OFFER
2008**

*One child free with two paying adults
Valid during 2008*

NOT TO BE USED IN CONJUNCTION WITH ANY OTHER OFFER

ESKDALE HISTORIC WATER MILL

**Mill Cottage, Boot, Eskdale,
Cumbria CA19 1TG
Tel: 019467 23335
e-mail: david.king403@tesco.net
www.eskdale.info**

Eskdale
Historic
Water Mill

**READERS'
OFFER
2008**

*Two children FREE with two adults
Valid during 2008*

NOT TO BE USED IN CONJUNCTION WITH ANY OTHER OFFER

CRICH TRAMWAY VILLAGE

**Crich, Matlock
Derbyshire DE4 5DP
Tel: 01773 854321 • Fax: 01773 854320
e-mail: enquiry@tramway.co.uk
www.tramway.co.uk**

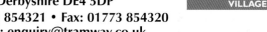

**READERS'
OFFER
2008**

*One child FREE with every full-paying adult
Valid during 2008*

NOT TO BE USED IN CONJUNCTION WITH ANY OTHER OFFER

DEVONSHIRE COLLECTION
OF PERIOD COSTUME

**Totnes Costume Museum,
Bogan House, 43 High Street,
Totnes,
Devon TQ9 5NP**

**READERS'
OFFER
2008**

*FREE child with a paying adult with voucher
Valid from Spring Bank Holiday to end of Sept 2008*

NOT TO BE USED IN CONJUNCTION WITH ANY OTHER OFFER

A collection of cars from film and TV, including Chitty Chitty Bang Bang, James Bond's Aston Martin, Del Boy's van, Fab1 and many more.

PETS MUST BE KEPT ON LEAD

Open: daily 10am-5pm.
Open February half term,
1st April to end November,
also weekends in December.

Directions: in centre of Keswick close to car park.

The oldest working mill in England with 18th century oatmeal machinery running daily.

DOGS ON LEADS

Open: 11am to 5pm April to Sept. (may be closed Saturdays & Mondays)

Directions: near inland terminus of Ravenglass & Eskdale Railway or over Hardknott Pass.

A superb family day out in the atmosphere of a bygone era. Explore the recreated period street and fascinating exhibitions. Unlimited tram rides are free with entry. Play areas, woodland walk and sculpture trail, shops, tea rooms, pub, restaurant and lots more.

Open: daily April to October 10 am to 5.30pm, weekends in winter.

Directions: eight miles from M1 Junction 28, follow brown and white signs for "Tramway Museum".

Themed exhibition, changed annually, based in a Tudor house. Collection contains items of dress for women, men and children from 17th century to 1980s, from high fashion to everyday wear.

Open: Open from Spring Bank Holiday to end September. 11am to 5pm Tuesday to Friday.

Directions: centre of town, opposite Market Square. Mini bus up High Street stops outside.

WOODLANDS
Blackawton, Dartmouth,
Devon TQ9 7DQ
Tel: 01803 712598 • Fax: 01803 712680
e-mail: fun@woodlandspark.com
www.woodlandspark.com

12% discount off individual entry price for up to 4 persons. No photocopies. Valid 15/3/08 – 1/11/08

READERS' OFFER 2008

NOT TO BE USED IN CONJUNCTION WITH ANY OTHER OFFER

KILLHOPE LEAD MINING MUSEUM
Cowshill, Upper Weardale,
Co. Durham DL13 1AR
Tel: 01388 537505
e-mail: killhope@durham.gov.uk
www.durham.gov.uk/killhope

One child FREE with full-paying adult
Valid April to October 2008

READERS' OFFER 2008

NOT TO BE USED IN CONJUNCTION WITH ANY OTHER OFFER

TWEDDLE CHILDREN'S ANIMAL FARM
Fillpoke Lane, Blackhall Colliery,
Co. Durham TS27 4BT
Tel: 0191 586 3311
e-mail: info@tweddle-farm.co.uk
www.tweddle-farm.co.uk

FREE bag of animal food to every paying customer.
Valid until end 2008

READERS' OFFER 2008

NOT TO BE USED IN CONJUNCTION WITH ANY OTHER OFFER

ST AUGUSTINE'S FARM
Arlingham
Gloucestershire GL2 7JN
Tel & Fax: 01452 740277
staugustines@btconnect.com
www.staugustinesfarm.co.uk

One child FREE with paying adult.
Valid March to October 2008.

READERS' OFFER 2008

NOT TO BE USED IN CONJUNCTION WITH ANY OTHER OFFER

All weather fun - guaranteed!
Unique combination of indoor/outdoor
attractions. 3 Watercoasters, Toboggan
Run, Arctic Gliders, boats, 15 Playzones
for all ages. Biggest indoor venture zone
in UK with 5 floors of play and rides.
New Big Fun Farm with U-drive Tractor
ride, Pedal Town and Yard Racers.
Falconry Centre.

Open: mid-March to November open daily at 9.30am. Winter: open weekends and local school holidays.

Directions: 5 miles from Dartmouth on A3122. Follow brown tourist signs from A38.

This award-winning Victorian mining
museum makes a great day out for
all the family. Hands-on activities
plus unforgettable mine tour.
Green Tourism Gold Award 2007.

Open: Easter weekend +April 1st to October 31st 10.30am to 5pm daily.

Directions: alongside A689, midway between Stanhope and Alston in the heart of the North Pennines.

Children's farm and petting centre
with lots of farm animals and exotic
animals too, including camels, otters,
monkeys, meerkats and lots more.
Lots of hands-on, with bottle
feeding, reptile handling and bunny
cuddling happening daily.

Open: March to Oct: 10am-5pm daily; Nov to Feb 10am to 4pm daily. Closed Christmas, Boxing Day and New Year's Day.

Directions: A181 from A19, head towards coast; signposted from there.

A real working organic dairy farm in
the Severn Vale. St Augustine's is a
typical dairy farm of over 100 acres
where the everyday farm life will go
on around you.

Open: March to October open daily 11am to 5pm (except term-time Mondays).

Directions: leave M5 by J13 to A38. Half a mile south turn right on B4071 and follow brown tourist signs.

191

 **READERS' OFFER 2008**

AVON VALLEY RAILWAY
Bitton Station, Bath Road, Bitton,
Bristol BS30 6HD
Tel: 0117 932 5538
e-mail: info@avonvalleyrailway.org
www.avonvalleyrailway.org

One FREE child with every fare-paying adult
Valid May - Oct 2008 (not 'Day Out with Thomas' events)

NOT TO BE USED IN CONJUNCTION WITH ANY OTHER OFFER

 **READERS' OFFER 2008**

EXPLOSION! MUSEUM OF NAVAL FIREPOWER
Priddy's Hard, Gosport
Hampshire PO12 4LE
Tel: 023 9250 5600 • Fax: 023 9250 5605
e-mail: info@explosion.org.uk
www.explosion.org.uk

SPECIAL OFFER 2008 - entry for just £1 per person.
One person per voucher. Not valid for events tickets.

NOT TO BE USED IN CONJUNCTION WITH ANY OTHER OFFER

 **READERS' OFFER 2008**

QUEX MUSEUM, HOUSE & GARDENS
Quex Park, Birchington
Kent CT7 0BH
Tel: 01843 842168 • Fax: 01843 846661
e-mail: enquiries@quexmuseum.org
www.quexmuseum.org

One adult FREE with each full-paying adult on
presentation of voucher. Valid until 31 December 2008

NOT TO BE USED IN CONJUNCTION WITH ANY OTHER OFFER

 **READERS' OFFER 2008**

CHISLEHURST CAVES
Old Hill, Chislehurst,
Kent BR7 5NB
Tel: 020 8467 3264 • Fax: 020 8295 0407
e-mail: info@chislehurstcaves.co.uk
www.chislehurstcaves.co.uk

FREE child entry with full paying adult.
Valid until end 2008 (not Bank Holiday weekends)

NOT TO BE USED IN CONJUNCTION WITH ANY OTHER OFFER

The Avon Valley Railway offers a whole new experience for some, and a nostalgic memory for others.

PETS MUST BE KEPT ON LEADS AND OFF TRAIN SEATS

Open: Steam trains operate every Sunday, Easter to October, plus Bank Holidays and Christmas.

Directions: on the A431 midway between Bristol and Bath at Bitton.

A hands-on interactive museum, telling the story of naval warfare from gunpowder to modern missiles. Also fascinating social history of how 2500 women worked on the site during World War II. Gift shop and Waterside Coffee Shop with stunning harbour views.

Open: Saturday and Sunday 10am to 4pm (last entry one hour before closing).

Directions: M27 to J11, follow A32 to Gosport; signposted.
By rail to Portsmouth Harbour, then ferry to Gosport.

World-ranking Museum incorporating Kent's finest Regency house. Gardens with peacocks, woodland walk, walled garden, maze and fountains. Children's activities and full events programme. Tearoom and gift shop.

Open: mid-March-Nov: Sun-Thurs 11am-5pm (House opens 2pm). Winter: Sundays 1-3.30pm (Museum and Gardens only).

Directions: A2 to Margate, on entering Birchington turn right at church into Park Lane; Quex Museum signposted.

Miles of mystery and history beneath your feet! Grab a lantern and get ready for an amazing underground adventure. Your whole family can travel back in time as you explore this labyrinth of dark mysterious passageways. See the caves, church, Druid altar and more.

Open: Wed to Sun from 10am; last tour 4pm. Open daily during local school and Bank holidays (except Christmas). Entrance by guided tour only.

Directions: A222 between A20 and A21; at Chislehurst Station turn into Station Approach; turn right at end, then right again into Caveside Close.

WINGHAM WILDLIFE PARK
Rusham Road, Wingham,
Canterbury, Kent CT3 1JL
Tel: 01227 720836
gabr@winghamwildlifepark.co.uk
www.winghamwildlifepark.co.uk

One FREE child entry with two full paying adults

NOT TO BE USED IN CONJUNCTION WITH ANY OTHER OFFER

THE HOP FARM AT THE KENTISH OAST VILLAGE
Beltring, Paddock Wood,
Kent TN12 6PY
Tel: 01622 872068 • Fax: 01622 870800
e-mail: info@thehopfarm.co.uk
www.thehopfarm.co.uk

THE HOP FARM

Admit one child HALF PRICE with a full paying adult.
Valid until March 2008.

NOT TO BE USED IN CONJUNCTION WITH ANY OTHER OFFER

MUSEUM OF KENT LIFE
Lock Lane, Sandling, Maidstone,
Kent ME14 3AU
Tel: 01622 763936 • Fax: 01622 662024
e-mail: enquiries@museum-kentlife.co.uk
www.museum-kentlife.co.uk

MUSEUM OF KENT LIFE

One child FREE with one full-paying adult
Valid during 2008

NOT TO BE USED IN CONJUNCTION WITH ANY OTHER OFFER

DOCKER PARK FARM
Arkholme, Carnforth,
Lancashire LA6 1AR
Tel & Fax: 015242 21331
e-mail: info@dockerparkfarm.co.uk
www.dockerparkfarm.co.uk

One FREE child per one paying adult (one voucher per child)
Valid from January to December 2008

NOT TO BE USED IN CONJUNCTION WITH ANY OTHER OFFER

Come and join us .. .take a walk on the wildside ... see meerkats, lemurs, reptile house, birds of prey, pet village, parrot house and much more. With an adventure playground and full facilities, you'll be sure to enjoy your day.

Open: daily 10am to 6pm or dusk (whichever is earlier). Guide dogs only.

Directions: on the A257 main Sandwich to Canterbury road, just outside the village.

FHG GUIDES, ABBEY MILL BUSINESS CENTRE, PAISLEY PA1 1TJ • www.holidayguides.com

---

Set in 400 acres of unspoilt Kent countryside, this once working hop farm is one of Kent's most popular attractions. The spectacular oast village is home to an indoor and outdoor play area, interactive museum, shire horses and an animal farm, as well as hosting special events throughout the year.

Open: 10am-5pm daily (last admission 4pm).

Directions: A228 Paddock Wood

FHG GUIDES, ABBEY MILL BUSINESS CENTRE, PAISLEY PA1 1TJ • www.holidayguides.com

---

Kent's award-winning open air museum is home to a collection of historic buildings which house interactive exhibitions on life over the last 150 years.

Open: seven days a week from February to start November, 10am to 5pm.

Directions: Junction 6 off M20, follow signs to Aylesford.

FHG GUIDES, ABBEY MILL BUSINESS CENTRE, PAISLEY PA1 1TJ • www.holidayguides.com

---

We are a working farm, with lots of animals to see and touch. Enjoy a walk round the Nature Trail or refreshments in the tearoom. Lots of activities during school holidays.

Open: Summer: daily 10.30am- 5pm. Winter: weekends only 10.30am-4pm.

Directions: Junction 35 off M6, take B6254 towards Kirkby Lonsdale, then follow the brown signs.

FHG GUIDES, ABBEY MILL BUSINESS CENTRE, PAISLEY PA1 1TJ • www.holidayguides.com

Well known for rescuing and rehabilitating orphaned and injured seal pups found washed ashore on Lincolnshire beaches. Also: penguins, aquarium, pets' corner, reptiles, Floral Palace (tropical birds and butterflies etc).

Open: daily from 10am. Closed Christmas/Boxing/New Year's Days.

Directions: at the north end of Skegness seafront.

A unique visitor attraction that transports you on an enlightening and atmospheric journey into the life, times, culture and music of the Beatles. See how four young lads from Liverpool were propelled into the dizzy heights of worldwide fame and fortune to become the greatest band of all time. Hear the story unfold through the 'Living History' audio guide narrated by John Lennon's sister, Julia.

Open: daily 10am to 6pm (last admisssion 5pm) all year round (excl. 25/26 December)

Directions: located within Liverpool's historic Albert Dock.

Explore one of Europe's leading steam collections, take a ride over 5 miles of narrow gauge steam railway, wander through beautiful gardens, or visit the only official 'Dads' Army' exhibition. Two restaurants and garden centre.

Open: Easter to October 10.30am - 5pm

Directions: 2½ miles west of Diss and 14 miles east of Thetford on the A1066; follow brown tourist signs.

Family-run farm park set in beautiful countryside next to river. 20-acre site with animal handling, large indoor soft play area, go-karts, trampolines, pedal tractors, swings, slides, zipline and assault course.

Open: daily 10am to 5.30pm April to end September. Closed Mondays except Bank Holidays and during school holidays. Please check for winter opening hours.

Directions: off A612 Nottingham to Southwell road.

NEWARK AIR MUSEUM
The Airfield, Winthorpe, Newark,
Nottinghamshire NG24 2NY
Tel: 01636 707170
e-mail: newarkair@onetel.com
www.newarkairmuseum.org

READERS' OFFER 2008

Party rate discount for every voucher (50p per person off normal admission). Valid during 2008.

NOT TO BE USED IN CONJUNCTION WITH ANY OTHER OFFER

THE TALES OF ROBIN HOOD
30 - 38 Maid Marian Way,
Nottingham NG1 6GF
Tel: 0115 9483284 • Fax: 0115 9501536
e-mail: robinhoodcentre@mail.com
www.robinhood.uk.com

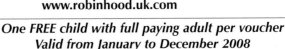

READERS' OFFER 2008

*One FREE child with full paying adult per voucher
Valid from January to December 2008*

NOT TO BE USED IN CONJUNCTION WITH ANY OTHER OFFER

DIDCOT RAILWAY CENTRE
Didcot,
Oxfordshire OX11 7NJ
Tel: 01235 817200 • Fax: 01235 510621
e-mail: info@didcotrailwaycentre.org.uk
www.didcotrailwaycentre.org.uk

READERS' OFFER 2008

*One child FREE when accompanied by full-paying adult
Valid until end 2008 except during Day Out With Thomas events*

NOT TO BE USED IN CONJUNCTION WITH ANY OTHER OFFER

HOO FARM ANIMAL KINGDOM
Preston-on-the-Weald-Moors
Telford, Shropshire TF6 6DJ
Tel: 01952 677917 • Fax: 01952 677944
e-mail: info@hoofarm.com
www.hoofarm.com

READERS' OFFER 2008

*One child FREE with a full paying adult (one child per voucher).
Valid until Sept 2008 (not Bank Holiday Mondays). Closed Jan-March*

NOT TO BE USED IN CONJUNCTION WITH ANY OTHER OFFER

A collection of 70 aircraft and cockpit sections from across the history of aviation. Extensive aero engine and artefact displays.

Open: daily from 10am (closed Christmas period and New Year's Day).

Directions: follow brown and white signs from A1, A46, A17 and A1133.

Travel back in time with Robin Hood and his merry men on an adventure-packed theme tour, exploring the intriguing and mysterious story of their legendary tales of Medieval England. Enjoy film shows, live performances, adventure rides and even try archery! Are you brave enough to join Robin on his quest for good against evil?

Open: 10am-5.30pm, last admission 4.30pm.

Directions: follow the brown and white tourist information signs whilst heading towards the city centre.

See the steam trains from the golden age of the Great Western Railway. Steam locomotives in the original engine shed, a reconstructed country branch line, and a re-creation of Brunel's original broad gauge railway. On Steam Days there are rides in the 1930s carriages.

Open: Sat/Sun all year; daily 21 June to 31 August + school holidays. 10am-5pm weekends and Steam Days, 10am-4pm other days and in winter.

Directions: at Didcot Parkway rail station; on A4130, signposted from M4 (Junction 13) and A34

A real children's paradise. A complete hands-on experience, from feeding the lambs and sheep, goat racing, petting the lizards and talking to the parrots to candle dipping, mini quad biking, pony rides and other craft activities. Hoo Farm has everything for a family day out.

Open: follow brown tourist signs from M54 J6, A442 at Leegomery or A518 at Donnington

Directions: 10am-6pm (last entries 5pm) Tues-Sun during term times and every day during school holidays and Bank Holidays.

EXMOOR FALCONRY & ANIMAL FARM
Allerford, Near Porlock, Minehead,
Somerset TA24 8HJ
Tel: 01643 862816
e-mail: exmoor.falcon@virgin.net
www.exmoorfalconry.co.uk

10% off entry to Falconry Centre
Valid during 2008

READERS' OFFER 2008

FLEET AIR ARM MUSEUM
RNAS Yeovilton, Ilchester,
Somerset BA22 8HT
Tel: 01935 840565
e-mail: enquiries@fleetairarm.com
www.fleetairarm.com

One child FREE with full paying adult
Valid during 2008 except Bank Holidays

READERS' OFFER 2008

THE HELICOPTER MUSEUM
The Heliport, Locking Moor Road,
Weston-Super-Mare BS24 8PP
Tel: 01934 635227• Fax: 01934 645230
e-mail: helimuseum@btconnect.com
www.helicoptermuseum.co.uk

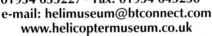

One child FREE with two full-paying adults
Valid from April to October 2008

READERS' OFFER 2008

YESTERDAY'S WORLD
High Street, Battle, E. Sussex TN33 0AQ
Tel: 01424 775378 (24hr info)
Enquiries/bookings: 01424 893938
e-mail: info@yesterdaysworld.co.uk
www.yesterdaysworld.co.uk

One child FREE when accompanied by one
full-paying adult. Valid until end 2008

READERS' OFFER 2008

Falconry centre with animals - flying displays, animal handling, feeding and bottle feeding - in 15th century NT farmyard setting on Exmoor. Also falconry and outdoor activities, hawk walks and riding.

Open: 10.30am to 5pm daily

Directions: A39 west of Minehead, turn right at Allerford, half a mile along lane on left.

Europe's largest naval aviation collection with over 40 aircraft on display , including Concorde 002 and Ark Royal Aircraft Carrier Experience. Situated on an operational naval air station.

Open: open daily April to October 10am-5.30pm; November to March 10am-4.30pm (closed Mon and Tues).

Directions: just off A303/A37 on B3151 at Ilchester. Yeovil rail station 10 miles.

The world's largest helicopter collection - over 70 exhibits, includes two royal helicopters, Russian Gunship and Vietnam veterans plus many award-winning exhibits. Cafe, shop. Flights.

PETS MUST BE KEPT UNDER CONTROL

Open: Wednesday to Sunday 10am to 5.30pm. Daily during school Easter and Summer holidays and Bank Holiday Mondays. November to March: 10am to 4.30pm

Directions: Junction 21 off M5 then follow the propellor signs.

The past is brought to life at one of the South East's best loved family attractions. 100,000+ nostalgic artefacts, set in a charming 15th century house and country garden. New attractions and tearooms.

Open: 9.30am to 6pm (last admission 4.45pm, one hour earlier in winter). Closing times may vary – phone or check website.

Directions: just off A21 in Battle High Street opposite the Abbey.

PARADISE PARK & GARDENS
Avis Road, Newhaven,
East Sussex BN9 0DH

Tel: 01273 512123 • Fax: 01273 616000
e-mail: enquiries@paradisepark.co.uk
www.paradisepark.co.uk

Admit one FREE child with one adult
paying full entrance price. Valid during 2008

READERS' OFFER 2008

NOT TO BE USED IN CONJUNCTION WITH ANY OTHER OFFER

WILDERNESS WOOD
Hadlow Down, Near Uckfield,
East Sussex TN22 4HJ
Tel: 01825 830509• Fax: 01825 830977
e-mail: enquiries@wildernesswood.co.uk
www.wildernesswood.co.uk

one FREE admission with a full-paying adult
Valid during 2008 (not for Special Events/Bank Holidays)

READERS' OFFER 2008

NOT TO BE USED IN CONJUNCTION WITH ANY OTHER OFFER

EARNLEY BUTTERFLIES & GARDENS
133 Almodington Lane, Earnley, Chichester,
West Sussex PO20 7JR
Tel: 01243 512637
e-mail: earnleygardens@msn.com
www.earnleybutterfliesandgardens.co.uk

£2 per person offer normal entry prices.
Valid late March to end October 2008.

READERS' OFFER 2008

NOT TO BE USED IN CONJUNCTION WITH ANY OTHER OFFER

STRATFORD BUTTERFLY FARM
Swan's Nest Lane, Stratford-upon-Avon
Warwickshire CV37 7LS

Tel: 01789 299288 • Fax: 01789 415878
e-mail: sales@butterflyfarm.co.uk
www.butterflyfarm.co.uk

Admit TWO for the price of ONE
Valid until 31/12/2008

READERS' OFFER 2008

NOT TO BE USED IN CONJUNCTION WITH ANY OTHER OFFER

Discover 'Planet Earth' for an unforgettable experience. A unique Museum of Life, Dinosaur Safari, beautiful Water Gardens with fish and wildfowl, plant houses, themed gardens, Heritage Trail, miniature railway. Playzone includes crazy golf and adventure play areas. Garden Centre and Terrace Cafe.

Open: open daily, except Christmas Day and Boxing Day.

Directions: signposted off A26 and A259.

Wilderness Wood is a unique family-run working woodland park in the Sussex High Weald. Explore trails and footpaths, enjoy local cakes and ices, try the adventure playground. Many special events and activities. Parties catered for. Green Tourism Gold Award.

Open: daily 10am to 5.30pm or dusk if earlier.

Directions: on the south side of the A272 in the village of Hadlow Down. Signposted with a brown tourist sign.

3 attractions in 1. Tropical butterflies, exotic animals of many types in our Noah's Ark Rescue Centre. Theme gardens with a free competition for kids. Rejectamenta - the nostalgia museum.

Open: 10am - 6pm daily late March to end October.

Directions: signposted from A27/A286 junction at Chichester.

Wander through a tropical rainforest with a myriad of multicoloured butterflies, sunbirds and koi carp. See fascinating animals in Insect City and view deadly spiders in perfect safety in Arachnoland.

Open: daily except Christmas Day. 10am-6pm summer, 10am-dusk winter.

Directions: on south bank of River Avon opposite Royal Shakespeare Theatre. Easily accessible from town centre, 5 minutes' walk.

READERS' OFFER 2008

HATTON FARM VILLAGE AT HATTON COUNTRY WORLD
Dark Lane, Hatton, Near Warwick,
Warwickshire CV35 8XA
Tel: 01926 843411
e-mail: hatton@hattonworld.com
www.hattonworld.com

Admit one child FREE with one full-paying adult day ticket. Valid during 2008 except Bank Holidays or for entrance to Santa's Grotto promotion.

NOT TO BE USED IN CONJUNCTION WITH ANY OTHER OFFER

READERS' OFFER 2008

AVONCROFT MUSEUM
Stoke Heath,
Bromsgrove,
Worcestershire B60 4JR
Tel: 01527 831363 • Fax: 01527 876934
www.avoncroft.org.uk

AVONCROFT
MUSEUM OF HISTORIC BUILDINGS

One FREE child with one full-paying adult
Valid from March to November 2008

NOT TO BE USED IN CONJUNCTION WITH ANY OTHER OFFER

READERS' OFFER 2008

EMBSAY & BOLTON ABBEY STEAM RAILWAY
Bolton Abbey Station, Skipton,
North Yorkshire BD23 6AF
Tel: 01756 710614
e-mail: embsay.steam@btinternet.com
www.embsayboltonabbeyrailway.org.uk

EMBSAY &
BOLTON ABBEY
STEAM RAILWAY

One adult travels FREE when accompanied by a full fare paying adult (does not include Special Event days). Valid during 2008.

NOT TO BE USED IN CONJUNCTION WITH ANY OTHER OFFER

READERS' OFFER 2008

WORLD OF JAMES HERRIOT
23 Kirkgate, Thirsk,
North Yorkshire YO7 1PL
Tel: 01845 524234
Fax: 01845 525333
www.worldofjamesherriot.org

HERRIOT

Admit TWO for the price of ONE (one voucher per transaction only). Valid until October 2008

NOT TO BE USED IN CONJUNCTION WITH ANY OTHER OFFER

Hatton Farm Village offers a wonderful mix of farmyard animals, adventure play, shows, demonstrations, and events, all set in the stunning Warwickshire countryside.

Open: daily 10am-5pm (4pm during winter). Closed Christmas Day and Boxing Day.

Directions: 5 minutes from M40 (J15), A46 towards Coventry, then just off A4177 (follow brown tourist signs).

A fascinating world of historic buildings covering 7 centuries, rescued and rebuilt on an open-air site in the heart of the Worcestershire countryside.

PETS ON LEADS ONLY

Open: July and August all week. March to November varying times, please telephone for details.

Directions: A38 south of Bromsgrove, near Junction 1 of M42, Junction 5 of M5.

Steam trains operate over a 4½ mile line from Bolton Abbey Station to Embsay Station. Many family events including Thomas the Tank Engine take place during major Bank Holidays.

Open: steam trains run every Sunday throughout the year and up to 7 days a week in summer. 10.30am to 4.30pm

Directions: Embsay Station signposted from the A59 Skipton by-pass; Bolton Abbey Station signposted from the A59 at Bolton Abbey.

Visit James Herriot's original house recreated as it was in the 1940s. Television sets used in the series 'All Creatures Great and Small'. There is a children's interactive gallery with life-size model farm animals and three rooms dedicated to the history of veterinary medicine.

Open: daily. Easter-Oct 10am-5pm; Nov-Easter 11am to 4pm

Directions: follow signs off A1 or A19 to Thirsk, then A168, off Thirsk market place

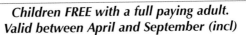

Visit the FHG website
www.holidayguides.com
for details of the wide choice of accommodation
featured in the full range of FHG titles

All types of birds of prey exhibited here, from owls and kestrels to eagles and vultures. Special flying displays 12 noon, 1.30pm and 3pm. Bird handling courses arranged for either half or full days.

GUIDE DOGS ONLY

Open: 10am to 4.30pm summer 10am to 4pm winter

Directions: on main A65 trunk road outside Settle. Follow brown direction signs.

FHG GUIDES, ABBEY MILL BUSINESS CENTRE, PAISLEY PA1 1TJ • www.holidayguides.com

---

Dinostar features an exhibition of dinosaurs and fossils. Highlights include a T-Rex skull, Triceratops bones you can touch, and our unique dinosaur sound box.

Open: 11am to 5pm Wednesday to Sunday.

Directions: in the Fruit Market area of Hull's Old Town, close to The Deep and Hull Marina.

FHG GUIDES, ABBEY MILL BUSINESS CENTRE, PAISLEY PA1 1TJ • www.holidayguides.com

---

A fascinating display of railway carriages and a wide range of railway items telling the story of rail travel over the years.

ALL PETS MUST BE KEPT ON LEADS

Open: daily 11am to 4.30pm

Directions: approximately one mile from Keighley on A629 Halifax road. Follow brown tourist signs

FHG GUIDES, ABBEY MILL BUSINESS CENTRE, PAISLEY PA1 1TJ • www.holidayguides.com

Please note

All the information in this book is given in good faith in the belief that it is correct. However, the publishers cannot guarantee the facts given in these pages, neither are they responsible for changes in policy, ownership or terms that may take place after the date of going to press.
Readers should always satisfy themselves that the facilities they require are available and that the terms, if quoted, still apply.

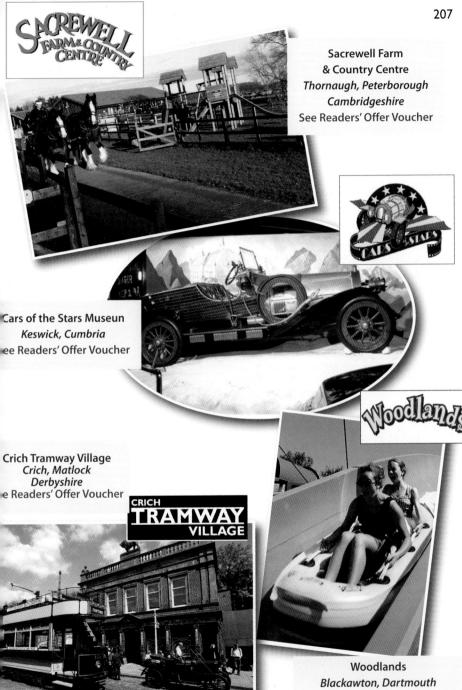

Sacrewell Farm
& Country Centre
Thornaugh, Peterborough
Cambridgeshire
See Readers' Offer Voucher

Cars of the Stars Museum
Keswick, Cumbria
ee Readers' Offer Voucher

Crich Tramway Village
Crich, Matlock
Derbyshire
e Readers' Offer Voucher

Woodlands
Blackawton, Dartmouth
Devon
See Readers' Offer Voucher

Hoo Farm Animal Kingdom
Preston-on-the-Weald-Moors
Telford, Shropshire
See Readers' Offer Voucher

Galloway Wildlife Conservation Park
Lochfergus, Kirkcudbright,
Dumfries & Galloway
See Readers' Offer Voucher

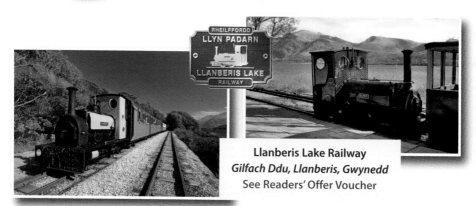

Llanberis Lake Railway
Gilfach Ddu, Llanberis, Gwynedd
See Readers' Offer Voucher

28-acre theme park with over 100 nursery rhyme characters, set in beautifully landscaped gardens. Shop and restaurant on site.

Open: 1st March to 31st October: daily 10am to 6pm; 1st Nov to end Feb: Sat/Sun only 11am to 4pm

Directions: 6 miles west of Aberdeen off B9077

FHG GUIDES, ABBEY MILL BUSINESS CENTRE, PAISLEY PA1 1TJ • www.holidayguides.com

---

Visitor Centre dedicated to the much-loved Scottish writer Lewis Grassic Gibbon. Exhibition, cafe, gift shop. Outdoor children's play area. Disabled access throughout.

Open: daily April to October 10am to 4.30pm. Groups by appointment including evenings.

Directions: on the B967, accessible and signposted from both A90 and A92.

FHG GUIDES, ABBEY MILL BUSINESS CENTRE, PAISLEY PA1 1TJ • www.holidayguides.com

---

19th century prison with fully restored 1820 courtroom and two prisons. Guides in uniform as warders, prisoners and matron. Remember your camera!

Open: April to October 9.30am-6pm (last admission 5pm); November to March 10am-5pm (last admission 4pm)

Directions: A83 to Campbeltown

FHG GUIDES, ABBEY MILL BUSINESS CENTRE, PAISLEY PA1 1TJ • www.holidayguides.com

---

Scotland's seafaring heritage is among the world's richest and you can relive the heyday of Scottish shipping at the Maritime Museum.

Open: 1st April to 31st October - 10am-5pm

Directions: situated on Irvine harbourside and only a 10 minute walk from Irvine train station.

FHG GUIDES, ABBEY MILL BUSINESS CENTRE, PAISLEY PA1 1TJ • www.holidayguides.com

211

FHG

·K·U·P·E·R·A·R·D·

READERS'
OFFER
2008

GALLOWAY WILDLIFE CONSERVATION PARK
Lochfergus Plantation, Kirkcudbright,
Dumfries & Galloway DG6 4XX
Tel & Fax: 01557 331645
e-mail: info@gallowaywildlife.co.uk
www.gallowaywildlife.co.uk

One FREE child or Senior Citizen with two full paying adults.
Valid Feb - Nov 2008 (not Easter weekend and Bank Holidays)

NOT TO BE USED IN CONJUNCTION WITH ANY OTHER OFFER

FHG

·K·U·P·E·R·A·R·D·

READERS'
OFFER
2008

MUSEUM OF SCOTTISH LEAD MINING
Wanlockhead,
Dumfriesshire ML12 6UT
Tel: 01659 74387 • Fax: 01659 74481
e-mail: miningmuseum@hotmail.co.uk
www.leadminingmuseum.co.uk

One FREE child with each full paying adult.
Valid April to October 2008.

NOT TO BE USED IN CONJUNCTION WITH ANY OTHER OFFER

FHG

·K·U·P·E·R·A·R·D·

READERS'
OFFER
2008

CREETOWN GEM ROCK MUSEUM
Chain Road, Creetown, Newton Stewart
Dumfries & Galloway DG8 7HJ
Tel: 01671 820357 • Fax: 01671 820554
e-mail: enquiries@gemrock.net
www.gemrock.net

10% discount on admission.
Valid during 2008.

NOT TO BE USED IN CONJUNCTION WITH ANY OTHER OFFER

FHG

·K·U·P·E·R·A·R·D·

READERS'
OFFER
2008

DALSCONE FARM FUN
Dalscone Farm, Edinburgh Road,
Dumfries DG1 1SE
Tel: 01387 257546 • Shop: 01387 254445
e-mail: dalscone@btconnect.com
www.dalsconefarm.co.uk

One FREE adult (16 years+)
Valid during 2008

NOT TO BE USED IN CONJUNCTION WITH ANY OTHER OFFER

212

The wild animal conservation centre of Southern Scotland. A varied collection of over 150 animals from all over the world can be seen within natural woodland settings. Picnic areas, cafe/gift shop, outdoor play area, woodland walks, close animal encounters.

Open: 10am to dusk 1st February to 30 November.

Directions: follow brown tourist signs from A75; one mile from Kirkcudbright on the B727.

Visitors can experience the thrill of a guided tour into an 18thC lead mine, explore the two period cottages, visit the second oldest subscription library and investigate the Visitor & Exhibition Centre. Taster sessions of gold panning available July and August.

Open: 1 April - 30 June: 11am-4.30pm July, August and Bank Holidays: 10am -5pm.

Directions: off M74. J14 if travelling north, J13 if travelling south.

A fantastic display of gems, crystals, minerals and fossils. An experience you'll treasure forever. Gift shop, tearoom and AV display.

Open: Summer - 9.30am to 5.30pm daily; Winter - 10am to 4pm daily. Closed Christmas to end January.

Directions: follow signs from A75 Dumfries/Stranraer.

Indoor adventure play area, farm park, toyshop and cafe. A great day out for all the family, with sledge and zip slides, mini-golf, trampolines, bumper boats, pottery painting and so much more.

Open: Monday to Saturday 10am-5.30pm.

Directions: just off the A75/A701 roundabout heading for Moffat and Edinburgh.

213

 **K·U·P·E·R·A·R·D**
READERS'
OFFER
2008

THE SCOTTISH MINING MUSEUM
Lady Victoria Colliery, Newtongrange,
Midlothian EH22 4QN
Tel: 0131-663 7519 • Fax: 0131-654 0952
visitorservices@scottishminingmuseum.com
www.scottishminingmuseum.com

One child FREE with full-paying adult
Valid January to December 2008

NOT TO BE USED IN CONJUNCTION WITH ANY OTHER OFFER

 **K·U·P·E·R·A·R·D**
READERS'
OFFER
2008

BUTTERFLY & INSECT WORLD
Dobbies Garden World, Melville Nursery,
Lasswade, Midlothian EH18 1AZ
Tel: 0131-663 4932 • Fax: 0131-654 2774
e-mail: info@edinburgh-butterfly-world.co.uk
www.edinburgh-butterfly-world.co.uk

One child FREE with full paying adult.
Valid during 2008.

NOT TO BE USED IN CONJUNCTION WITH ANY OTHER OFFER

 **K·U·P·E·R·A·R·D**
READERS'
OFFER
2008

BO'NESS & KINNEIL RAILWAY
Bo'ness Station, Union Street,
Bo'ness, West Lothian EH51 9AQ
Tel: 01506 822298
e-mail: enquiries.railway@srps.org.uk
www.srps.org.uk

FREE child train fare with one paying adult/concession. Valid 29th
March-26th Oct 2008. Not Thomas events or Santa Steam trains

NOT TO BE USED IN CONJUNCTION WITH ANY OTHER OFFER

 **K·U·P·E·R·A·R·D**
READERS'
OFFER
2008

MYRETON MOTOR MUSEUM
Aberlady,
East Lothian
EH32 0PZ
Tel: 01875 870288

MYRETON MOTOR MUSEUM

One child FREE with each paying adult
Valid during 2008

NOT TO BE USED IN CONJUNCTION WITH ANY OTHER OFFER

visitscotland 5-Star Attraction with two floors of interactive exhibitions, a 'Magic Helmet' tour of the pithead, re-created coal road and coal face, and new Big Stuff tour. Largest working winding engine in Britain.

Open: daily. Summer: 10am to 5pm (last tour 3.30pm). Winter: 10am to 4pm (last tour 2.30pm)

Directions: 5 minutes from Sherrifhall Roundabout on Edinburgh City Bypass on A7 south

See free-flying exotic butterflies in a tropical rainforest paradise, iguanas roaming free in jungle flora, and small birds darting in and out of the flowers. Have close encounters of the crawly kind in the 'Bugs & Beasties' exhibition that includes arrow frogs, tarantulas, amazing leaf-cutter ants and a unique Scottish Honey Bee display.

Open: daily. 9.30am-5.30pm summer, 10am-5pm winter.

Directions: located just off the Edinburgh City Bypass at the Gilmerton exit or Sherrifhall roundabout.

Steam and heritage diesel passenger trains from Bo'ness to Birkhill for guided tours of Birkhill fireclay mines. Explore the history of Scotland's railways in the Scottish Railway Exhibition. Coffee shop and souvenir shop.

Open: weekends Easter to October, daily July and August.

Directions: in the town of Bo'ness. Leave M9 at Junction 3 or 5, then follow brown tourist signs.

On show is a large collection, from 1899, of cars, bicycles, motor cycles and commercials. There is also a large collection of period advertising, posters and enamel signs.

Open: March-November - open daily 11am to 4pm. December-February - weekends 11am to 3pm or by special appointment.

Directions: off A198 near Aberlady. Two miles from A1.

CLYDEBUILT SCOTTISH MARITIME MUSEUM
Braehead Shopping Centre, King's Inch Road,
Glasgow G51 4BN
Tel: 0141-886 1013 • Fax: 0141-886 1015
e-mail: clydebuilt@scotmaritime.org.uk
www.scottishmaritimemuseum.org

READERS'
OFFER
2008

HALF PRICE admission for up to 4 persons.
Valid during 2008.

SPEYSIDE HEATHER GARDEN & VISITOR CENTRE
Speyside Heather Centre, Dulnain Bridge,
Inverness-shire PH26 3PA
Tel: 01479 851359 • Fax: 01479 851396
e-mail: enquiries@heathercentre.com
www.heathercentre.com

Speyside
HEATHER
GARDEN

READERS'
OFFER
2008

FREE entry to 'Heather Story' exhibition
Valid during 2008

LLANBERIS LAKE RAILWAY
Gilfach Ddu, Llanberis,
Gwynedd LL55 4TY
Tel: 01286 870549
e-mail: info@lake-railway.co.uk
www.lake-railway.co.uk

READERS'
OFFER
2008

One pet travels FREE with each full fare paying adult
Valid Easter to October 2008

ANIMALARIUM
Borth,
Ceredigion
SY24 5NA
Tel: 01970 871224
www.animalarium.co.uk

READERS'
OFFER
2008

FREE child with full paying adult.
Valid during 2008.

The story of Glasgow and the River Clyde brought vividly to life using AV, hands-on and interactive techniques. You can navigate your own ship, safely load your cargo, operate an engine, and go aboard the 130-year-old coaster 'Kyles'. Ideal for kids young and old wanting an exciting day out. New - The Clyde's Navy.

Open: 10am to 5.30pm daily

Directions: Green Car Park near M&S at Braehead Shopping Centre.

Award-winning attraction with unique 'Heather Story' exhibition, gallery, giftshop, large garden centre selling 300 different heathers, antique shop, children's play area and famous Clootie Dumpling restaurant.

Open: all year except Christmas Day.

Directions: just off A95 between Aviemore and Grantown-on-Spey.

A 60-minute ride along the shores of beautiful Padarn Lake behind a quaint historic steam engine. Magnificent views of the mountains from lakeside picnic spots.

DOGS MUST BE KEPT ON LEAD AT ALL TIMES ON TRAIN

Open: most days Easter to October. Free timetable leaflet on request.

Directions: just off A4086 Caernarfon to Capel Curig road at Llanberis; follow 'Country Park' signs.

A collection of unusual and interesting animals, including breeding pairs and colonies of exotic and endangered species whose natural environment is under threat. Many were unwanted exotic pets or came from other zoos.

Open: 10am - 6pm April to October

Directions: only a short walk from the railway station and beach in Borth, which lies between Aberystwyth and Machynlleth.

Visit the FHG website
www.holidayguides.com
for details of the wide choice of accommodation
featured in the full range of FHG titles

Mini-rainforest full of tropical plants and exotic butterflies. Personal attention of the owner, Mr John Devereux. Gift shop, cafe, video room, exhibition. Suitable for disabled visitors. VisitWales Quality Assured Visitor Attraction.

PETS NOT ALLOWED IN TROPICAL HOUSE ONLY

Open: daily Easter to end October 10.30am to 5pm

Directions: West Wales, 7 miles north of Cardigan off Aberystwyth road. Follow brown tourist signs on A487.

Journey through the lanes of cycle history and see bicycles from Boneshakers and Penny Farthings up to modern Raleigh cycles. Over 250 machines on display

PETS MUST BE KEPT ON LEADS

Open: 1st March to 1st November daily 10am onwards.

Directions: brown signs to car park. Town centre attraction.

Make a pit stop whatever the weather! Join an ex-miner on a tour of discovery, ride the cage to pit bottom and take a thrilling ride back to the surface. Multi-media presentations, period village street, children's adventure play area, restaurant and gift shop. Disabled access with assistance.

Open: Open daily 10am to 6pm (last tour 4pm). Closed Mondays Oct - Easter, also Dec 25th to early Jan.

Directions: Exit Junction 32 M4, signposted from A470 Pontypridd. Trehafod is located between Pontypridd and Porth.

Please note

All the information in this book is given in good faith in the belief that it is correct. However, the publishers cannot guarantee the facts given in these pages, neither are they responsible for changes in policy, ownership or terms that may take place after the date of going to press.

Readers should always satisfy themselves that the facilities they require are available and that the terms, if quoted, still apply.

Index of Towns and Counties

Visit the FHG website
www.holidayguides.com
for details of the wide choice of accommodation
featured in the full range of FHG titles

ico chic — croatia chic — tokyo chic — newzealand chic — beijing chic — italy chic

9781857334203 £12.95 (9814155014)
ISBN 13: 9781857334128 New £12.95
ISBN 13: 9781857334173 NEW £12.95
ISBN 13: 9781857334197 Sept 2007 £12.95
ISBN 13: 9781857334180 Sept 2007 £12.95
ISBN 13: 9781857334210 Jan 2008 £12.95

...hic series are the definitive guides to the world's most luxurious and alluring hotels. The ...rties featured—whether a city hotel, a beachside resort or a rustic hacienda—have been ...en for their individuality and chic appeal.

...its into the essence of each property help readers decide on the one that best suits their needs ...references. A fact-packed panel summarises each hotel's facilities and nearby attractions.

thechicseries

...raordinary destinations. Incomparable accommodations. Exceptional advice. ...n discerning travellers who have found everything they desire in the chic series ...el guides: hot properties, stunning photography and brilliant tips on where to go ...l how to do it in some of the worlds chicest locations.

apore chic — india chic — thailand chic — morocco chic — caribbean chic

3: 9781857334159 — ISBN 13: 9781857334104 — ISBN 13: 9781857334081 — ISBN 13: 9781857334067 — ISBN 13: 9781857334135

nghai chic — southafrica chic — bali chic — spain chic — hongkong chic

3: 9781857334111 — ISBN 13: 9781857334050 — ISBN 13: 9781857334098 — ISBN 13: 9781857334166 — ISBN 13: 9781857334142

Order any chic guide via the Kuperard website and receive free postage on any quantity of guides. Visit www.kuperard.co.uk to see the full range in the series and type in the following promotional code chic2. Or call us on 0208 446 2440 and quote the same code.

All titles are paperback priced £12.95

222

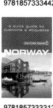     

FHG Guides Ltd have a large range of attractive
oliday accommodation guides for all kinds of holiday opportunities throughout Britain.
They also make useful gifts at any time of year.
ur guides are available in most bookshops and larger newsagents but we will be happy
o post you a copy direct if you have any difficulty. POST FREE for addresses in the UK.
We will also post abroad but have to charge separately for post or freight.

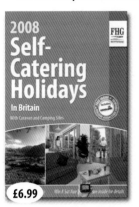

**SELF-CATERING HOLIDAYS
in Britain**
Over 1000 addresses throughout
for self-catering and caravans
in Britain.

**Recommended
INNS & PUBS of Britain**
Pubs, Inns and small hotels.

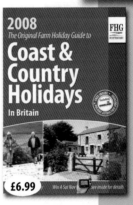

**The original
Farm Holiday Guide to
COAST & COUNTRY HOLIDAYS**
in England, Scotland, Wales,
Ireland and Channel Isles. Board,
Self-catering, Caravans/Camping,
Activity Holidays.

**The Original
PETS WELCOME!**
The bestselling guide to
holidays for pet owners
and their pets.

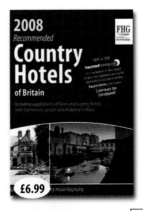

**Recommended
COUNTRY HOTELS
of Britain**
Including Country Houses, for the
discriminating.

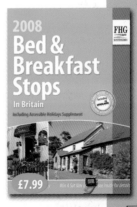

BED & BREAKFAST STOPS
Over 1000 friendly and
comfortable overnight stops.
Non-smoking, Disabled and
Special Diets Supplements..

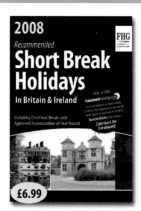

CHILDREN WELCOME!
Family Holidays and
Days Out guide.
Family holidays with details of
amenities for children and
babies.

The FHG Guide to
CARAVAN & CAMPING
HOLIDAYS
Caravans for hire, sites and
holiday parks and centres.

Recommended
SHORT BREAK HOLIDAYS
IN BRITAIN & IRELAND
"Approved" accommodation for
quality bargain breaks.

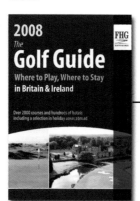

The GOLF GUIDE – *Where to play Where to stay*
In association with GOLF MONTHLY. Over 2800 golf
courses in Britain with convenient accommodation.
Holiday Golf in France, Portugal, Spain, USA and Thailand.

Tick your choice above and send your order and payment to

FHG Guides Ltd. Abbey Mill Business Centre
Seedhill, Paisley, Scotland PA1 1TJ
TEL: 0141- 887 0428 • FAX: 0141- 889 7204
e-mail: admin@fhguides.co.uk

Deduct 10% for 2/3 titles or copies; 20% for 4 or more.

Send to:　　NAME ....

ADDRESS ....

....

....

POST CODE ....

I enclose Cheque/Postal Order for £ ....

SIGNATURE ....DATE ....

Please complete the following to help us improve the service we provide.
How did you find out about our guides?:

☐ Press　　☐ Magazines　　☐ TV/Radio　　☐ Family/Friend　　☐ Other